JAPANESE POLITICS TODAY

JAPANESE POLITICS TODAY

FROM KARAOKE TO KABUKI DEMOCRACY

Edited by
Takashi Inoguchi
and
Purnendra Jain

JAPANESE POLITICS TODAY
Copyright © Takashi Inoguchi and Purnendra Jain, 2011.

First published in 2011 by
PALGRAVE MACMILLAN®
in the United States—a division of St. Martin's Press LLC,
175 Fifth Avenue, New York, NY 10010.

Where this book is distributed in the UK, Europe and the rest of the world,
this is by Palgrave Macmillan, a division of Macmillan Publishers Limited,
registered in England, company number 785998, of Houndmills,
Basingstoke, Hampshire RG21 6XS.

Palgrave Macmillan is the global academic imprint of the above companies
and has companies and representatives throughout the world.

Palgrave® and Macmillan® are registered trademarks in the United States,
the United Kingdom, Europe and other countries.

ISBN: 978–0–230–11796–9

Library of Congress Cataloging-in-Publication Data

Japanese politics today: from karaoke to kabuki democracy / edited by
Takashi Inoguchi and Purnendra Jain.
    p. cm.
    ISBN 978–0–230–11796–9 (alk. paper)—ISBN 978–0–230–11797–6 (alk.
paper) 1. Japan—Politics and government—1989– 2. Democracy—Japan.
I. Inoguchi, Takashi. II. Jain, Purnendra.

JQ1631.J363 2011
320.952—dc22   2011014002

A catalogue record of the book is available from the British Library.

Design by Newgen Imaging Systems (P) Ltd., Chennai, India.

First edition: October 2011

10 9 8 7 6 5 4 3 2 1

Printed in the United States of America.

CONTENTS

Figures, Graph and Tables

Figures

Graph

Tables

PREFACE

This book on contemporary Japanese politics aims to capture important aspects of the political life of the nation at a significant historical moment, given the geostrategic shifts under way regionally in Northeast Asia and in a global context. The book is unusual in two senses, both of which we recognize as strengths of this volume.

First is the diversity of contributors in terms of their national origin and training in Japanese politics—from the United States, England, Australia, China, India, Israel, and Japan. With complex dramas reshaping the nation's political life at the dawn of the twenty-first century, the broader range of analytical lenses presented here provides valuable insight and useful comparative perspective.

Second is appraisal of the sweep of change in recent years, alongside the continuity that has marked some aspects of Japan's political life for the past half century. Between our initial conception for a collected volume at a workshop in Tokyo in mid-2008 and receiving the final revised manuscripts in early 2011, many largely unexpected developments have unfolded in Japanese politics. Our contributors have been culturally sensitive and operationally dexterous in preparing their contributions to analyze, synthesize, and contextualize these recent unexpected developments alongside the continuities that we would usually expect in discussion of Japanese politics.

Thinking about the study of Japanese politics and the influences upon its intellectual traditions, we would like to express sincere gratitude to those who inspire and enrich our thinking. Here Takashi Inoguchi gratefully acknowledges the contributions of the late Lucian Wilmott Pye, formerly of MIT and a veteran Asian politics analyst. Our book highlights the political transformation in Japan from what we call karaoke democracy to kabuki democracy. Whereas our book identifies the present state of Japanese politics as "kabuki" democracy, Pye would have insisted it is more like another highly codified Japanese dramatic form, the noh play. A noh player's face is still for quite a long time while the player slowly articulates flat-sounding statements. But it changes dramatically when the noh player suddenly bursts into words full of emotion and moves his feet fast and adroitly, while still holding his face tightly. Japanese traditional dramas from centuries past serve us well as metaphor for understanding developments in Japanese politics today.

We are both indebted to those who provided administrative and intellectual support in preparing this book: particularly, Kimiko Goko, Kiyoko

Hoshino, Akiko Kanatani, and Wataru Numata in Japan; Maureen Todhunter, Joel Rathus, and Midori Kagawa-Fox in Australia. We appreciate and thank them for their contributions. We also appreciate contributions from Palgrave Macmillan, and particularly thank Farideh Koohi-Kamali and Robyn Curtis, whose efforts have brought this project to a tangible reality. Finally, we each acknowledge the support of our families whose patience and understanding are always vital to us.

Japanese politics is still in a state of flux in this transition period, as the chapters in this book explain. Certainly we can expect more drama on the national political stage—with the shift from "Karaoke" to "Kabuki" democracy reminding us of the distinctive style of Japan's political system and the importance of the past to understand the present.

TAKASHI INGOUCHI
PURNENDRA JAIN
Tokyo/Adelaide, January 2011

Contributors

Jennifer Chan is Associate Professor in the Department of Educational Studies at the University of British Columbia in Vancouver, Canada. She is the author of *Gender and Human Rights Politics in Japan* (Stanford University Press, 2004) and editor of *Another Japan Is Possible: New Social Movements and Global Citizenship Education* (Stanford University Press, 2008). She has published numerous articles and book chapters on social movements, human rights, gender, and multiculturalism. Her current project looks at the role of transnational advocacy networks in HIV/AIDS in reforming global health governance.

Ofer Feldman is Professor of Political Psychology and Behavior at Doshisha University, Kyoto, Japan. He holds a PhD in Social Psychology from the University of Tokyo, Japan. He is the author, editor, and coeditor of 14 books and monographs in English and Japanese, and the author and coauthor of more than 80 journal articles and book chapters, and more than 100 encyclopedia items, in the fields of political behavior/psychology, communication studies, and Japanese politics. Most recently, during 2009–2010, he received a grant from the Lady Davis Foundation and held a teaching and research position at the Hebrew University of Jerusalem, Israel.

Kentaro Fukumoto is Professor of Political Science and Chair of the Department of Political Science, Faculty of Law at Gakushuin University. His research interest lies in legislative studies and political methodology. He is the author of *Politics in the Japanese Diet: A Statistical Analysis of Postwar Government Legislation* (University of Tokyo Press, 2000, in Japanese) and *Legislative Institutions and Process* (Bokutaku Sha, 2007, in Japanese). His articles appeared in *American Journal of Political Science* and *Japanese Journal of Political Science*. He also serves on the editorial board of *American Journal of Political Science*.

Aurelia George Mulgan is Professor of Politics in the School of Humanities and Social Sciences, University of New South Wales, Australian Defence Force Academy. She is the author of a number of books including *The Politics of Agriculture in Japan* (Routledge, 2000), *Japan's Failed Revolution: Koizumi and the Politics of Economic Reform* (Asia Pacific Press, 2002), *Japan's Interventionist State: MAFF and the Agricultural Policy Regime* (RoutledgeCurzon, 2005) and *Japan's Agricultural Policy*

Regime (Routledge, 2006). Her articles have appeared in *Foreign Affairs, The Washington Quarterly, Government and Opposition, Political Studies, Australian Journal of Political Science, Asian Survey, Pacific Affairs, Journal of Japanese Studies,* and other such journals.

Helen Hardacre earned her doctorate from the University of Chicago in 1980, studying with Professor Joseph Kitagawa. She has done extended field study on contemporary Shinto, Buddhist religious organizations, and the religious life of Japan's Korean minority. She has also researched State Shinto and contemporary ritualizations of abortion in Japan. Before moving to Harvard in 1992, she taught at Princeton University (1980–1989) and Griffith University (Australia) (1990–1991). Her publications include *The Religion of Japan's Korean Minority* (University of California Press, 1984), *Lay Buddhism in Contemporary Japan: Reiyukai Kyodan* (Princeton University Press, 1984), *Kurozumikyo and the New Religions of Japan* (Princeton University Press, 1986), *Shinto and the State, 1868–1988* (Princeton University Press, 1989), *Marketing the Menacing Fetus in Japan* (University of California Press, 1997), and *Religion and Society in Nineteenth-Century Japan: A Study of the Southern Kanto Region, Using Late Edo and Early Meiji Gazetteers* (University of Michigan Press, 2002). Her current research projects include a study of Shinto history and the issue of constitutional revision in Japan and its effect on religious groups.

Takashi Horie is Associate Professor of Social Policy and Welfare at Tokyo Metropolitan University. He is the author of *Gendai Seiji to Josei Seisaku* [Politics and Gender Policies in Contemporary Japan] (Keiso Shobo, 2005), and the coeditor of *Seiji o Toinaosu 1: Kokumin Kokka no Kyokai* [Reexamining Politics 1: The Boundaries of Nation States] (Nihon Keizai Hyoronsha, 2010) and *Mosakusuru Seiji: Daihyosei Minshushugi to Fukushi Kokka no Yukue* [Revitalising Politics: The Search for New Ideas beyond Representative Democracy and the Welfare State] (Nakanishiya Shuppan, 2011). He received his PhD in Political Science from Hitotsubashi University in 2002.

Hiroaki Inatsugu is Professor of Public Administration at the faculty of Political Science and Economics, Waseda University, Japan. He specializes on public management, public personnel administration, and local government management. He has published a number of books in these fields.

Takashi Inoguchi, PhD (MIT), Professor Emeritus, University of Tokyo and President, University of Niigata Prefecture, specializes in Japanese politics and international relations and has published over 85 books and numerous articles both in English and in Japanese. Amongst them are *Japanese Politics: An Introduction* (Trans Pacific Press, 2005), *Political Cultures in Asia* and *Europe and Citizens and the State* (both coauthored with Jean Blondel, Routledge, 2006 and 2008 respectively), *Federalism in Asia* (coedited with Baogang He and Brian Galligan, Edward Elgar, 2007), *American Democracy Promotion* (coedited with Michael Cox and G. John Ikenberry,

Oxford University Press, 2000), *Reinventing the Alliance* and *The Uses of Institutions*(both coedited with G.John Ikenberry, Palgrave Macmillan, 2003 and 2007 respectively) and *Alliance Constrained* (coedited with G. John Ikenberry and Yoichiro Sato, Palgrave Macmillan, October 2011). He directs the AsiaBarometer project and is Founding Editor, *The Japanese Journal of Political Science* (Cambridge University Press, 1999–) and *International Relations of the Asia Pacific* (Oxford University Press, 2000–).

Purnendra Jain is Professor of Japanese Studies in the Centre for Asian Studies at Australia's University of Adelaide. Author and editor of 12 books and numerous scholarly articles on contemporary politics and foreign policy of Japan, his book *Japan's Subnational Governments in International Affairs* (Routledge, 2006) was translated in Japanese under the title *Nihon no jichi-tai gaiko* (Keibundo, 2009). His latest coedited book is *Japan in Decline: Fact or Fiction?* (Global Oriental, 2011). He is currently President of the Asian Studies Association of Australia.

Gregory J. Kasza is Professor of Political Science and East Asian Languages & Cultures at Indiana University. He is the author of *The State and the Mass Media in Japan, 1918–1945* (University of California Press, 1988), *The Conscription Society* (Yale University Press, 1995), and *One World of Welfare: Japan in Comparative Perspective* (Cornell University Press, 2006). Professor Kasza received his PhD in political science from Yale University in 1983, and he has held research appointments at Tokyo University, Kyoto University, Hitotsubashi University, Oxford University, and Harvard University. His research on the Japanese welfare system was supported by a grant from the Japan Foundation and an Abe Fellowship from the Center for Global Partnership and the Social Science Research Council.

Steven R. Reed is Professor of Modern Government at Chuo University in Japan, where all of his classes are taught in Japanese. His major areas of research are parties, elections, electoral systems, and Japanese politics. He recently coedited *Political Change in Japan: Electoral Behavior, Party Realignment, and the Koizumi Reforms* (Brookings, 2009) with Kenneth Mori McElwain and Kay Shimizu. He has published articles in *The British Journal of Political Science, The American Journal of Political Science, The Journal of Japanese Studies, Comparative Politics, Comparative Political Studies, Party Politics, Electoral Studies*, and several Japanese journals.

Professor **J. A. A. Stockwin** was born in Britain, has a first degree in Philosophy, Politics and Economics from the University of Oxford and a doctorate in international relations from the Australian National University, Canberra. Between 1964 and 1981 he taught in the Department of Political Science of the Australian National University. Between 1982 and his retirement in 2003, he was Nissan Professor of Modern Japanese Studies and Director of the Nissan Institute of Japanese Studies at the University of Oxford. In 1994–1995 he was President of the British Association of Japanese Studies. He is now an Emeritus Fellow of St. Antony's College,

University of Oxford. His publications include *The Japanese Socialist Party and Neutralism* (1968), *Japan and Australia in the Seventies* (editor, 1973), *Dynamic and Immobilist Politics in Japan* (editor and part author, 1988), *Dictionary of the Modern Politics of Japan* (2003), *Collected Writings of J.A.A. Stockwin: The Politics and Political Environment of Japan* (2004), *Governing Japan: Divided Politics in a Resurgent Economy* (4th rev. ed., 2008).

INTRODUCTION

FROM *KARAOKE* TO *KABUKI* DEMOCRACY: JAPANESE POLITICS TODAY

Takashi Inoguchi and Purnendra Jain

Our 1997 book, *Japanese Politics Today: Beyond Karaoke Democracy?*[1] questioned the nature of contemporary Japanese politics in the closing years of the twentieth century. In this book, after a decade into the twenty-first century, we return to the political stage. We find much has changed in the structures and processes that characterized Japanese politics in the 1980s and most of the 1990s. Japanese politics has moved beyond *karaoke* democracy. The performers, their performances, and purposes have changed dramatically, with analogies that cleave closely to a very different type of Japanese drama: *kabuki*. Now we see a transition under way, from a *karaoke* style of democracy to one that we believe is well captured in the label "*kabuki* democracy."

What is "*kabuki*" about current Japanese politics? How and why has the performance on the nation's political landscape transformed from the *karaoke* style we observed in the late 1990s? In this introduction we provide a brief overview. The ensuing chapters provide the details.

Kabuki as traditional performance art has itself undergone transformation since its genesis in seventeenth-century Japan. And as with life on the national political stage, *kabuki* will always be subject to different interpretations, appreciations, and appraisals depending on the observer's perspective. However, we see the essence of the resemblance with contemporary political life in the nature of the performance: who it reaches and how. *Kabuki* in its modern form is exciting, a show of drama and extravagance, not for the narrow elite but broadly for the hoi polloi. Its players perform a skillful dance to an original script that strikes a deep emotional chord with audiences. In *kabuki* democracy, political leaders bring personality and emotions to their role on the national political stage. This direct and wider engagement with the ordinary people makes national politics more interesting and vibrant.

In *karaoke* democracy, bureaucrats provided political leaders with scripts on policy statements. Leaders generally rendered those statements as their own and tried to convince voters that they deserved to be returned to power on the basis of their ideas and policies that delivered successful outcomes. Thus, although prime ministers and cabinet ministers changed frequently in a single party-dominated system, policy directions only mildly changed, determined largely by bureaucrats who preferred incremental change to keep the national ship steady. Deep, substantive reform, no matter how much it may have augured economic, social, and political improvement for the nation, was not on the political agenda. Similar to a *karaoke* stage, the singers behind the microphone came and went but the song sheets remained unchanged.

Under *kabuki* democracy, politics becomes more interesting and colorful because political leaders seek—and bring—change to the political agenda. They have their own distinctive personal style, and consciously express their human qualities—emotions, personal preferences, and vulnerabilities—to skillfully connect with the people. In their political performances leaders are eager to have an emotional connection and to strike a deep chord with audiences. Junichiro Koizumi, Japan's Liberal Democratic Party (LDP) prime minister (2001–2006), clearly captures this *kabuki* style.[2] In this sense Koizumi was somewhat exceptional as an LDP prime minister, moving away dramatically from the *karaoke* song sheet of policy. The three years of post-Koizumi political confusion confirmed Koizumi's style as exceptional, with a succession of three LDP leaders who metaphorically and in practice appeared to have lost the plot line. *Kabuki* style disappeared as quickly as Koizumi had swept it in; *karaoke* democracy returned to the political stage as the microphone was passed from one new prime minister to the next.

Defeat over the LDP would not come till the August 2009 general election. Trouncing of the severely weakened LDP by the Democratic Party of Japan (DPJ) ousted the conservative party, after 38 years of unbroken rule, from parliamentary power.

Many observers expected that the defeat of the LDP at the 1993 general election would usher in a new era of politics in Japan, shifting away from *karaoke* style to one more appropriate to the popular participatory style of democracy transforming political systems in many countries.[3] But that hope faded quickly. The unwieldy eight-party coalition government under first Morihiro Hosokawa and then very briefly Tsutomu Hata could not endure internal division among coalition members. As a result, the LDP bounced back quickly into the ruling seat and Japan returned to business as usual: faction-based LDP politics with bureaucrat-dependant and interest-group-oriented policymaking.

Although the 1993–1994 coalition governments were short-lived, the Hosokawa government set in motion fundamental changes in the electoral system that would eventually bring competition and alternation between parties in power, ending the LDP's one-party dominance that long characterized Japan as an "uncommon democracy."[4] This possibility remained elusive, though, even after a new electoral system was put in place. Partly it was because the opposition remained weak and divided following the LDP's return to government in 1994, in coalition with a number of political parties including, briefly, its former archrival the Japan Socialist Party.[5] But six years later, the LDP itself was clearly in decay.

During Yoshiro Mori's prime ministership from April 2000, the LDP became the least-favored party in Japan. The party was increasingly fragile, facing the prospect of defeat at the forthcoming upper house (House of Councilors) elections in July 2001, while the opposition led by the DPJ gathered momentum.[6] To prevent electoral catastrophe, the LDP forfeited the traditional factional considerations and methods of selecting party president. Popular leader Junichiro Koizumi was chosen as party president and thus Japan's prime minister in April 2001. A new and maverick LDP leader, Koizumi undertook the daunting task of rescuing the party and the LDP leadership from ever more dismal electoral prospects. The national political stage was set for drama, for reengaging the deeply disillusioned constituency. Koizumi delivered, in unprecedented *kabuki* style.

Koizumi swiftly engineered a remarkable turnaround in public reception, with his own popularity soaring above an unprecedented 80 percent. He had been chosen to lead the nation without the binding ties of allegiance that had hamstrung his predecessors to factional groups within the LDP, to special interest groups, and to other LDP leaders. Koizumi was free to do as he thought best to rescue the party, govern the nation, and, importantly, reengage the people. He came as an unconventional LDP leader, at a time when LDP conventions—especially the service of entrenched interests—had manifestly led the party into political morass. Takashi Inoguchi refers us to *zeitgemaessheit*: "political leaders in harmony with the political environment of the time."[7]

Koizumi used his personal skills of cultivating popularity and engaging the people so masterfully that he freed his leadership and office from the traditional constraints of party and bureaucracy. He selected cabinet members without factional consideration and locked horns with party bigwigs as occasion demanded. The source of his political strength was his direct rapport with Japanese voters, particularly through policy pronouncements and his media-savvy appearance. He could, and he did, emotionally connect with the people. In local elections in June, two months after he became prime minister, Koizumi led the party to win in key areas such as the Tokyo Metropolitan Assembly. In the following month's upper house elections in which his party was slated for defeat, the LDP lost seats but won the election.

His personality and ability to communicate with the electorate to build support for his political convictions eclipsed the political space long dominated by factions, bureaucracy, and special interest groups. Koizumi had set the national political stage to move beyond *karaoke* democracy into the more populist and engaging style of *kabuki*. In consummate Koizumi style, the song sheets he did later choose to sing from, during a prime ministerial visit to the United States in July 2006, were none other than Elvis Presley's.[8] This was a classic display of the populist politics and emotional connection that Koizumi played out on the national, and sometimes international, stage.

A hard act to follow, and not simply because of his personal charismatic style, Koizumi public leadership qualities had shifted the ground on which Japanese prime ministers would exercise national leadership and the Japanese public would expect to engage with their national leader. In an era of globalization, he had pulled the nation toward the populist, participatory modes reshaping political life in countries across the globe.

As public dissatisfaction deepened with the LDP and its leaders after Koizumi's departure, and as the opposition DPJ gathered political momentum with its solid performance at the 2007 House of Councilors election, the political climate was right for a seismic shift in Japanese politics.[9] Here was a political environment seeking strong and popular leadership. The August 2009 general election produced a landslide victory for the DPJ and a crushing defeat for the LDP.

The DPJ under Hatoyama entered a political stage already prepared for *kabuki*-style leadership by Koizumi. Hatoyama's administration began on a high note because of its *kabuki*-style political promises of direct communication and populist outreach. Key goals resonated well with ordinary Japanese people, particularly emphasis on governance and leadership by politicians instead of dependence on bureaucrats, and pledges to cut back on unnecessary and unproductive public works projects, and to distance government from special interest groups. Public outreach included the DPJ's well-received promises of care, for those with special needs. The new government's honeymoon was, however, brief. Within months of the DPJ coming to power, media reported that not only Ichiro Ozawa, the chief party strategist and secretary general renowned for "political dealings," but also the new prime minister himself were involved in "money politics."

We contend that this style of personal, populist politics is likely to continue in Japan for some time. The advent of DPJ government replacing the LDP signals a major shift in conditions on the national political stage and within the electorate, conditions that now enable and promote the populist kabuki approach. National leaders' direct connections with the people make for a more engaged and participatory political system—an important component of democracy as the nation's economic, political, and social transition proceeds alongside globalization.

Today Japanese people no longer accept the cozy relationship between political leaders, bureaucracy, and big business that entrenched exclusive interests within the political system and produced the political malaise.[10] Public will has shifted and political players know it. Political executives and governing parties understand that intrinsic to their hold on power now is capacity to control and direct bureaucracy rather than follow policies made by bureaucrats. Instead of factional politicking, party leaders themselves are expected to take responsibility, to be accountable, and to connect directly with the people. These new protocols and expectations have excised much of the political turf on which business organizations operated, rendering *their voices* much weaker in political decision making. The steady tide of globalization appears to have reduced the role and influence of social intermediary organizations and the state itself.

Addresses to the National Diet provide insight into the evolution from *karaoke* to *kabuki* democracy.[11] Instead of representatives from bureaucratic agencies, business sectors, personal support organizations, and other organized groups, individual actors can now appear on center stage without the organizational and financial strength that was needed earlier. Now the requirement is to strike a chord among audiences. Oratorical excellence, rhetorical brilliance, and support mobilization are vital. In delivering a Diet speech, the presenter must now create a context in which audience members become coactors with the presenter. This can make *kabuki* democracy erratic on the Diet floor as few leaders are to make the needed emotional connection with their audience.

At this point, it is useful to consider the etymology of *kabuki*. The word "*kabuki*" derives from *kabuku*, which means "lean in a certain direction." Some say the word is related to *katamuki*, which means "slanted" and "strongly inclined." Both meanings refract the lens through which we can understand *kabuki* democracy.

Koizumi certainly leaned in a particular direction as prime minister and the particular policies he pushed may be regarded as slanted and strongly inclined. His controversial postal reform is a classic example. In pushing postal reform, Koizumi alienated a strong group of LDP supporters and colleagues who identified with the postal lobby group. His slant so strongly toward postal reform led to party breakaways and, some say, ultimately caused the defeat of the LDP in 2009. A similar slant can be seen within the DPJ, with its move to reduce the influence of bureaucrats in policymaking. The move receives widespread accolades for the DPJ, but the party understands that it is unwise to alienate the bureaucracy whose tradition not only reaches back to the Tokugawa period but remained untouched during the postwar Occupation period (1945–1952).[12]

We also see signs of lopsidedness emerging in the national political arena in areas beyond policy. One is in the parties themselves, or at least the LDP. The once invincible LDP has today become a fragile political party, rudderless and without direction. It seems to be fragmenting as senior members leave the party to form their own parties.[13] The party has yet to learn how to be an effective opposition. The DPJ, despite its troubles and the controversies surrounding its key leaders, remains strong and is hardly in danger of being swept out of power anytime soon. If the LDP continues to weaken and remains dysfunctional in opposition, the stage is set for a return to lopsided politics with a single dominant party (now the DPJ). However, this scenario is less than acceptable to any democratic nation in the twenty-first century.

The new political era in Japan today is leaning toward *kabuki* democracy. The transition has not yet truly lifted Japan from its long political morass, but it has moved the country a step forward into the new century. The recent move toward *kabuki* democracy is not of itself dramatic, but it indicates that voters no longer endorse the old ways of karaoke democracy. Japanese voters seek leadership that promises and delivers new political approaches and directions appropriate for today.[14] Even while Japanese politics has changed, much remains the same. Ongoing change is likely as Japan's democratic system transforms itself in response to the needs of society in a rapidly evolving globalized world. This volume records both the changes and the stagnation over the past decade in a range of political structures, processes, and policies. The chapters also discuss ways forward as the nation moves further toward—then ultimately beyond—*kabuki* democracy.

Our theme is that the key feature of Japanese politics has been changing from *karaoke* to *kabuki* democracy. The political manifestation of this transition is characteristically Japanese. Yet the shift is not necessarily confined to Japan. The shift is very closely related to the changing nature of democracy worldwide. This global shift as labeled by John Keane is from representative to monitory democracy.[15] By representative democracy, Keane means the type whereby people's deputies are electorally selected and with people's mandate they carry out the task of government according to their understanding of people's preference. Representative democracy is sometimes called classical democracy. Whereas people give legitimacy to government through democratic election, government tries to affect positively the lives of people. By monitory democracy, Keane means the type whereby the conduct of government is watched carefully and the explanation of government conduct intermittently required. Monitory democracy is sometimes called digital democracy. Not only is government conduct digitalized for popular scrutiny but also popular feedbacks to government are digitalized in such forms as leader's popularity, ups and downs of company stocks and government bonds, and protest movements. For government to initiate and implement policy action, imaginatively crafted policy statements and a set of policy measures are required to strike a chord among people. Whereas representative democracy has intermediary institutions between government and people, monitory democracy makes it critical for government and people to interact directly and intermittently with limited interference by intermediate-level social groups. Under monitory democracy leaders are required to have a much better instinctive sense of popular preference and discomfort, to express passion and determination to match people's mood, to mobilize and move people with oratorical finesse, and to avoid faux pas, gaffes, mishaps, and so on. *Karaoke* politics is about making the best use of bureaucracy, whereas *kabuki* politics is about reducing mediation and appealing directly to the public. *Karaoke* politics is primarily about securing organized votes, whereas *kabuki* politics is primarily about securing floating votes. *Karaoke* politics is a Japanese version of representative democracy; *kabuki* politics is a Japanese version of monitory democracy. Monitory democracy is defined as the politics of mutual monitoring of government and citizens evolving around transparency and accountability. Its Japanese version is *dadamore minshushugi* (leaking democracy).[16]

The chapters in this book are actor oriented and fall under the above two distinctive regime environments. After this introduction, Inoguchi describes and illustrates the prime ministers—Shigeru Yoshida, Kakuei Tanaka, and Junichiro Koizumi—in three distinctive periods of Japanese politics. The shift from *karaoke* to *kabuki* democracy is vividly illustrated. Hiroaki Inatsugu presents a fairly schematized picture of Japanese bureaucracy in terms of its size, its mission, its location in, and relation to, society, its employment, and its payment. In other words, how a small-sized bureaucracy exercizes substantial influence in policymaking and legislation. However, how it metamorphoses under *kabuki* democracy remains to be seen. Kentaro Fukumoto gives a daily time-spending pattern of legislators and legislative outputs of the 1955–1993 prereform period and the 1993–2009 postreform period. Reform refers to legislative reform in 1993 governing political money and electoral system. Steven Reed describes the electoral and political reform enacted in 1994 and analyzes the electoral ups and downs of political parties under a new electoral environment. The 2009 victory of Democrats is closely analyzed in the two-party system framework. Arthur Stockwin gives a masterly story of Japanese party politics from the Occupation period through the 2009 political earthquake—victory of Democrats. Aurelia George Mulgan examines interest groups. She singles out the farm lobby, richly detailing how it exerts great influence despite a small agricultural population. Although many social intermediate organizations reduce their size and activity, they still constitute a strong wing of Japanese protectionism. Jennifer Chan portrays and analyzes civil society from the postmodern perspective, tackling citizens frontally but not in relation to the state. Rather than state-subject and state-citizen relationship perspectives, which have dominated discourses on Japanese civil society, she adopts a global citizenship perspective in her examination. Gregory Kasza and Takashi Horie examine social policy, the "issue of all the issues." After tracing the historical evolution of social policy from the prewar period, they examine how the current predicament of social policy arose and annoys the government and people as direct participants of social policy under the policy environment of low fertility rates and rising inequalities. Purnendra Jain describes how subnational governments try to activate the policy direction they deem important: greater decentralization and political participation from the nadir of their profile. Ofer Feldman examines mass media in terms of dissemination of political information. The media is characterized as concentrated, under indirect government control, commercialized, and self-censored. Feldman focuses on how these features are changing under globalization and government deregulation. Helen Hardacre tackles constitutional revision, an issue that the long-governing LDP includes as one of the political missions in their party constitution. She focuses on the legislation of an administrative law that in her view would produce a similar effect to constitutional revision on government capacity in legislation in issues such as education and the rising of the national flag and singing of the national anthem.

Our collective hope is that readers find the volume important and interesting: important in understanding how kabuki democracy requires astuteness and agility; and interesting in realizing how a cleverly crafted speech moves people and changes politics overnight.

The present volume is a product of our continuing interest in, and questioning of, Japan's contemporary political system. In our several meetings as editors of *Japanese Politics Today: Beyond Karaoke Democracy?* we began to rethink our characterization of Japanese politics in the context of the changes reconfiguring the national political landscape, especially since the emergence of the Koizumi administration. With this in mind, we asked leading international political scientists on Japan to present their research at a Tokyo workshop in mid-2008. Since this meeting, Japanese politics has undergone further transformation through the historical shift in August 2009. Each author has revised their respective chapters in light of the changes since the Hatoyama government took office in September 2009.

NOTES

1. Purnendra Jain and Takashi Inoguchi, eds., *Japanese Politics Today: Beyond Karaoke Democracy?* (Melbourne: Macmillan 1997).
2. Takashi Inoguchi, "Japan: The Personalisation of Politics-Koizumi and Japanese Politics," in Jean Blondel and Jean-Louis Thiébault with Katarzyna Czernicka, Takashi Inoguchi, Ukrist Pathmanand, and Fulvio Venturino, *Political Leadership, Parties and Citizens: The Personalisation of Leadership* (London: Routledge, 2009), pp. 209–228.
3. Purnendra Jain, "A New Political Era in Japan: The 1993 Election," *Asian Survey*, 33, no. 11 (November 1993): 1071–1082. Takashi Inoguchi, "Japanese Politics in Transition: A Theoretical Review," *Government and Opposition*, 28, no. 4 (Autumun 1993): 443–455; "The Rise and Fall of 'Reformist Governments': Hosokawa and Hata 1993–1994," *Asian Journal of Political Science*, 2, no. 2 (December 1994): 73–88.
4. Takashi Inoguchi, "The Political Economy of Conservative Resurgence under Recession: Public Policies and Political Support in Japan, 1977–1983," in T. J. Pempel, ed., *Uncommon Democracies: The One-Party Dominant Regimes* (Ithaca: Cornell University Press, 1990), pp. 189–225.
5. See Ethan Scheiner, *Democracy without Competition in Japan: Opposition Failure in a One-party Dominant State* (Cambridge: Cambridge University Press, 2006).
6. Chao-Chi Lin, "How Koizumi Won," in Steven R. Reed, Kenneth Mori McElwain, and Kay Shimuzu, eds., *Political Change in Japan: Electoral Behaviour, Party Realignment and the Koizumi Reforms* (Standford: Walter H. Shorenstein Asia-Pacific Research Center, 2009), p. 112.
7. See Inoguchi, "Prime Ministers" in this volume, and Inoguchi, "Japan: the Personalisation of Politics—Koizumi and Japanese Politics," in Jean Blondel and Jean-Louis Thiebault with Katarzyna Czernicka, Takashi Inoguchi, Ukrist Pathmanand, and Fulvio Venturino, *Political Leadership, Parties and Citizens: The Personalisation of Leadership* (London: Routledge, November 2009), pp. 209–228.
8. As reported, Koizumi "delighted the president, first lady Laura Bush and tour guides Priscilla and Lisa Marie Presley . . . With the pack of media in the room entreating him, Koizumi delivered a teasing cabaret of tunes," http://www.elvis.com/news/full_story.asp?id=1050 (accessed May 18, 2010).
9. Arthur Stockwin has called it "political earthquake in Japan." See his "Political Earthquake in Japan: How Much of a Difference Will It Make?" in Purnendra Jain and Brad Williams, eds., *Japan in Decline: Fact or Fiction?* (Folkestone: Global Oriental, 2011).

10. See Inoguchi's characterization of the last of the three periods of Japanese politics since 1945, that is, military rule, strong economic growth, and steady globalization in Takashi. Inoguchi, "Japanese Contemporary Politics: Towards a New Interpretation," in Kay Lawson, Anatoly Kulik, and Baogang He, eds., *Political Parties and Democracy: Post-Soviet and Asian Political Parties* (New York: Praeger, 2010), pp. 173–189, 261–263.

11. See Takafumi Suzuki, "Investigating Japanese Government's Perceptions of the Postwar World as Revealed in Prime Ministers' Diet Addresses: Focusing on East-West and North-South Issues," *International Relations of the Asia-Pacific* (2009), 9, no. 2: 317–338.

12. Takashi Inoguchi, "The Pragmatic Evolution of Japanese Democratic Politics," in Michele Schmiegelow, ed., *Democracy in Asia* (New York: St. Martin's, 1997), pp. 217–231; Inoguchi, "Political Parties and Democracy in Japan," in *Political Parties and Democracy*, pp. 173–189, 261–263, and Takashi Inoguchi, "Japanese Contemporary Politics: Towards a New Interpretation," in Rien Segers, ed., *A New Japan for the Twenty-First Century: An Inside Overview of Current Fundamental Changes and Problems* (London: Routledge, 2008), pp. 67–86.

13. For example, former health minister Yoichi Masuzoe, now heads Shinto Kaikaku, which includes five other upper house lawmakers. Other new parties include Yoshimi Watanabe's Your Party and the Sunrise Party of Japan led by former ministers Takeo Hiranuma and Kaoru Yosano.

14. Takashi Inoguchi, "Japanese Contemporary Politics: Towards a New Interpretation," in Rien Segers, ed., *A New Japan for the Twenty-First Century: An Inside Overview of Current Fundamental Changes and Problems* (London: Routledge, 2008), pp. 67–86.

15. John Keane, *The Life and Death of Democracy* (London: Simon & Schuster, 2010).

16. Takashi Higaki, *Dadamore minshushugi* (Leaking Democracy) (Tokyo: Kodansha, 2010).

1

PRIME MINISTERS

Takashi Inoguchi

INTRODUCTION: ARE JAPANESE PRIME MINISTERS INHERENTLY WEAK?

When Prime Minister Shinzo Abe was abruptly hospitalized for two weeks in September 2007, the *Financial Times* commented that Japan might be able to function without a prime minister because Abe had not even appointed an acting prime minister. Abe's chief cabinet secretary provided bedside briefings to him for two weeks, at the end of which Abe resigned from office.[1] This event and other similar examples of Japanese prime ministers give sometimes the impression that Japan is a country without a leader. Karel Van Wolferen's writings exemplify this view well.[2] In examining three recent Japanese prime ministers—Shigeru Yoshida, Kakuei Tanaka, and Junichiro Koizumi—I make two points:

1. That the political system of Japan carries heavy legacies from the early modern period and that the floundering of Japanese-style absolutism in the late sixteenth century paved the course of Japanese political development in a fragmented and fissiparous fashion.[3]
2. That the effectiveness of a prime minister to forge a solid coalition in harmony with the spirit of his time while in office is key to his ability to overcome the limited constitutional and institutional authority allocated to the Office of Prime Minister.

I chose Yoshida, Tanaka, and Koizumi because they represent the three distinctive periods since 1945 and thus need to be examined carefully according to historical contextual differences:[4]

1. Military occupation and economic reconstruction (1945–1960);
2. Strong economic growth (1960–1985); and
3. Globalization (1985–2010).

First, I summarize the early modern legacies of the Japanese political system pointing to the quasi-federal nature of bureaucratic dominance.[5] Then I characterize the three periods of the post-1945 Japanese political system, focusing on the support base, priority policies, the predominant government ministry, public sentiment and concerns, and reasons for supporting opposition parties.[6] Third, I depict Yoshida, Tanaka, and Koizumi as prime ministers representing each of these three periods, illustrate how effective coalition formation strategies do make a difference to the strength and weakness of prime ministers, irrespective of constitutionally prescribed, institutionally embedded, and historically carried-over structures within which each prime minister has to act.

Japan's Early Modern Legacies

By early modern legacies, I refer to the unsuccessful attempt in Japan to establish an absolute monarchy as done in early modern Europe. Instead, the Japanese political system retained the late medieval, feudalistic fragmentation of power during the early modern period (1603–1867) and the modern period (1868–1985).[7] Ieyasu Tokugawa, prevailed over 300 domains with a quasi-monopoly on external commerce, diplomacy, and defense in his hands. The era of Pax Tokugawa (1603–1867) was achieved through a quasi-federalist scheme, Japanese style. A sharp distinction among the four classes—warriors, peasants, artisans, and merchants—existed, with the warriors mostly disarmed and assembled into the castle towns of domains where their duties were defined primarily as bureaucratic. The key feature of domain governance is bureaucratic authoritarianism that was clannish in nature. Each domain was headed by a domain lord who organized his bureaucracy based on the idea of the extended family with warriors-cum-bureaucrats capping the structure of the domain.[8] Another key feature is the democratizing potentials of bureaucratic authoritarianism in the domain.[9] As the task of governance in the domain expanded gradually in tandem with the rise of the population and increased agricultural production, the warrior class category loosened to include rich peasants and merchants, especially as domain finance was intermittently tight and lending to the domain became a common business of rich merchants. In 1603 the warrior population accounted for 3 percent of the population, but in 1867, this class accounted for 7 percent. More important to the democratic potentials of this type of bureaucratic authoritarianism in a domain is the decision-making mode of collective discussion among senior bureaucrats whose highest priority was the protection and promotion of organizational dignity and interests, but not necessarily loyalty to the domain chief.[10]

Quasi-federalism, organizational decision making based on the conception of an extended clan, and inclusive authoritarianism are the three central features of early modern, modern, and postmodern Japanese politics. These features have manifested themselves time and again. Quasi-federalism metamorphoses itself into a federation of bureaucratic agencies. Each bureaucratic agency is semisovereign, although not necessarily the Office of the

Prime Minister. Organizational decision making based on the concept of an extended clan is succeeded by each bureaucratic agency, not necessarily the prime minister's decision. The scope of power available to the prime minister is considerably limited and occasionally only slightly more than nominal. The same holds true for inclusive authoritarianism. Although authoritarianism metamorphosed into democracy through the years, the impetus to include more clients under its umbrella did not decline under democracy.[11]

In 1868 and the ensuing years, quasi-federalism and organizational decision making with extended clan conception and inclusive authoritarianism were retained in modified forms. The transition of *haihan-chiken* (abolish domains, establish prefectures) into more or less semisovereign bureaucratic agencies is important. Replacing domains and centralizing prefectures came naturally. Semisovereign, bureaucratic agencies came, at least, initially in the form of Meiji Restoration leaders capturing government posts and positions and attracting like-minded people or nonstrangers from their home domains to work with them. For instance, the army was heavily Choshu-dominant and the navy was Satsuma-dominant. Even with the equalization of the four classes after 1868, the former warrior class dominated government. Up until the 1920s, more than one-half of upper stream civil servants came from warrior families.

In 1945 Japan unconditionally surrendered to the Allied Powers led by the United States. The United States wanted Japan to rule itself under the general direction of the Supreme Commander of the Allied Powers, General Douglas MacArthur. With the exception of the army, the navy, the Internal Security Police, and some war-tainted politicians and high-ranking bureaucrats, much of the imperial service was retained. The emperor's status was changed dramatically from a sovereign king to a living national symbol through the abolishment and replacement of the Imperial Constitution with a new constitution. Quasi-federalism among bureaucratic agencies did not change at all with each agency remaining broadly semisovereign in its policy area.

Core elites of the bureaucracy continued to be from the warrior class of the early modern period. The modern Japanese political system evolved around the bureaucracy. That explains why the modern Japanese political system has been fragmented, fissiparous, and decentralized at the very top level of government by semisovereign bureaucratic agencies, why prime ministers (or domain lords) have never been like the descendants of absolutist monarchs in Europe or autocrats in China, and why the modern Japanese political system has been able to adapt to environmental changes at home and abroad without jeopardizing its basic continuity. Yet the three features (quasi-federalism and organizational decision making with extended clan conception, and inclusive authoritarianism) have not changed as much for the bureaucracy. From the prime ministers' perspective, the three features manifest themselves as follows: that is, prime ministers are like domain chiefs. They do not necessarily enjoy the power of the highest authority. Prime ministers are constitutionally and institutionally weak. Prime ministers give broad directives to cabinet ministers but not detailed instructions. Prime ministers must obtain consensus from all cabinet ministers before cabinet-sponsored bills are sent to the National Diet. If a cabinet member resists signing a proposed bill, then she or he must resign from office or the entire cabinet. The prime minister is no exception to this rule. Only when the prime minister exercises his authority with exceptional tact and good timing, can he be very powerful. Yet his power is never guaranteed.[12]

The path dependence of the modern Japanese political system is underlined in this chapter and book with some inevitable dissonance from what the more conventional view of modern Japanese history would suggest, that is, modernization and centralization in 1868 and thereafter and democratization and centralization in 1945 and thereafter. Until recently, the bureaucracy has enjoyed dominance. As globalization permeated society and reduced mediating institutions' weight, bureaucracy entered a period of slow decline as a key political actor. During the post-1985 period, the bureaucracy has become less of a predominant political force and prime ministers have had to experience some daunting change in their political environment.

THREE PERIODS OF POST-1945 JAPANESE POLITICS

Before examining our three prime ministers and their style and performances, I provide brief accounts of each period in which each prime minister was a key actor. In the first period after World War II, the period of occupation and reconstruction (1945–1960), the government's emphasis and orientation was on pacifism and economic growth. This two-prong policy focus came to be known as the Yoshida Doctrine, after the prime minister was credited with its creation and implementation. Renouncing war in its postwar constitution, Japan followed a pacifist military and foreign policy that was possible because of the Japan-U.S. Security Treaty. The treaty left Japan significantly dependent on the United States for its security; yet the arrangement allowed Tokyo to focus on the second prong of the doctrine— economic reconstruction and growth.

Fueled by deep poverty for the vast majority of the Japanese population in the immediate years after World War II, political emotions and opposition to the government ran high. The political tension and sentiments of the electorate shifted as the economy started to grow and reconstruction ensued. In 1955, two conservative parties joined together to form the Liberal Democratic Party (LDP). Sparked by the growing power of the center-right and growing support from the self-employed, the LDP electoral power base continued to expand into rural areas that had witnessed, under the U.S. occupation, farmland reforms and the creation of a large class of landowning farmers. The economic programs and initiatives of government sponsored an ongoing expansion of support from the self-employed business sector. The Economic Planning Agency, known then as the Headquarters for Economic Stability, led Japan's efforts at economic reconstruction.

In the years after World War II, political tempers ran high. The Japan-U.S. Security Treaty served as a lightning rod, with the loudest political voices warning that U.S. military installations on Japanese soil would only hasten Japan into another war. The Japan Socialist Party (JSP) and the Japanese Communist Party (JCP) were among those voices. Conversely, those who argued that such a security arrangement would deter any military threats resonated less well among the public. The LDP, or at least the party that would eventually become it, supported this viewpoint. The other point of contention was how the government should proceed economically: should the emphasis be on promoting economic recovery through reconstruction and building fundamental economic strength or should the emphasis be more at a microlevel, at the level of the individual and individual family. The LDP supported the former economic approach; the JSP and JCP supported the latter.

Strong economic growth characterized the second period under consideration (1960–1985) in this chapter. The Japanese bureaucracy together with the LDP and business formed a powerful tripartite structure that propelled the Japanese economy to grow and expand at an unprecedented rate. Although all three actors are credited, the model of development is viewed as bureaucracy driven. The bureaucracy directed and managed the development of the national economy: from the administration of research and development subsidies seeking technological innovation to subsidies for less competitive industries to corporate financing. The bureaucracy provided the budgets for industrial infrastructure and gave direction on fiscal and financial policy.

The primacy of the bureaucracy in the Japanese policy process has led to the characterization that "government overrules politics." Indeed, the guiding principles behind a policy are frequently drafted by government agencies for governing parties and business leaders to review. The historical roots of this bureaucracy-driven political structure can be found in the periods of early modern (1603–1867) and modern (1868–1985) Japan.

Farmers and self-employed businessmen formed the initial base of support for the LDP, but their importance to the party diminished as a new body of LDP support appeared from the new middle class and "new middle-class masses" that emerged with economic growth.

In the postwar years, the overarching policy objectives of the LDP were to provide the conditions for stable and competitive economic growth, that is, conditions that led to Japan resuming its position among the advanced countries. To reach those objectives, the policy priorities focused on the obvious area of macroeconomic management and the, not so obvious, area of social policy. Concerned by downward trends in its support base, the LDP sought to strengthen and expand its support among the new middle-class masses by prioritizing social policy.

The government ministries central to Japan's policy aspirations during the period of reconstruction and economic growth were those that had the portfolios for international trade and industry (MITI), finance (MoF), and health and welfare. With regard to budget allocation and size of population, the Ministry of Health and Welfare would not appear to be a key ministry, however, its significance was soon to be realized. The increasing recognition of the growing middle-class masses and their importance in enhancing and securing LDP support translated into a mounting awareness about the significance of social policy.

Over the years, the governing party and opposition parties have experienced several ups and downs in their respective support base. Rising income levels and lower worker participation in labor unions did not correlate directly to a shrinking support base for opposition parties. LDP political gaffes and scandals certainly worked in favor of the opposition parties' support base. At times the opposition parties also garnered substantial support among the segment of the new middle-class masses that supported stronger social policies, pacifism, and equality. To reclaim this block of votes, the LDP responded by placing a greater emphasis on social policy and alliances with other countries. This block of votes also shifted away from the opposition parties as pressure for market liberalization intensified and principles, such as pacifism, became linked to protectionism.

Aided by technology, globalization gained considerable momentum at the end of the twentieth century. This phenomenon divides national economies and seeks to merge and reintegrate the most competitive industries. This is a constant process. Those who are less competitive see their income levels drop.

Globalization affects all areas of policy. To secure their support base, governing parties must have as their primary concern those companies that compete internationally. The organizational structure to support these companies must be astutely and adroitly readjusted to changing market and other forces and must be a priority for governing parties. The catch phrases for the governing parties must be continuous technology innovation, improved efficiency, and increased competitiveness.

How the LDP responds to the tide of globalization will largely impact its support base. The LDP decided to present an optimistic and aggressive approach to tackling uncertainties presented by globalization. This message resonated with parts of the electorate who believe that although government deregulation and market liberalization negatively affect their employment and lives, the future would be bleaker if this path was not followed. This electorate is further fortified by Prime Minister Koizumi's own show of enthusiasm and courage in facing these risks himself. Therefore, the support base of the LDP during this period of globalization comes from those Japanese citizens who share their leaders' belief that the uncertainty of the future is best faced with optimism, strong resolve, and a bold approach.

Globalization presents challenges and forces states to refocus their policies. Waning economic growth, changing demographics, and gender inequality also pose challenges. Globalization prompts the Japanese governing party to shift from policies of macroeconomic management to those that can ameliorate economic standards and alter regulations. Those who are less competitive look to the government for financial assistance. Japan does not have a safety net. Social policies are under financial strain as demographics change to a predominantly aging population and economic growth remains poor. Gender equality is also weak, but here it is the corporate culture that must first change.

Since 2005 Japan's population has been in decline. Reversing this trend will do much to abet the above issues. Yet the high rate of childless couples has much to do with the conditions of economic uncertainty, strained social policies, and the lack of a safety net. Increased government allocation of funds will not resolve these issues. Globalization spotlights issues not previously considered serious, but all the same must be addressed for actors to be competitive. Policy emphasis is on deregulation and reducing government expenditures. Those ministries given large portions of the budget (e.g., Ministry of Land, Infrastructure, and Transport) are no longer a policy priority. That said, individual ministers can highlight specific policies and issues. The shift in the working dynamics of ministries has met resistance that is twofold. First, the bureaucracy of large ministries and agencies oppose political maneuvering; second, government bureaucratic culture does not endorse swift actions or quick decisions. To overcome the lack of bureaucratic will for policy redesign, the prime minister and his cabinet ministers are increasingly needed to be the driver of government policy.

Globalization makes the role of the Japanese prime minister and his cabinet indispensable to the political process. If the office of the prime minister serves only a symbolic role, then ministerial secretaries, campaign strategists, and political consultants are behind-the-scene workhorses on globalization-related issues. Any outgoing political statements must be carefully considered. The more critical the public, the more likely government's policies will be negatively received. The 2006 by-election in Chiba prefecture revealed that Ichiro Ozawa, the new president of the Democratic Party of Japan (DPJ), had outmaneuvered Koizumi with an emphasis on voter mobilization and the human touch over Koizumi's bold and carefully crafted messages.

The opposition parties must also strive to connect with their support base. Both globalization and reform of the lower house electoral system have changed the political landscape. Government spending habits have also changed. Pork-barrel projects are gone. A prolonged recession has drastically limited the government spending for large-scale public works, central government grants to the local government, and large-scale social policy projects. Moreover, voters are no longer swayed by Diet members' promises to secure central government funding.

Given the changed circumstances, how can a politician win the electorate's support? It is now the political message that mobilizes voter support. To rally support, Ozawa had face-to-face meetings with each organization in his district, cycled around his district to meet people, and when campaigning used a pile of crates as his podium. This approach is known as street-side campaigning, and was once the forte of the LDP. In contrast, Koizumi made campaign speeches from the top of a campaign truck and depended on his use of bold, skilful rhetoric to win the voters. At one time, the opposition parties were content to make grand overstatements, knowing that power was not within their reach. Today, the political environment has changed. The LDP attracts voters who are worried about the future and feel reassured by the party's bold, optimistic message. The LDP has chosen to employ courageous rhetoric over a detailed outline of specific policies. Conversely, opposition parties have relinquished their traditional strategy of overstatement, and instead have focused on presenting themselves as the real representatives of the people. Their emphasis is to shake hands, meet people, and be the sympathetic ear, ultimately stressing that they are the ones with the human touch.

THREE PRIME MINISTERS: YOSHIDA, TANAKA, AND KOIZUMI

Yoshida, Tanaka, and Koizumi are perfect profile as Japanese prime ministers who, to prove powerful, must act within the above summarized parameters.[13] In my scheme of analysis, Yoshida represents the period of military occupation as an authoritarian diplomat of aristocratic heritage. Tanaka represents the period of strong economic growth as captured in his bestselling book, *Remolding the Japanese Archipelagoes*. And Koizumi represents the period of globalization, focused on the deregulation and privatization of (semi)governmental firms. The period of military occupation extends till 1960 when Japan and the United States revised the Security Treaty, whereby the asymmetric alliance was moderated in the direction of more symmetry. The period of strong economic growth ends in 1985 with the signing of the Plaza Accord, designed to accelerate qualitatively and quantitatively the tide of globalization through deregulation of currency trade.

Yoshida

Shigeru Yoshida was a professional diplomat.[14] He was bold and self-confident, and, at the same time, arrogant and abrasive. In the 1940s he acted against the military to facilitate the termination of war against the United States. Because of his actions he was constantly monitored by internal security police, culminating in de facto house arrest for the remaining part of the war. Incoming General Douglas MacArthur purged from office many professional politicians for being tainted with wartime activities. Yoshida was selected as the leader of a newly established, conservative, pro-American political party. The country's surrender and the conclusion of the peace treaty had been handled by prime ministers very close to the Imperial House. But Yoshida handled the security treaty between the United States and Japan. Yoshida was articulate and decisive and at the same time thoughtful. Yoshida reasoned that since Japan had been completely defeated by the United States that wanted to retain and use all the military bases and facilities in Japan, it would not be a bad decision for Japan to conclude an alliance treaty in which the United States guarantees Japan's defense while Japan abandons its right to build its own armed forces to defend the country as outlined in the famous Article 9. Critics of Yoshida were abundant. The National Diet was not always well controlled by the governing coalition. Public opinion overwhelmingly opposed Yoshida's decision. Yet Yoshida was determined and decisive. He argued that a completely defeated Japan should make the best use of the situation, gallantly accepting the terms of the alliance and with determination focusing on recovering from the war to develop a highly industrialized country without the burden of building its own armed forces to cope with the Cold War confrontation.

In retrospect, Yoshida was the best man for the task. Among the conservatives the overriding propensity was to be exceedingly nationalistic, stressing patriotism and armed buildup even under the military occupation. The presence and power of such sentiments should not be underestimated. Yoshida had the audacity to go it alone with his decision. He persuaded the governing party even though the bulk of party members and supporters did not like what they viewed as a submissive position taken by the Japanese government. His characteristic aloofness and arrogance played well in this situation. Yoshida, not being a professional politician or a publicly elected figure, asked party leaders not to give him the task of intraparty persuasion when he accepted his party presidency. In return Yoshida said he would single-handedly deal with MacArthur. Vis-à-vis MacArthur, Yoshida was a good match. MacArthur tended to be overly self-confident and arrogant. MacArthur was both the United Nations commander in chief of its forces in Korea and the Supreme Commander of the Allied Powers in Japan. To handle MacArthur, a task critical to Japan's recovery, was best left to Yoshida. A single and simple message (complete obedience to power) sent by Yoshida resonated well with MacArthur. Moreover, Yoshida was aristocratic. When he signed documents, it was not Prime Minister Shigeru Yoshida but His Majesty's subject Shigeru.

In terms of the needs of both Yoshida and MacArthur, Yoshida was fortunate. Yoshida was not interested in the day-to-day handling of many administrative matters and the consensus-building mechanisms of party politics and formation of public opinion, and MacArthur was also equally indifferent to the task of day-to-day administration, which was left mostly to two key bureaucratic groups within the occupation authorities, those New Dealers carried over from the 1930s and those Cold War confrontationists. MacArthur was relieved by the U.S. role in what was called indirect rule. The longstanding Japanese bureaucracy continued to work tirelessly under Yoshida without many complicated daily problems arising because of the direct rule of the Japanese leadership. MacArthur's primary focus was the Cold War; Yoshida's was swift economic recovery and political stability for Japan.

In sum, Yoshida was a perfect fit for the type of Japanese politics under military occupation. His diplomatic career helped him to deal with MacArthur. Yoshida represented the dignity of a nation and sense of independence when foreign military forces occupied the country. Yoshida was a national savior in that he taught the Japanese people that they could be proud even at the nadir of their nation's existence, if one is proud of the nation and confident in the nation's ability to recover and grow.

Here, it is important to note that the steady work by the national bureaucracy during the period helped the military occupation to become a far less traumatic experience to the nation and helped the economic recovery and development to proceed amazingly smoothly.

Tanaka

Kakuei Tanaka was a professional politician.[15] A son of a horse dealer, he was a self-made man. Since he was a graduate from a technical engineering school, the training helped him immensely later in his political life when redesigning the Japanese economy and society. He acquired valuable experience in construction and in doing land deals with the government, small and large, and with financing sources.

His expertise was honed in his early days in Manchukuo (1932–1945) and wartime and immediate postwar time business activities when near chaos prevailed and a small dint of entrepreneurship mattered immensely in the near-complete vacuum. Tanaka's book *Reconstructing the Japanese Archipelago* lays out his longtime dreams with many concrete examples of the direction in which Japan should proceed as a highly industrialized country without many natural resources but a well-educated population with a strong work ethic. His strength was his ability to make use of the legislative drafting process and to forge a policy-focused coalition based on his own solid understanding of local folks' grievances and their resentful attitude toward the state and of his remarkable familiarity with numerous laws regulating infrastructural, industrial, and agricultural development in those less developed areas.

Tired of bureaucratic leaders who preceded him, the electorate saw Tanaka as a national hero-to-be at the time of his ascent to power. However, the first oil crisis of 1973–1974 dashed that expectation. Yet being articulate, aggressive, and agile, Tanaka was the best leader for the crisis. He assured the nation that they need not worry about petroleum shortages as the government was committed to vigorously accelerating the construction of oil tank bases and the exploration and exploitation of petroleum supply lines. When the United States made rapprochement with China amid the turmoil of the Vietnam War, Tanaka moved swiftly to do the same and more. In 1971 the United States realized rapprochement with China, best characterized as diplomatic normalization. Japan followed the United States but moved beyond diplomatic normalization to make peace, followed quickly by a combination of business and war reparation initiatives to help China in its modernization. Henry Kissinger raised concern that Tanaka could endanger U.S. national interest by acting so recklessly, so swiftly, and so independently.

Domestically, Tanaka was a perfect fit to Japanese politics during the period of strong economic growth. His vigor in moving himself upward was resonant with the national rise in the ranking of Gross National Product and economic growth rate. He was one of the youngest cabinet ministers and one of the youngest to become prime minister (1972–1974). What was striking about him was his encyclopedic knowledge of names and faces, and sometimes birthdays, of civil servants that impacted his policy interests and met his supporters'/clients' interests. He represented the focal points of business, bureaucracy, and the LDP.[16] Through his vigorous interactions with people from every walk of life he made his bureaucratic networks function in their most visible, tangible, and effective way. Important to stress here also is that his strength was in making and maintaining the national bureaucracy his close assistant. For that purpose, he interacted with bureaucrats intensely and extensively to give his directives on issues over cabinet ministers in charge of that portfolio. His knowledge of policy issues and bureaucrats' names was most remarkable. He was definitely hyperactive in policy areas. He symbolized the nation's immersion in high economic growth.

In terms of the governing party, his grip of power was near perfect. He outpaced his rivals on all fronts. When the economy grew by leaps and bounds, government revenue grew proportionately. Thus policy ideas and initiatives found numerous opportunities to be materialized. The governing party is made up of factions, each led by a faction leader. The Tanaka faction grew and grew because of his charisma, his financial assistance to faction members for their campaign money and other purposes, and his political tact in getting high-ranking posts in the party and the cabinet for his faction members, all of which culminated in the Tanaka faction being the predominant faction of the governing party. Yet power degenerates once it reaches its pinnacle. Tanaka was indicted by the prosecutors' office for bribery related to the Lockheed aircraft company and found guilty. While in the process of appealing the lower court sentence through a higher court, Tanaka passed away.

Koizumi

Junichiro Koizumi is a third-generation politician of a political dynastic family.[17] Koizumi was a lone wolf. He did not like meetings and dining with fellow politicians. Although he belonged to the Fukuda faction, he did not attend its meetings assiduously. After serving the country as prime minister for five years (2001–2006), he was alone with no followers. He did not speak much in meetings or in tête-a-têtes. Thus, he did not collaborate much with others. When he acted, he acted alone. When he acted, he surprised because he did not consult anyone beforehand. Throughout his career, two people stood out for their communications with this lone wolf. First, one of his three sisters, Nobuko, has been his secretary throughout his political career. Second, his secretary, Isao Iijima, was his right-hand man and a shrewd and strong gatekeeper for Koizumi. Most importantly, Koizumi did not visit his district often and did not bring pork-barrel projects to his district. Roads in the district are in poor condition. Public transportation to Tokyo is not very convenient.

His early political career was overshadowed by the predominance of the Tanaka faction. His lone wolf style was nurtured and honed during this period. Only after the strong economic growth period and the Cold War were over, did opportunities arrive. The first chance went to the opposition parties that took over power briefly in 1993–1994. Koizumi's chances came only after the Takeshita faction (successor of the Tanaka faction) enfeebled itself slowly with the onset of a long recession (1991–2006). The Tanaka faction was predominant from the time that Eisaku Sato appointed Tanaka secretary-general of the LDP in the mid 1960s till 2000 when Keizo Obuchi, the last prime minister of the Tanaka faction, suddenly passed away. Yoshinori Mori, the leader of the Fukuda faction, then captured power. Accordingly, members of the Fukuda faction were in the spotlight from 2000. Koizumi was one of them. In 2001 Mori was forced to resign due, in part, to his poor relationship with the mass media. Koizumi beat his rivals in the 2001 presidential election.

The 1985 Plaza Accord heralded in the period of globalization. The tide of globalization started to permeate every area of the globe. The much-vaunted national unity and solidarity was steadily undermined by deregulation and market liberalization that accompanies this tide of integration. Most directly, mediating institutions that include bureaucracy, political parties, trade unions, and interest groups are reduced in terms of their role and weight. Koizumi's politics of deregulation and remediation was his response to that tide and was meant to activate the economy. Koizumi politics means less mediation between the public and leaders. Hence his deregulatory legislations. Hence his kabuki performance. The strategy of pushing populism and raising participatory modes is adopted worldwide. In an era of globalization, of more floating votes, of less mediation, and of more digitalization, the transition from representative to monitory democracy has been taking place universally as the tide of globalization reduces the power of organized interests and bureaucratic fortresses.

Symbolic of his distaste for mediation is his style of decision making within the constitutional constraints and institutional framework.[18] When government discussions focused on how to reform and reduce the local transfer portion of national tax revenue to local governments, Koizumi brusquely advised the three ministers, who favored their pet projects to the exclusion of other bureaucratic interests, that if they did not come up with an integrated plan, he would make the decision. He avoided intervening in their discussions, knowing too well that bureaucrats act as representatives of a semisovereign entity. In order to dilute their self-claimed semisovereignty, the best he could do was not to assert prime minister's sovereignty but to force them to come up with the best option among themselves. If Koizumi meddled, he would only make more enemies by revealing his preferences. Once a final decision was made, Koizumi deleted all the phrases outlining the causes and reasons for adopting that policy, saying that every and each policy action had so many causes and reasons and that picking one or two of them only created more enemies and confusions. Only the content of the policy decision mattered. Hence his politics of privatizing postal service and encouraging farmers and small business to stand on their own feet. Whether prime ministers are able to exercise their power effectively depends on many factors. Koizumi would have been unsuccessful in an era of high economic growth, organized interests, and bureaucratic dominance. He was successful in the era of globalization because he had a flair for politics that befits the times, of less mediation, of more floating voters, and of far too long an economic depression.

It is important to note that since 1945, the majority of prime ministers were not able to exercise much power because of constraints and lack of knowledge, skills, flair, and fortune. The three prime ministers I examined are rare because they fit their time. The LDP was an exemplifier of such an organic entity in politics. To add salt to the wound, Japan's economic development momentum was lost, registering at best a 1–2 percent annual growth rate. Koizumi fitted the political environment perfectly. First, he was a lone wolf, an ultimate individualist. He was never too dependent on organizational backings, whether in his district, in his party politics, or in national politics. Second, he was a believed in small government, whether it was for his district or for the entire nation. Third, he believed in free trade at home and abroad. Fourth, he believed in the power of words and prose. He was astute in using the mass media. His language was combative, forceful, and determined, yet lasting no more than 10 minutes. His speech immediately preceding his call for a general election on August 8, 2005, was fierce, forceful, and tactful, arguing that because his postal liberalization bill was denied in the House of Councilors, he could not proceed with it in the National Diet and that he must ask the entire nation to give a respectful judgment as to whether the nation has confidence in Koizumi or not.

In terms of policy, he distinguished himself from other prime ministers. His instinct for right directions was apparent in policies that sought economic renewal through privatization and liberalization and diplomacy that leaned to one side at a time of crisis. The collapse of the economic bubble in 1991 brought Japan into an unprecedented long recession. Koizumi was assisted by cabinet minister Heizo Takenaka in his economic policy of recovery through innovation, including at the organizational level. By the time Koizumi's tenure ended and he retired as prime minister and member of the National Diet in 2006, the economy was showing signs of recovering. It is unfortunate that in 2008 the Lehman Brothers triggered the great global recession that hit Japan also hard. Koizumi privatized and liberalized a couple of semigovernmental enterprises, including postal services. The other pillar of his policy was leaning to one side at a time of global war against terrorism. His pro-U.S. policy was perfect in terms of timing, a minimum commitment of troops sent and withdrawn.

Koizumi declared full support for Bush's war against global terrorism but sent troops to Iraq only after Bush declared victory! Koizumi interpreted the constitutional ban on sending troops abroad that once the war was declared over, Japan could then send troops to help in reconciliation and recovery.

ZEITGEMAESSHEIT A STRONG LEADERSHIP REQUIREMENT

Zeitgemaessheit occurs when political leaders are in harmony with the political environment of the time. Yoshida was a perfect leader to deal with Douglas MacArthur, and he did not have to invest much energy in domestic rivals and other politicians and bureaucrats. Therefore, Yoshida's authoritarian personality did not hinder him from exercising his leadership; rather it helped him to do so. It was a simple hierarchical world. The United States was *supremo* bar none. Its representative was, therefore, supreme. Yoshida played the role of a sergeant who carried out decisions on behalf of the commander in chief. Some accused Yoshida of being a comprador, to which Yoshida rebuffed that those vanquished must act with a sense of dignity vis-à-vis those victors. He was fond of saying that taking up a prime ministership is what only the fool does.

Tanaka was a perfect leader to make the best use of bureaucrats to envision the policy direction and draft legislative bills, because he was experienced in finding solutions to those problems raised by clients and district people by connecting himself within a myriad of interactions among bureaucrats, politicians, and business leaders. Tanaka was a political entrepreneur in a complex organic whole. Just like karaoke, the button you push determines the political action. Every morning at his home he met dozens of people who sought his help in fixing their problems. Tanaka, after listening to them each for a couple of minutes, directly called someone who he believed would play a key role in resolving the situation. Needless to say, the larger the repertoire of karaoke, the better, and the more effective one becomes. Tanaka had the largest repertoire and he sang karaoke most effectively.

Koizumi was a perfect leader as a lone wolf who took risks and played the most effective roles on the basis of calculated moves. Koizumi is fond of kabuki, Japanese opera, and amid his most hectic times watched it. His motivation came from a desire to convey his message in the most effective and succinct prose by learning and emulating relevant scenes. When he called for a general election on August 8, 2005, he was rehearsing the passages from the *Man from La Mancha* (Don Quixote). When he publicly announced his soon-to-be resignation toward the end of his party's presidential tenure at the prime ministerial garden party in the Shinjuku-gyoen in spring 2006, he sang the short poem composed by Hosokawa Garasha, wife of a leader, who was besieged in her husband's absence for war assignment elsewhere by his enemy in the warring period of the late sixteenth century, and who committed suicide after singing the poem. Koizumi learned from drama and acted dramatically.

CONCLUSION

Japanese prime ministers are constrained by constitutional and institutional setups. The point I make is simply that with the parameters of the time well grasped and placed in control, Japanese prime ministers can be very powerful. I briefly examined the nature of those parameters in the three periods since the end of World War II—the period of military occupation, the period of strong economic growth, and the period of globalization. Then I examined the three prime ministers who fitted those parameters of the time—Yoshida, Tanaka, and Koizumi. It is not that every prime minister is a good fit for his time; rather the opposite is more often true. This is why the phenomenon of leadership deficit is often observed. Yoshida was perfect in that he was self-confident. His time was that of military occupation by foreigners. He had to act with dignity to uphold the nation's pride despite all the wounds and humiliation. Tanaka was the best man for his time. As long as he knew which button in the karaoke machine to push, karaoke democracy worked well. The politics of this period was based on the tightly knit organic whole often scripted by the bureaucratic corps. Tanaka was articulate in policy thinking, aggressive in persuasion, and agile in action. Koizumi was superb for his time. His obsession with pithy prose and sentences drawn from *kabuki* and *noh* (another traditional form of Japanese theater) was effective in an era of globalization and digitalization. *Zeitgemaessheit* cannot be underestimated when political leadership is examined.

The dramatic power change from the LDP to the DPJ on August 30, 2009, may be attributed in part to the lack of *Zeitgemaessheit* in the leadership style of Shinzo Abe (2006–2007), Yasuo Fukuda (2007–2008), and Taro Aso (2008–2009), the three prime ministers who succeeded Koizumi. They all lacked charismatic appeal and critical public leadership qualities. That said, the global economic recession triggered by the Lehman Brother's default meltdown and its negative consequences on the government and the legitimacy deficit, in part fed by the three successive leadership changes (all untested by popular vote) since 2005, did make an enormous difference. Yet none of the three ensuing national leaders after Koizumi had the leadership requirements for a period of globalization.[19] The DPJ understands now that *seiji shudo* (Politics take command!) does not work well once in power. MP Yukio Edano of the DPJ, for one, keeps repeating this message. The DPJ as an opposition kept criticizing the LDP government, arguing that the LDP government was too dependent on bureaucracy and too subservient to bureaucratically formulated policy packages and that the DPJ, once in power, would practice the politics of *seiji shudo*. But negating karaoke politics does not necessarily help the DPJ to play kabuki politics better. It must be noted that democracy is in transition. I argue that the type of democracy has been in great transition from karaoke to kabuki democracy in Japan, with many other versions of transitions occurring in many other democracies, but all in basic harmony with the argument made by John Keane, that is, the transition from representative democracy to monitory democracy is increasingly and ubiquitously unfolding and deepening around the globe. Tanaka and Noboru Takeshita relied heavily on bureaucracy and worked closely with it to mediate interests. Koizumi's practice was no mediation. He did not like bureaucracy or his own party, the LDP. Yoshida's style was that of a subject, a subject both to General MacArthur and Emperor Hirohito. His time was neither that of state sovereignty (Japan was occupied) nor that of globalization (Japan was recovering from war). Whether prime ministers fit the time is most critical. With regard to the post-Koizumi landscape, being a second or third generation politician, Abe, Fukuda, or Aso did not master a wide range of karaoke songs unlike Kakuei Tanaka. Prime Ministers and prime ministerial aspirants of the Democratic Party seem to be desired in terms of flair befitting an era of Kabuki democracy as long as they refuse to be a puppet of bureaucracy. It is important to note that the DPJ's 2009 victory was obtained by Ichiro Ozawa more than by Hatoyama. Ozawa represents a good mix of karaoke democracy, taking care of critical organized voters called rengo (federation of trade unions), and kabuki democracy, attacking bureaucracy and stressing livelihood first with his characteristically "good country folk" style of speaking clearly, directly but somewhat slowly, and with pauses placed between sentences.

NOTES

1. Inoguchi, "Japanese Contemporary Politics: Towards a New Interpretation," pp. 67–86; Inoguchi, "Can the LDP Survive Globalization?" pp. 45–49.
2. Van Wolferen, *The Enigma of Japanese Power*.
3. Inoguchi, "The Ghost of Absolutism"; Inoguchi, *Tokugawa Moderu o Sutekirenai Nihonjin* (The Japanese Who Cannot Throw Away the Tokugawa Model).
4. Inoguchi, "Japanese Contemporary Politics."
5. Inoguchi, "The Pragmatic Evolution of Japanese Democratic Politics"; Inoguchi, "Federal Traditions and Quasi-Federalism in Japan," pp. 216–289.
6. Inoguchi, "Japanese Contemporary Politics"; Inoguchi, "Parliamentary Opposition under (Post-) One-Party Rule: Japan," pp. 113–132.
7. Inoguchi, "The Pragmatic Evolution of Japanese Democratic Politics"; Inoguchi, "Federal Traditions and Quasi-Federalism in Japan."
8. Murakami et al., *Bunmei toshite no Ie-shakai* (The Ie-Society as Civilization).
9. Inoguchi, "The Pragmatic Evolution of Democratic Politics."
10. Kasaya, *Shukun Oshikome no Kozo* (The Structure of Placing a Domain Lord under Home Arrest). Ikegami, *The Taming of the Samurai: Honorific Individualism and the Making of Modern Japan*.
11. Inoguchi, "Japan: The Personalization of Politics-Kozumi and Japanese Politics."
12. Van Wolferen, *The Enigma of Japanese Power*.
13. As for all the prime ministers in Japanese modern history, see Toriumi, *Rekidai Naikaku Shusho Jiten* (Encyclopedia of Prime Ministers).
14. Kosaka, *Saisho Yoshida Shigeru*; Hara, *Yoshida Shigeru*; John Dower, *Empire and Aftermath Yoshida Shigeru and the Japanese Experience 1878–1954*.
15. Iwami, *Tanaka Kakuei: Seiji no Tensai* (Genius of Politics); Shigezo, *Seijika Tanaka Kakuei* (The Politician Tanaka Kakuei).

16. *Asahi Shimbun*, January 5, 2010.
17. Shimizu Masato, *Kantei Shudo:Koizumi Junichiro no Kakumei* (Prime Minister's Leadership: The Revolution of Koizumi Junichiro); Inoguchi, "Japan: The Personalization of Politics-Kozumi and Japanese Politics," pp. 209–227.
18. Private conversation with a high-ranking bureaucrat who participated in this high-level policymaking on the reduction of the local transfer. (December 21, 2010, in Tokyo)
19. Inoguchi, "Political Parties and Democracy: Japan."

Bibliography

Asahi Shimbun, January 5, 2010.

Dower, John, *Empire and Aftermath Yoshida Shigeru and the Japanese Experience 1878–1954* (New York: Harvard University Asia Center, 1988).

Hara, Yoshihisa, *Yoshida Shigeru—Sonno no Seijika* (A Imperial Subject as a Politician) (Tokyo: Iwanami Shoten, 2005).

Hayasaka, Shigezo, *Seijika Tanaka Kakuei* (The Politician Tanaka Kakuei) (Tokyo: Chuokoronsya, 1987).

Ikegami, Eiko, *The Taming of the Samurai: Honorific Individualism and the Making of Modern Japan* (Cambridge, MA: Harvard University Press, 1997).

Inoguchi, Takashi, "The Pragmatic Evolution of Japanese Democratic Politics," in Michele Schmiegelow, ed., *Democracy in Asia* (New York: St. Martin's, 1997).

———, "Federal Traditions and Quasi-Federalism in Japan," in Baogang He, Brian Galligan, and Takashi Inoguchi, eds., *Federalism in Asia* (London: Edward Elgar, 2007).

———, "The Ghost of Absolutism," paper presented at the Anglo-Japanese Daiwa Fund Lectures, London, November 22, 2007.

———, "Can the LDP Survive Globalization?" *Education about Asia*, 12, no. 3 (2008): 45–49.

———, "Parliamentary Opposition under (Post-) One-Party Rule: Japan," *The Journal of Legislative Studies*, 14, no. 1/2 (2008): 113–132.

———, "Japanese Contemporary Politics: Towards a New Interpretation," in Rien Segers, ed., *A New Japan for the Twenty-First Century: An Inside Overview of Current Fundamental Changes and Prospects* (London: Routledge, 2008), pp. 67–86.

———, "Japan: The Personalization of Politics-Kozumi and Japanese Politics," in Jean Blondel and Jean Louis-Thiebault, eds., *Political Leadership, Parties and Citizens: The Personalization of Leadership* (London: Routledge, 2009), pp. 209–228.

———, *Nihon seiji no nazo: Tokugawa model o sutekirenai Nihonjin* (The Enigma of Japanese Politics: The Japanese Who Cannot Throw Away the Tokugawa Model) (Tokyo: Nishimura shoten, 2010).

———, "Political Parties and Democracy: Japan," in Kay Lawson and Baogang He, eds., *Political Parties and Democracy: Eurasia and Asia* (New York: Praeger, 2010), pp. 173–189, 261–263.

Iwami, Takao, *Tanaka Kakuei: Seiji no Tensai* (Tanaka Kakuei: Genius of Politics) (Tokyo: Gakuyo shobo, 1998).

Kasaya, Kazuhiko, *Shukun Oshikome no Kozo* (The Structure of Placing a Domain Lord under Home Arrest) (Tokyo: Heibonsha, 1988).

Keane, John, *The Life and Death of Democracy* (London: Simon and Schuster, 2009).

Kissinger, Henry A., *Does America Need a Foreign Policy?: Towards a Diplomacy for the 21st Century* (New York: Simon and Schuster, 2001).

Kosaka, Masataka, *Saisho Yoshida Shigeru* (Prime Minister Shigeru Yoshida) (Tokyo: Chuokoronshinsha, 2006).

Krauss, Ellis and Robert Pekkanen, *The Rise and Fall of Japan's LDP* (Ithaca, New York: Cornell University Press, 2010).

Murakami, Yasusuke Shunpei Kumon, and Seizaburo Sato, *Bnmei toshite no Ie-shakai* (The Ie-Society as Civilization) (Tokyo: Chuo koronsha, 1979).

Shimuzu, Mahito, *Kantei Shudo:Koizumi Junichiro no Kakumei* (Prime Minister's Leadership: The Revolution of Koizumi Junichiro) (Tokyo: Nihon Keizai Shinbunsha, 2005).

Toriumi, Yasushi, ed., *Rekidai Naikaku Shusho Jiten* (Encyclopedia of Prime Ministers) (Tokyo: Yoshikawa Kobunkan, 2009).

Van Wolferen, Karel, *The Enigma of Japanese Power* (New York: Alfred Knopf, 1989).

Whiteley, Paul, "Is the Party Over? The Decline of Party Activism and Membership across the Democratic World," *Party Politics*, September 2010.

2

The System of Bureaucrats in Japan

Hiroaki Inatsugu

Introduction

Bureaucrats and civil servants play an extremely important role in the contemporary welfare state, and the ultimate governmental capacity to solve various problems is dependent on the quality of its staff. How to recruit such talents, train, select, and motivate them are perpetual themes for the study of personnel and public administration. As Herman Finer said 70 years ago, "The question of personnel . . . , that is the heart of the administration."[1]

In Japan, a total of 3.61 million people work in the public sector, of which 0.66 million work for the national government and 2.95 million for local governments.[2] This is about 5.5 percent of the working population of Japan, which is extremely low compared to the percentages in other advanced industrialized countries (22 percent in France, 28 percent in Sweden, 11 percent in Germany, and 14 percent in the United States).[3]

If we look at the number of public employees per every thousand people of the population, Japan has only 33.1 personnel, even including the armed forces. This is extremely low compared to 79.5 in the UK, 87.6 in France, 78.1 in the United States, and 55.8 in Germany.[4]

It is said that the resources of the relatively low number of government employees are fully committed by the administrative activities conducted in Japan.[5]

Small Number of Employees and Huge Amount of Governmental Work

Meanwhile, some argue that in Japan the administrative branch is excessively powerful compared to legislative or judicial branches of government. Many political scientists in the United States have characterized Japan as a "state-led country" or a "developmental state."

For example, Chalmers Johnson described the bureaucrats as the central power of the Japanese government, which has fostered Japanese economic growth to the extent that it has been called a "miracle."[6] It was Johnson who named Japan a developmental state, thereby emphasizing the bureaucratic importance in leading the Japanese economy:

> Although it is influenced by pressure groups and political claimants, the elite bureaucracy of Japan makes most major decisions, drafts virtually all legislation, controls the national budget, and is the source of all major policy innovations in the system.[7]
>
> The political system of the developmental state covertly separates reigning and ruling: the politicians reign and the bureaucrats rule.[8]

I do not intend to discuss here whether or not this is an accurate description. However, the truth is that the Japanese administrative sector has handled massively diverse and complex administrative work with a relatively small number of employees.

Moreover, Japanese civil servants are devoted to their work, and loyal to the ministries for which they work. Normally *Kasumigaseki* (the headquarters of the government ministries) bureaucrats work from 9:00 a.m. to midnight or later every day.

People have paid great respect to the efficiency of the public administration of the Japanese government for a long time. However, recently in some quarters the prestige of central bureaucracies is decreasing. Since the 1990s in particular, mass media and political scientists have repeatedly criticized managerial issues in the central ministries for holding up, for example, scandals involving their elite bureaucrats. People are criticizing the inefficiencies of civil servants and calling for restructuring.

In response to such public criticisms, the Shinzo Abe government introduced comprehensive civil service reform in 2008. Although the final picture is not yet clear at the time of writing in 2011, I mention, in the final section of this chapter, the direction and summary of intended reforms.

There are several excellent studies about bureaucrats in Japan.[9] Most of them have focused on the social origin or strata of higher civil servants, the relations between bureaucrats and politicians, and so on. However, a few studies examine how civil servants are trained and promoted, what their pay scales are like, and especially how noncareer bureaucrats are treated.

In this chapter, after reviewing the history I examine the above-mentioned issues and make the following argument. Although Japan's civil service is based on a "career system," a personnel/wage system—which emphasizes intraorganizational balance—has been adopted to "mobilize to the maximum" not just the career bureaucrats but civil servants as a whole, the majority of whom are in the noncareer stream. The Japanese central ministries have also adopted an efficient personnel/wage system, which mobilizes the resources of their employees to the maximum via the "slow promotion" (late selection) system and the "accumulated awards" system. This personnel/wage system, along with the physical environment (*ohbeyashugi*), ambiguous job division, and the practice of working cooperatively, all of which are mutually complementary, has made the Japanese public sector efficient.[10]

The civil service reform under discussion brings in partial, but major, alterations to this system. A possible outcome may be that the mutual inter-dependence of the entire system is lost, and, as a result, the adage of "small in numbers but huge in workload" may no longer apply to Japanese bureaucrats in the near future.

A BRIEF HISTORY OF JAPAN'S CIVIL SERVICE SYSTEM

Merit System and Internal Promotion System

The current system is merit based, that is, all positions from administrative vice minister to rank-and-file workers are filled by regular service employees, hired according to the results of their civil service examinations.

The rigid structure of internal promotions is key to understanding the Japanese civil service system. In pre- and postwar periods, this was a system in which, no matter how capable a worker may be, all the same-year entrants were promoted at the same speed (simultaneous entry, simultaneous promo-tion system to a certain rank). No one can be promoted to a higher rank unless he or she goes through certain stages. Only those who observe this rule and succeed in the competition can reach the highest positions. This rule has prevented political parties from intervening and selectively promot-ing certain bureaucrats. Let us review the evolution of this system.

The Early Period of the Civil Service System

Under the Imperial Constitution of 1889, sovereign power was vested in the emperor. The Diet, the cabinet, and the courts were established. Even though these three organs of government (legislative, executive, and judicial) were set up as independent bodies, the emperor had supreme authority over them. The emperor was also commander in chief of the armed forces and was responsible for the appointment of senior officials in the civil service.

Before the promulgation of the Imperial Constitution, the Meiji govern-ment introduced in 1887 a system of civil service examinations, with reference to Prussia as its model. In the previous year, the government announced the ordinance to establish the Imperial University. Tokyo Imperial University was established with the expectation that it would play a substantial role in the training of civil servants, and those who graduated from this institution would constitute the main body of the civil service. This examination-based system was introduced at a fairly early stage for a late-developer country.

Personnel administration was first established at this time. Two open civil service examinations were held for the positions of *koutou-kan* (elite bureaucrat) and *han'nin-kan* (lower bureaucrat) grades, and a rigid distinc-tion between the two existed. Below the *han'nin-kan* category, there were the *koin* (rank-and-file employee) and *youjin* (custodial service employee) categories, with each ministry responsible for hiring employees under these categories through private contracts.

The Elimination of the Spoils System

In 1898 the Ohkuma-Itagaki cabinet, which was the first party cabinet in Japan, assigned many party members to become officials of imperial appointment, such as administrative vice minister, bureau chiefs of ministries, and governors of prefectures.

This indicates a shift toward a spoils system. However, this cabinet collapsed within four months, and the second cabinet led by Yamagata was formed. Under the Yamagata cabinet, the ordinance for the employment of civil servants was revised to abolish the free appointment of imperial-appointee civil servants and to impose strict constraints on the revision process thereafter. This ordinance limited, as much as possible, the influence of party politics on the bureaucracy. However, even after this, disputes between the bureaucracy and the politicians over the range of free employment continued, and the elitist government leaders tried to prevent the advancement of party and private sector power into the bureaucracy.

The idea of upholding the neutrality of the bureaucracy through a complete internal promotion system was maintained as a bulwark against political interference.

The Differences between Elite Bureaucrats and Others under the Imperial Constitution

Unlike the higher officials, the noncareer civil servants or employees belonged to a different class, and their promotion and advancement were governed by a totally different rule. Even the cafeteria and restroom for this stream of employees were separate. The ministries were keen on maintaining the morale of the high officials, but were indifferent about lower officials and regular employees. In the prewar period, the range of government activity was not as extensive, and motivation of the noncareer officials was considered to be unnecessary. Consequently, the intraorganizational difference in wages corresponding to status stratification was fairly large throughout most of the prewar period. In this sense, the prewar civil service system belonged to the elitist model found typically in the French personnel administration.

New Constitution and Reform

Defeat in World War II brought sudden and sweeping changes to Japan, comparable to those of the Meiji Restoration. Under the guidance of General Douglas MacArthur and his staff, a new constitution, replacing the Imperial Constitution, was promulgated in 1947. This was followed by enactment of the National Public Service Law (hereinafter NPSL), which brought about major reforms in public administration.

Since the constitution and the NPSL were based on the principles of democratic government and respect for fundamental human rights, public administration had to adjust both institutionally and functionally. The reform of the personnel system can be characterized as a radical transformation of civil servants from government officials of the emperor to servants of the whole nation based on the enactment of the NPSL. In the original NPSL, the position of administrative vice minister was deemed to be one of free appointment; however, after the following year's revision it was again changed so as to be treated as part of a career service position.

Following these battles to achieve neutrality, the current system was established. As I pointed out earlier, the thoroughness of internal promotion is the key to understanding the Japanese civil service system.

The Establishment of the NPA

The National Personnel Authority (NPA) was established in 1948 after the revision of the NPSL, reflecting the strong leadership of the General Head Quarters (GHQ).

At first, the GHQ's intention of comprehensive reform via the NPA was not accepted by other ministries, which especially disliked the introduction of the position classification system. This fundamentally changed personnel from being person-centered into being work-centered. The involved actors opposed such initiatives on the basis of not being suitable for the human resource practices of Japan.

Severe political battles between the NPA and other ministries also marked this time period. Although the ministries tried to abolish the NPA several times, they failed. During these struggles, the NPA gave up on executing a comprehensive package of civil service system reforms.

Yet certain ministries were eventually satisfied that they could maintain the same highflyer system and recruit the same type of newly graduated employees through the maintenance of the prewar examination system, and subsequently stopped their attacks on the NPA. Bureaucrats then became busy with the introduction of economic policies and other public duties. Finally, the NPA was able to establish its role in the maintenance and development of the national public service system, which included the right to enact NPA rules concerning the arbitration of fairness and behavioral norms for public officials.[11] Overall, the NPA worked for the expansion of noncareer employee benefits; however, little complaint was heard from the highflyers. This was because wages increased every year for all workers, and the wages of younger employees never surpassed those of their seniors. This was possible because the government budget expanded along with the rapid growth of the Japanese economy.

THE CIVIL SERVICE SYSTEM AFTER WORLD WAR II UNTIL 2009

In the case of national civil service entrance examinations, employees are initially appointed, in principle, through a competitive examination conducted by the NPA, which is open equally to all citizens. However, since the ultimate appointing power is vested in the head of each ministry, final selections are made after each ministry has comprehensively evaluated eligible applicants who passed the NPA entrance examination.

NPA civil service examinations are categorized into Classes 1, 2, and 3. Those who are employed through the Class 1 examination (formerly called the Senior A Class examination; renamed in 1985), who are reputed to be the best and the brightest elite bureaucrats, are called the "career group" or "careers."

It is extremely difficult to pass this examination; for example, in 2008, only 1,545 out of 21,200 applicants, or 1 in 13.7, passed. (Among these, if we look only at the examination categories of administration, law, and economics, taken by those desiring to follow a typical career track, only 752 out of 13,646 applicants, or 1 in 18.1, passed.) Successful NPA examination candidates have to face a final selection by the ministry he or she would like to join. Fewer than 40 percent of the successful NPA examination candidates can join one of the ministries.

Those who passed the other two types of examination, Class 2 (four-year college graduates, mainly) and Class 3 (high-school graduates, mainly) are generally called "noncareers." The career group comprises 4.3 percent (15,356 persons) of the total number of employees (359,659).[12] Career group members, however, account for more than 80 percent of all executive positions (departmental division director, *honshokacho* or above) within ministries' head offices.

On entry, personnel administration is conducted under the authority and responsibility of each ministry, in particular by the personnel division of each minister's secretariat. In general practice, employees are rotated to different positions every few years under the personnel division initiative. After someone moves to a new position, he or she develops the necessary knowledge and skills on the job, under the guidance of the supervisor and supporting assistance from colleagues or subordinates.

Each person's specialty is flexible. After being appointed to a ministry, the individual is trained and rises within the hierarchy of the organization, utilizing job rotation, which is applied periodically. Both the management and employees accept the principle of lifetime employment and personnel administration throughout their working lives from the day they are appointed to their retirement, including the seniority system and job rotation.

Under lifetime employment, the system of promotion is one of the most important factors in personnel administration. Promotion is decided on a merit basis. No examination is conducted regarding promotion.

Promotion Management of Elite Bureaucrats

If we look at the promotion management of career bureaucrats, those who are hired in the same year and follow almost identical career paths until their mid-thirties, or when they become acting directors, their ranks and wages are basically the same.

About the time they turn 40 and become directors, the differences eventually become apparent, and while some are promoted to a higher rank (such as deputy director-general or *kyoku-ji-cho/shingikan*), others retire and start a new life, as they "golden parachute" into related organizations and private companies (*amakudari*, literally means "descent from heaven"). Such a policy is designed to avoid having people of the same start year with the same number of years of experience positioned in different ranks within the hierarchy. Such an "up-or-out" policy is made possible by the ample source of *amakudari* as occurs in public corporations, business organizations, and the private sector.

To reiterate, career bureaucrats of the central ministries are subject to strict selection when they are first hired, and then are promoted at the same pace until they reach 40 years or so of age, a procedure essentially similar to "sponsored mobility." However, internally this leads to fierce competition for advancement, and rigorous selection is conducted thereafter in the process of promotion. This system can be described as a "tournament" (an elimination series), in which long-term competition takes place.

Evaluations for promotion are based on a comprehensive assessment of the employee's accumulated achievements, and such a selection process continues for promotions up to the highest rank, the position of administrative vice minister. This system conforms to the slow promotion policy, a practice long adopted by typical Japanese corporations and described below.

A characteristic of the promotion management of Japanese corporations is the so-called slow promotion system or late selection model, in which workers who join large Japanese firms are typically not differentiated from their cohort until 10 to 15 years after they join, after which there is considerable differentiation according to ability. This practice is in contrast with the typical American fast track or early selection system.

Corporations give various reasons for adopting this practice, such as "it permits the accurate evaluation of an employee's ability," "it increases the motivation of employees," or "it permits employees to better develop their abilities."

Pay of Elite Bureaucrats

At most of the larger Japanese corporations, the personnel system is structured in line with the practice of longterm employment. As for salaries, a senioritybased system has been adopted, which takes living costs into account. However, differences in pay gradually emerge among those who are hired in the same year, depending on whether or not one has been promoted in position or salary grade. Economists argue that "it is the substantial lifetime pay differences stemming from different rates of promotion that motivate employees in the Japanese firm."[13]

This salary system has also been adopted by the public sector. The following is a closer look at the public sector's salary scale, which determines not only an individual's monthly pay but also bonus and retirement compensation directly, and pension indirectly. A new career member is graded at Step 1 of Pay Grade 3 when first hired, and is quickly elevated to a higher pay grade under the rule of "simultaneous entry, simultaneous promotion." After being upgraded from Pay Grade 3 to Grade 4 (the grade of senior section chiefs) in the fifth year of employment, further upgrades occur every two years, finally reaching Grade 10 (the grade of head office division directors or *honshokacho*) at 40 years of age. Those who fail in the competition for promotions begin to retire when they are around 47 years old. The winners, meanwhile, receive substantial increases in pay when they are promoted to the so-called designated posts (such as *kyoku jicho* or deputy director-general of the bureau), whose pay grades are much higher than Grade 11.

When some are promoted to *kyokucho* or director-general of the bureau, those who are not promoted retire; and when the most successful person is promoted to *jimujikan* or administrative vice minister, the other *kyokucho* retire and start a new life outside the ministry.

The wage differentials resulting from differences in position and rank are relatively small, compared to other countries. The pay raises associated with promotions are not very large either, except when the promotion is an upgrading to a designated post. Seniority-based factors, such as periodical pay raises and wage revisions, are more significant.

As explained above, all higher bureaucrats who entered the ministry in the same year advance simultaneously until they are 40 or so years old, or when they reach the level of division director, with no visible difference in their compensation. Since those who are not promoted to a higher position must retire under the uprout personnel policy, whether or not one is promoted after a certain age and beyond the position of division director results in considerable differences in lifetime earnings, depending on variations in actual retirement age, retirement allowances, and places where they may *amakudari* or descend with a golden parachute.

First of all, a bureaucrat's retirement age is delayed the higher he or she is promoted, which means a salary for that much longer.[14] Besides, the salary is paid on a designated salary scale, set at as high a standard as that of board members in the private sector.

Second, the bureaucrat's retirement allowance grows larger the longer he or she remains in the civil service. This allowance is calculated by multiplying the monthly wage at the time of retirement by a certain number of months. The number of months rises sharply with the years spent in service, particularly if it is greater than 25, up to a maximum of about 60 months. The monthly wage, which is the basis of this calculation, also increases according to seniority, and it increases sharply when the employee is promoted to a designated position. Thus, as these two considerations have an overlapping effect when applied together, those who work for a longer period of time receive much higher retirement allowances. Those who advance to the position of administrative vice minister can receive a much greater amount than those who failed earlier in the competition for success. (For example, a 59yearold administrative vice minister receives 70 million yen [about US$850,000] in retirement allowances, compared to a 47yearold division director who receives only 20 million yen [about US$245,000].)

Third, a bureaucrat's final post affects the place where one can parachute or the treatment received once there. Takenori Inoki has proven, by analyzing the data that the more successful one has been in competition within a ministry at the time of retirement, and the higher the final post, the higher the position in a public corporation will be and the longer the stay after parachuting there.[15] In addition, such a bureaucrat is able to *amakudari* to a public corporation of higher status, and receives better pay there than would otherwise be the case. From this standpoint, Inoki argues that *amakudari* can be considered as a form of "deferred compensation" whose content (in terms of pay and treatment) is determined on the basis of the retiree's actual performance while an active member of a ministry. In addition, he argues that *amakudari*, with its integral mechanisms of deferred pay and early retirement, both of which seem to provide strong incentives enabling the potentially rich resources of the Japanese bureaucracy to be realized, energizes human resources in the bureaucracy.

Thus, depending on how far a bureaucrat is promoted, there are substantial differences in lifetime earnings among those who are hired in the same year, caused by resulting differences in retirement age, retirement allowance, and conditions after *amakudari*. Such promotions are based on the collective effect of evaluations over a long period of time. Past contributions are gradually accumulated and used as the basis for determining job transfers and promotions. In short, the accumulated achievements (most of which are not recorded formally on personnel files, but are "recorded" as reputations or in the memories of members of the ministry) of a bureaucrat over the years determines whether or not he or she is promoted after the age of 40. Those who are defeated in the competition for success must leave at a younger age, receive lower retirement allowances, and accept lesser treatment at a second, post*amakudari* job. Those who can advance to a much higher position can stay longer in the ministry, receive higher retirement allowances, and parachute to higher positions in other corporations. In addition, they can stay in their post*amakudari* jobs longer, and continue to receive deferred compensation. It can, therefore, be said that one of the characteristics of the Japanese public personnel system is the accumulated awards or accumulated merit system.

Promotion Management of Noncareer Bureaucrats

It is often said that the relationship between the career and noncareer groups is akin to the relationship between the *Shinkansen* or bullet train and the standard-line trains. Noncareer bureaucrats are promoted to section chief only after they turn 30 and to acting director in the main ministry only after they turn 40 years of age, at the earliest. Among them, very few reach departmental division director within the head office, and even if they are lucky enough to be promoted to that level, it would be after their fiftieth birthday.

If only the speed of promotion of the two groups is looked at, there is a great difference between the noncareer and the career groups, the latter being promoted almost simultaneously up to division director within the head office. However, positions in the regional offices or agencies are open to the noncareer group as well. In order to raise the morale of the noncareer stream, "stars" among them are occasionally promoted to major posts such as deputy director-general of the bureau. Thus, relatively high "target grades" are set for the noncareer group.

Seniority-based advancement is carried out among the the noncareer segment, and according to the NPA study, simultaneous entry, simultaneous promotion is implemented in 80 percent of all ministries up to the position of section chief, with differences becoming apparent only from the time they are promoted to acting director.[16] This usually occurs when they are in their mid-forties.[17] One survey conducted by the NPA shows that 40 percent of the noncareer group reached Grade 8 (acting director within the head office, or division director in a regional office), and 10 percent reached Grade 10 (division director within the head office, or deputy director-general of a regional office).[18]

Therefore, although their career paths are different from those of the career bureaucrats group, the noncareer stream as a category also go through the simultaneous entry, simultaneous promotion system until their early forties, and are subjected to intense competition among themselves thereafter. (In the case of the noncareer group, however, those who are not promoted can wait for the next opportunity, since they are not forced into retirement as are the career group under the up-orout policy.)

Pay of Noncareer Bureaucrats

A noncareer bureaucrat (who is typically a highschool graduate and has passed the Class 3 examinations) is initially graded at Grade 1, which is the lowest end of the pay scale. After staying there for five years, he or she advances to Grade 2 and stays there for three years, after which he or she advances to Grade 3. (Up to this point, all those in the noncareer group that took the Class 3 examination and are hired in the same year are basically promoted together.) After four years or more at Grade 3, the individual may be promoted to section chief and advance to Grade 4. From that point onward, the noncareer group hired in the same year is promoted at different paces from one another, with resulting differentials in pay, which gradually grow larger; by the time they retire, there are substantial differences in monthly wages among them. When the extra amounts of managerial allowance and bonus are added, there is a difference of more than 50 percent per year. Their retirement allowances also differ.

Moreover, *amakudari* positions are often prepared by the ministry for those in the noncareer stream who are ultimately promoted to high positions.[19] Promotions, or the lack thereof, thus have a considerable effect, even among the noncareer group.

Those in the noncareer group who entered the service in the same year thus receive the same pay until a certain level. Beyond that level, fierce competition for the next promotion appears, and with it wage differences start to appear, which gradually become substantial by the time of retirement. This reflects differences in promotion or advancement based on accumulated merit or contributions. The differences in accumulated talents and efforts, built up over many years, are evaluated and used when determining advancements or promotions. The structure of the pay system, therefore, enables the accumulation of compensations, or in other words, the incentives provided by the accumulated awards system.

Intraorganizational Balance Between Elites and Nonelites

1. *"Double Shogi's Piece" Type of Promotion Management*

Figure 2.1 displays the characteristics of the promotion management of Japan's national civil service employees, outlined above. First, career workers and noncareer workers are subject to a strict selection process, and the promotion management applied differs completely. The career and noncareer groups are also promoted at a different pace. Career bureaucrats are promoted simultaneously, as one class, up to the position of division director, reached around 40 years of age. This kind of group promotion is possible because of the existence of the noncareer category, which makes up the majority of bureaucrats. Those in the career group among the same entry class are promoted together until the position of acting director and division director, positions to which few in the noncareer group are promoted. This aspect is essentially similar to sponsored mobility.

After those in the career group attain the position of division director, however, fierce competition for further promotions await them, and since an uporout policy is applied from this stage onward, those who fall out of the competition must leave the ministry. Such an up-or-out policy is made possible by the ample availability of places to where dropouts from the competition may *amakudari*, such as public corporations, business organizations, the private sector, and local governments.

As for the noncareer group, they are promoted simultaneously as one class up to the rank of section chief, which they typically attain in their mid-thirties. However, they compete for promotions thereafter, in the lower part of the pyramid. Those in the noncareer group who succeed in reaching the rank of acting director then compete even more fiercely among themselves,

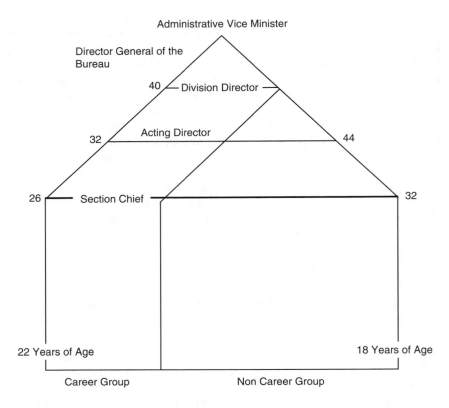

Figure 2.1 "Double Shogi-Piece" Type of Promotion Management.

with a very small number managing to reach the position of division director in the head office of the ministry. In this selection process, those who are defeated are not forced out of the ministry. In other words, the up-or-out policy is not applied here, and those who are not promoted stay at their current grade and rank. However, since the "Japanese public organization is formed giving sensitive consideration to noncareers' position and role,"[20] those less successful suffer no loss of morale, and continue working hard until retirement while maintaining their dignity. However, if they wish, the noncareer group can remain in the region of their choice until retirement, an option not available to the career group. Thus various arrangements are made to increase the internal drive of the noncareer group.

As we have seen, both the career and noncareer groups, up to a certain level, are promoted simultaneously (the slow promotion or late selection system) within each category, and beyond a certain level, a fierce, pyramid-shaped competition takes place. This is a "Shogi's piece" type of promotion management in which the two categories, career and noncareer, are treated as one from the standpoint of such management. It could be said that an "overlapping Shogi's piece" is the main characteristic of the promotion management of national civil service employees as a whole. To put it another way, a slow promotion system is applied in each category, and "compartmentalized competition," or a compartmentalized slow promotion system exists for the system as a whole.

2. *Accumulated Awards System (or Accumulated Merit System)*

On paper, nonaccumulated awards, that is, payments, which are directly linked with short-term evaluations, may have been made in Japan as part of bonuses or as a special pay raise. However, this has been unpopular, because "in actual practice, it would be difficult because the subjectivity of the evaluator inevitably interferes."[21] Such payments have, therefore, been made equally to all employees, without differentiating them.

As a result, no short-term differences in pay, based on achievements, have been evident in Japan's civil service remuneration system until recently; rather, winners are determined via a long-term competition, and the differences show in their lifetime earnings. As explained above, in the case of the career group, promotions (or the lack thereof) to designated posts such as bureau chief and administrative vice minister determine retirement age, retirement allowance, and the location and conditions of their *amakudari*. In the case of the noncareer group, those who entered the service in the same year gradually find differences in their pay, prompted by promotions and pay raises, or the lack thereof. The chief characteristic of the pay system of Japan's national civil service is that each arrangement functions as an accumulated awards incentive system.

3. *Personnel and Pay Policies that Produce Intraorganizational Balance*

The promotion systems currently used by the civil service of various countries can be broadly categorized into what Peter Self calls a "closed career system" and an "open career system."[22] West European countries and Japan belong to the former, whereas the United States belongs to the latter. According to Self, the chances of recruiting talented personnel who remain strongly committed to their work are higher in a closed career system.

The key characteristic of the personnel administration of the French system is the conspicuous difference in positions between various categories. A bureaucrat's starting and final ranks differ greatly depending on whether or not the individual attended the École Nationale d'Administration (ENA). Subsequently, the class ranking on graduation from the ENA carries great weight in determining whether or not the graduate is admitted to the Grands Corps, which creates further differences among bureaucrats. This is a typical example of the "early promotion" system, in which elites are selected at a very early stage. Wages are paid to guarantee an appropriate lifestyle for the rank of the recipient, and the differences among the various categories in wages are substantial. In the French public service system, the walls between different categories and groups of workers are indestructible, and the starting position and wages of an ENA graduate are higher than the final (i.e., at the time of retirement) position and wages of those in the lower categories. Internal examinations for advancement to a higher category also exist; however, the success rate is low. Therefore, workers in the lower category tend to be frustrated, and it is easy for morale problems to emerge.[23]

In contrast to France, where a significant gap in terms of promotion and wages between career and noncareer employees exists, full consideration is paid to the noncareer group in Japan with respect to personnel management, with emphasis placed on intraorganizational balance. Everyone, including the career officials, starts from the very bottom rank of the organization when they enter the ministry. And those in the noncareer group also have the opportunity for promotion to a high position, which most career bureaucrats cannot even reach.

Attention to such intraorganizational balance has also been paid in the wage structure. Differences in pay between the career and noncareer streams are small when both are still relatively young, although a difference does gradually develop. An employee in the career group earns only 25–30 percent more than another employee of a similar age in the noncareer group, that is, up to the time the person in the career stream is eligible for promotion to a designated position. Although the difference in pay between a noncareer and a successful career bureaucrat who has risen to director-general of the bureau or administrative vice minister is relatively large, a noncareer employee earns more in total pay and retirement allowances than a less successful career bureaucrat who was forced to retire after attaining the rank of division director. Each pay grade is subdivided into pay steps, which permits a person to continue receiving seniority-based pay raises until retirement, even if he or she stays at the same pay grade, thereby avoiding the problem of declining morale caused by the lack of further opportunity for pay raises. Japan's civil service pay system makes considerations for the noncareer stream and has adopted a pay structure characterized by intraorganizational balance.

To summarize, the Japanese national civil service system has adopted an intraorganizationally balanced personnel and pay system, which takes into consideration the need to achieve balance between the career and noncareer categories, and which consists of an arrangement whereby gradual differences in promotion and pay within the same category are produced as the result of long-term evaluations. This is a device that provides incentives enabling the resources of the civil service as a whole, including the noncareer group who make up the overwhelming majority (more than 95 percent) of the service, to be mobilized to the maximum extent.

In other words, Japan adopted an elite system that has never been put completely into practice. In the sense that elites compromise themselves against the nonelites to ensure overall harmony, this system can be called "compromising elitism" in terms of pay and promotion.[24]

Traditional Job Divisions, Workplace Structures, and On-the-Job Training (OJT)

As I have already shown, a strict job classification system does not fit the practices of the Japanese workplace, in which job duties are carried out as a group, with the job responsibilities of individuals remaining flexible and management and labor cooperating in the execution of duties. As a result, job categories within an organization are defined only ambiguously.

In addition, the socalled large roomism or open officeism (*ohbeyashugi*) is a physical characteristic of the Japanese workplace. Employees who are involved in the same task work together in the same room, and those below the rank of division director are rarely given their own office. The *ohbeyashugi* has several merits, including the lack of any need for secretaries, messengers, or unnecessary memos. Also, it allows telephones and many other facilities to be shared, and it encourages cohesion and teamwork among the members. Furthermore, *ohbeyashugi* enables members to evaluate the work of others (Figure 2.2).[25]

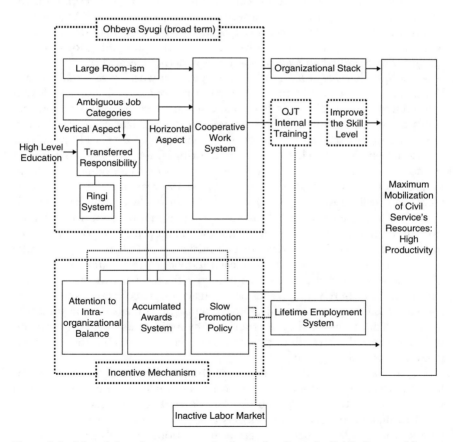

Figure 2.2 Mutual Complement among Attributes that Comprise Public Personnel System and Working Form.

In such a physical work environment, everyone in the same room divides jobs among themselves while at the same time they cooperate with, and cover for, each other. Over time, coworkers naturally learn the job duties of his or her neighbors. By clustering each work section as an "island," and by assigning one phone for several employees, the foundations for cooperative work are laid. Add to this scenario the "ambiguous job categories" mentioned above. In the regulations defining the division of labor and the assignment of responsibilities, job categories are defined only down to section or branch level, and job assignments to individual employees are made flexible by the appropriate supervisor, based on employee workloads at the time and individual abilities. Job categories are not clearly defined either horizontally, among employees of the same rank, or vertically, among superiors and subordinates. Together with the knowledge that each responsible employee (section chief or the responsible nonranked employee) possesses information, responsibility can be transferred to lowerranked personnel.[26] This is the basis of the *ringi* (bottom-up and collective decision-making) system. (In addition, the high level of Japanese education can be cited as a necessary condition for the transfer of such authority to lowerranked employees.) Job categories are ambiguous because of the *ohbeyashugi* (and vice versa), necessitating joint work horizontally. The "cooperative work" system, and ambiguous job categories, can be called an *ohbeyashugi* broadly defined as a whole.

Although the *ohbeyashugi* and the cooperative work system make it difficult to evaluate the achievements and contributions of individual employees (the contribution individuals have made toward the execution of the section's duties as a whole), employees are able to evaluate each other, both horizontally and vertically, permitting the creation of a "market price" for individual employees. This mutual monitoring among employees helps to formulate such a market price. As a result of this mutual evaluation system, longterm objective evaluations of individual employees' abilities and achievements can be accumulated, which form the basis of the accumulated awards or accumulated merit system. By avoiding shortterm linkage between evaluations and remuneration and by forming the market price, the possibilities for unwelcome influencing activities or behindthescenes bargaining (side trade) is reduced. Objective evaluations of each individual are accumulated, creating a longterm market price, which is then reflected back to the individual through longterm rewards. By adopting an accumulated awards system, personnel transfers among sections, departments, or bureaus can be smoothly made, and the accumulating of experience by individuals, through onthejob training received with each of the many transfers, can also be cited as a positive effect of such a system.

On the other hand, the formation of the "market" takes a certain number of years, and the adoption of a slow promotion system operates within a mutually supportive relationship via the cooperative work system. It is difficult to make transfers or promotions that go against the market, and the people who decide on such transfers or promotions must observe the objective evaluations, which are founded on unspoken agreements. Conversely, joint work within sections can be smoothly carried out because of the adoption of the slow promotion system. OJT within sections, in which the essential job techniques that cannot adequately be printed in manuals are transferred from more experienced to less experienced employees, can also be conducted smoothly. Although numerous administrative rules and directives exist, many activities and job techniques cannot adequately be printed in instruction manuals, given today's frequently changing administrative environment; examples include the methods of planning and organizing work, the peculiarities of the persons and organizations to which the civil service relates, and the methods of bargaining with various other sections needed to facilitate one's own work. Such knowledge and techniques can be transferred only through OJT. However, if Japan adopted a fast promotion (early selection) system, older employees would have to worry about the threat of being overtaken, in rank, by younger employees, giving the former an unreasonable cause for hiding from the latter the "essence" of carrying out their duties. By adopting a slow promotion system, such a possibility is reduced.

This long-term evaluation process, consisting of the accumulated awards and the slow promotion systems, provides individual civil service employees with the greatest amount of incentive possible. This is beneficial for the organization as a whole too, because the *ohbeyashugi* permits (in comparison with an individual office arrangement) a more flexible response to social and economic changes, and the development of the skill base of the organization as a whole, through the passing down of knowledge and skills via OJT. An increase in the level of skills within the organization as a whole is necessary for any improvement. To achieve this, employees must learn the various unwritten skills and techniques, which cannot adequately be explained in manuals. It seems that OJT and the *ohbeyashugi* are most appropriate for the transfer of such unwritten skills and techniques. It should also be noted that the *ohbeyashugi* produces organizational slack or surplus.[27]

In this way, the incentive-providing mechanisms of Japan's civil service organizations are characterized by pay and personnel systems, which motivate all employees (the career and noncareer groups, paying attention to intraorganizational balance), along with a workplace and work styles consisting of an ambiguous job categorization, a cooperative work system, and the *ohbeyashugi*. These collectively improve the skill level of the organization as a whole and the productivity of the entire civil service, permitting the mobilization of the civil service's resources to the maximum extent.

Ongoing Drastic Reform of the Civil Service System after 2009

Since the 1990s, the voice of the civil servant critic has grown. Responding to this situation, several study groups were set up, one after another, during the 1990s by the government and the NPA for the purpose of investigating Japan's civil service system.

In December 2000 the cabinet decided on an outline for administrative reform. Since then the Cabinet Secretariat's Office for Administrative Reform has led the planning for civil service reform. The Office tackled the problem using different methods and perspectives taken from the debate of the 1990s, and this led to the cabinet approving the outline for the reform of the civil service system in December 2001. In this outline, a bill was scheduled to be submitted during the 2003 fiscal year and to be enacted in 2006.

However, the reform has not advanced. This is because related actors, such as the unions and the NPA, opposed the reform plan. Moreover, opinion in the ruling party was also divided. Some argued that comprehensive reform would affect the merit system, and others claimed that the plan was very complicated.

Other reform items, such as the privatization of the postal services and of the Japan Public Highway Corporation, were given greater priority under the Junichiro Koizumi administration (2001–2006).

However, the civil service reform moved forward rapidly after Koizumi was succeeded by Shinzo Abe in the autumn of 2007, and Yoshimi Watanabe was subsequently appointed as an administrative reform minister.

At that time, the opposition party (Democratic Party) was strongly critical of *amakudari* to public corporations and private companies. Examples of receiving hefty rewards and retirement allowances after senior bureaucrats had retired and retired bureaucrats' involvement with public corporations were frequently pointed out. It became common for these public corporations to receive public financing, and the ruling Liberal Democratic Party could no longer avoid the placement of restrictions on the *amakudari* system in an effort to increase the approval rating of the government. As I already mentioned in this chapter, *amakudari* has offered various advantages, such as the mobilization of the ministries. However, this did not stop a wholesale attack on *amakudari*.

Finally, the NPSL amendment bill was put on the agenda of the Diet in the spring of 2007. According to this bill, encouragement of retirement and outplacement by each ministry is prohibited. Instead, it was decided that the cabinet would take care of the reassignment of each ministry's bureaucrats.

Following the NPSL revision in 2007, the ruling and opposition parties of the Diet reached a mutual agreement in 2008 on the fundamental law targeting a drastic reform of the national government employee system.

According to this law, the entrance examination system will be reorganized, and the career system may be abolished. The simultaneous entry, simultaneous promotion system will be erased, and replaced with the ability and merit system. A junior employee overtaking a senior will become natural and accepted. As for payment, salaries will include a greater element of performance-related scale.

The full reform is just beginning at the time of writing this chapter even after the change of government from Liberal Democratic Party (LDP) to Democratic Party of Japan (DPJ). However, these reforms contain the possibility of revolutionizing the national government employee system, which has remained unaltered over several decades.

NOTES

1. Finer, *The British Civil Service: An Introductory Essay*, p. 25.
2. National Personnel Authority, *2008 Profile of National Public Employees*, NPA, p. 3.
3. OECD, *The State of the Public Service*, OECD, 2008, p. 13, Figure 1.1.
4. National Personnel Authority, p. 3
5. Muramatsu, *Nihon no Gyousei* (Japanese Public Administration).
6. Johnson, *MITI and the Japanese Miracle: The Growth of Industrial Policy, 1925–1975*.
7. Ibid., pp. 20–21.
8. Ibid., p. 316.
9. See, for example, Kubota, *Higher Civil Service in Postwar Japan*; Muramatsu, *Sengonihon no Kanryousei* (The Postwar Japanese Bureaucracies).
10. Inatsugu, *Nihon no Kanryo Jinji System* (Public Personnel System in Japan).
11. Muramatsu, *Nihon no Gyosei* (Japanese Public Administration), p. 41.
12. NPA, *Ippanshoku no Kokka koumuin no Nin'youjoukyou Chousa, 19 Nendo* (Report on the Investigation of the Appointment Situation of the Regular Government Service, Fiscal Year 2007).
13. Itoh, "Japanese Human Resource Management from the Viewpoint of Incentive Theory."
14. The legal retirement age is 60, and noncareers normally continue working until this age. Since an uporout policy is implemented with respect to careers, however, those who could not be promoted to a higher position are given recommendations that they retire, which are usually followed. In such cases, the ministry finds a place for them to *amakudari*.
15. Inoki, "Japanese Bureaucrats at Retirement: The Mobility of Human Resources from Central Government to Public Corporations."
16. Nakajima, "Kokka Koumuin no Shousinkanri ni Tuite" (On Promotion Management of National Civil Servants).
17. Of course, persons are permitted to drop out of the competition from the time promotions to Section Chief are made (e.g., when one does not wish to be promoted to Section Chief because it would entail a geographical transfer). Such dropouts increase when promotions for Assistant Manager are up for consideration.
18. NPA, *Shogai Kyuyo Mondai Kenkyukai Houkokusho* (Official Report on Comparative Lifetime Payment between Public Employment and Private Employment).
19. Takamoto, *Ohkura Kanryo no Keifu* (Genealogy of MoF's Bureaucrats).
20. Muramatsu, *Nihon no Gyosei* (Japanese Public Administration).
21. Jichi-ro, ed., *Jichitai Roudousha no Chingin* (The Wage of Workers of Local Government) (Tokyo: Jichiro, 1992).
22. Self, *Administrative Theories and Politics*.
23. Page, "France: From l'Etat to Big Government," pp. 97–125.
24. Muramatsu and Inatsugu, "Compromising Elitism in Japanese Public Personnel Administration," pp. 243–260.

25. Ohmori, *Jititai Gyouseigaku Nyuumon* (Introduction to the Public Administration of Local Government).
26. Aoki, *Information, Incentives, and Bargaining in the Japanese Economy,* Chapter 3.
27. Muramatsu, *Nihon no Gyosei* (Japanese Public Administration).

BIBLIOGRAPHY

Aoki, Masahiko, *Information, Incentives, and Bargaining in the Japanese Economy* (Cambridge: Cambridge University Press, 1988).

Finer, Herman, *The British Civil Service: An Introductory Essay* (London: Fabian Society, 1927).

Inatsugu, Hiroaki, *Nihon no Kanryo Jinji System* (Public Personnel System in Japan) (Tokyo: Touyo Keizai Shinpo Sha, 1996).

Inoki, Takenori, "Japanese Bureaucrats at Retirement: The Mobility of Human Resources from Central Government to Public Corporations," in Hyung-Ki Kim, Michio Muramatsu, T.J. Pempel, and Kozo Yamamura, eds., *The Civil Service and Economic Development: Catalysts of Change* (Oxford: Oxford University Press, 1995).

Itoh, Hideshi, "Japanese Human Resource Management from the Viewpoint of Incentive Theory," in M. Aoki and R. Dore, eds., *The Japanese Firm: Sources of Competitive Strength* (Oxford: Oxford University Press, 1994).

Jichitai Roudousha no Chingin (The Wage of Workers of Local Government), Jichi-ro, ed., *Jichitai Roudousha no Chingin* (The Wage of Workers of Local Government) (Tokyo: Jichiro, 1992).

Johnson, Chalmers, *MITI and the Japanese Miracle: The Growth of Industrial Policy, 1925–1975* (Stanford: Stanford University Press, 1982).

Kubota, A., *Higher Civil Service in Postwar Japan* (Princeton: Princeton University Press, 1969).

Muramatsu, Michio, *Sengonihon no Kanryousei* (The Postwar Japanese Bureaucracies) (Tokyo: Touyo Keizai Shinpo Sha, 1981).

———, *Nihon no Gyousei* (Japanese Public Administration) (Tokyo: Chuo Koron Sha, 1994).

Muramatsu, Michio and Hiroaki Inatsugu, "Compromising Elitism in Japanese Public Personnel Administration," in F. Horie and M. Nishio, eds., *Future Challenges of Local Autonomy in Japan, Korea, and the United States: Shared Responsibilities between National and Sub-national Governments* (Tokyo: NIRA, 1997).

Nakajima, Sachiko, "*Kokka Koumuin no Shousinkanri ni Tuite*" (On Promotion Management of National Civil Servants), *Kikan Jinji Gyosei*, no. 28 (1984).

———, *Shogai Kyuyo Mondai Kenkyukai Houkokusho* (Official Report on Comparative Lifetime Payment between Public Employment and Private Employment), NPA, Tokyo, 1987.

———, *Ippanshoku no Kokkakoumuin no Nin'youjoukyou Chousa, 19 Nendo* (Report on the Investigation of the Appointment Situation of the Regular Government Service, Fiscal Year 2007), NPA, Tokyo, 2008.

———, *2008 Profile of National Public Employees,* NPA, Tokyo, 2009.

OECD, *The State of the Public Service,* OECD, Paris, 2008.

Ohmori, Wataru, *Jititai Gyouseigaku Nyuumon* (Introduction to the Public Administration of Local Government) (Tokyo: Ryosho Hukyukai, 1987).

Page, Edward, "France; From l'Etat to Big Government," in Richard Rose, ed., *Public Employment in Western Nations* (Cambridge: Cambridge University Press, 1985).

Self, Peter, *Administrative Theories and Politics,* 2nd ed. (London: George Allen and Unwin, 1977).

Takamoto, Mitsuo, *Ohkura Kanryo no Keifu* (Genealogy of MoF's Bureaucrats) (Tokyo: Nihon Shoseki, 1979).

3

LEGISLATORS

Kentaro Fukumoto

INTRODUCTION

In this chapter I summarize recent findings about contemporary Japanese legislators (members of the House of Representatives, unless otherwise noted). In particular, I focus on the postelectoral reform politics after 1996 and compare it with that of the prereform "1955 system," which spanned from 1955 to 1993.[1] Many (young) scholars have already published excellent studies on this field. Unfortunately, if they are written in Japanese, they are not necessarily known to English readers, even to experts of Japanese politics. Thus, I intend to "export" the literature abroad. I also utilize a few data sets I collected. To make the argument clear, some analyses deal with Liberal Democratic Party (LDP) members only, in which case that restriction is clearly stated.

The title of this chapter is individual "legislators," not collective bodies such as legislature, committee, party, or faction. Hence, I organize this chapter from the legislators' point of view. The first half deals with their life from a long-term perspective. Before coming to the Diet, what were they? How did they become and remain legislators? Why do they leave? The second half examines lawmakers' behavior from the short-term angle. What do they talk about and with whom in the districts? How about in Tokyo?

LONG-TERM VIEW: ENTRY AND EXIT

To start, I consider the career of former prime minister, Junichiro Koizumi. Although he is notoriously "a strange guy" in one sense, he is a typical LDP legislator in the other sense. He was born in 1942, as the son of Representative Jun'ya Koizumi, who was the son-in-law of Representative Matajiro Koizumi. All of them were elected from almost the same district in Kanagawa prefecture. Thus, Junichiro Koizumi is a *dynastic* legislator. Indeed, after he retired in 2009, his second son, Shinjiro Koizumi, succeeded him.

In 1967, Junichiro Koizumi graduated from a high-ranking, private *university*, Keio University. In 1969, after his father died, he ran and lost his

Table 3.1   The Career of Junichiro Koizumi

Term	Year	P	F	D	G	Post
1	1972					
	1973	P				Deputy Director, PR Bureau
2	1976	P				Deputy Director, Finance Division
	1977	P				Member of General Council
		P				Deputy Director, Education Bureau
	1979				G	Parliamentary Vice Minister of Finance
3						
	1980	P				Director, Finance Division
		P				Director-General, Treasury Bureau
4						
	1981	P				Vice Chairman, National Organization Committee
	1983	P				Deputy Secretary-General
5						
	1984	P				Vice Chairman, National Organization Committee
	1986			D		Chairman, Finance Committee
		P				Deputy Chairman, Policy Research Council
6						
	1987	P				Chief Deputy Chairman, Diet Affairs Committee
	1988				G	Minister of Health and Welfatre
	1989	P				Chairman, National Organization Committee
		P				Chairman, Research Commission on Fundamental Policies for Medical Care
	1990		F			Deputy Secretary-General
7						
	1991	P				Chief Deputy Secretary-General
	1992				G	Minister of Posts and Telecommunications
8	1993					
	1994		F			Deputy Chairman
	1996		F			Chief Director
9					G	Minister of Health and Welfatre
	1998		F			Deputy Chairman
	2000		F			Chairman
10						
	2001	P			G	Prime Minister (President of LDP)

P = Party.
F = Faction (Fukuda → Abe → Mitsuzuka → Mori).
G = Government.
D = Diet.

Source: Kabasima seminar (2008, pp. 293–294) and Prime Minister's Office Home Page, http://www.kantei.go.jp/foreign/koizumiprofile/2_milestones.html.

first election bid for the Diet. Then, he became a *secretary* to a LDP faction leader, Takeo Fukuda, who would become prime minister in 1976. When Koizumi won the election in 1972 at the age of 30, unusually young age for such an accomplishment, he was affiliated with Fukuda's faction whose heads were Shintaro Abe (father of Prime Minister Shinzo Abe), Hiroshi Mitsuzuka, and Yoshiro Mori (prime ministe) in the order of succession. Koizumi was *reelected* nine consecutive times.

Table 3.1 illustrates Koizumi's career as a legislator. Most of the posts he held were within the LDP. In the second term, he became parliamentary vice minister *(seimu jikan)*. In the fifth term, he assumed the chairmanship of a Diet committee. In the sixth term, he obtained a ministerial position for the first time. After that, Koizumi occupied posts in his faction. His next step included two additional ministerial posts before reaching the Office of the Prime Minister in the tenth term. He also accumulated expertise on finance in LDP Finance Division and Diet Finance Committee.

LIFE BEFORE POLITICS

Prior Occupation

What kind of occupations did legislators hold prior to being elected? Below I present the background history of the winners of the 1996 election.[2] For comparison, the corresponding values for the legislators in the prereform era (1947–1990) are indicated in parenthesis.[3]

Of the representatives, 33.3 percent (33.0 percent) have experience as local politicians. To give further details, 26.4 percent (22.0 percent) were members of prefectural assemblies; 12.2 percent (15.2 percent) were members of municipal assemblies; 3.8 percent (6.2%) were mayors; and 1.0 percent (2.4 percent) were governors. During the postwar period, the presence of prefectural assembly members increased.

Of the legislators, 29.4 percent (10.1 percent) were secretaries to other legislators. Unlike other occupations, the proportion of ex-secretaries skyrocketed. Of the ex-secretaries, 42.9 percent were dynastic legislators (to be explained in detail shortly).[4] They become Diet members at a younger age (on average, 44.8 years old) than others (50.7 years old).[5]

Of Diet members, 16.0 percent (13.3 percent) were bureaucrats. Until the 1950s, bureaucrats were the main source of legislators. But now, not so many follow this career path. Moreover, promising bureaucrats resign their position at a younger age than before so that they can serve in the Diet for a longer period.

Of lawmakers, 9.2 percent (10.6 percent) came from labor unions; 13.0 percent (13.8 percent) were executive officers; and 3 percent (8.2 percent) were teachers.

Of all party representatives, only 4.2 percent (1.8 percent) were women. The corresponding percentages were 20.0 percent (15.8 percent) for the Japanese Communist Party (JCP); 15.4 percent for the Social Democratic Party (SDP); 5.8 percent for the Democratic Party of Japan (DPJ); 1.7 percent (1.6 percent) for LDP; and 9.1 percent for independents. Left parties tend to have more female lawmakers.

Dynastic Politics

Some Diet members come from political families. Typically, a son "inherits" his father's seat and supporters' group in the same district when his father retires or dies. These "dynastic" legislators (in Japanese, *nisei* [second generation] or *seshu* [hereditary]) consist of around 30 percent of all legislators and 40 percent of LDP members.[6]

Dynastic legislators inherit three sources necessary for election, 3-*bans*. The first is *jiban*, that is, a group of supporters. As explained below, lawmakers organize their own "campaign club" (*koenkai*). When they retire, some "bequeath" it to a family member. In particular, when several ambitious candidates are trying to succeed a retiring legislator's campaign club, a son is the one easiest to attain the club's support. In fact, family members "inherit" 80 percent to 90 percent of votes their predecessor had obtained in the last election, while nonrelative successors win 60 percent to 70 percent of those votes.[7] The second source is *kamban* or name recognition. Because a successor has the same family name as the predecessor, it is easy for voters to know the name of that dynastic candidate. The third reason is *kaban*, namely, money. Retiring legislators contribute their political funds to their (political and biological) successors without inheritance tax. For example, when the head of a faction, Michio Watanabe, died in 1995, his son, Yoshimi Watanabe, received 500 million yen from his father's political fund groups (Yoshimi established Your Party in 2009).[8] In general, dynastic legislators have more assets than the others. If a family member succeeds a retiring incumbent, creditors are assured their loan will be repaid because of the political power of the inheritor.

Since dynastic legislators do not have to build their own electoral machine from scratch, they are more likely to win. Their victory percentage is in the 70s, whereas the total victory percentage is in the 20s. Even when focusing on newcomers only, the corresponding figure is around 40 percent. In particular, children who succeed their parent have an advantage over grandchildren, spouses, brothers, and sisters who try to enter political office. Daughters- and sons-in-law do much worse at elections. If dynastic candidates run for the same district as their family predecessor who won the last election, the successors will gain more votes. Dynastic legislators are more likely to be elected from rural districts. They are also good at bringing pork barrel projects to their districts.[9]

WHEN ELECTED FOR THE FIRST TIME

Age

The average age of freshmen is 44.7 years for 1996 through 2005; from 1983 to 1993 it was 46.8 years.[10]

Party Endorsement

Most viable nonincumbent candidates earn party endorsement, which serves as a cue of the candidates' quality for (unfamiliar) voters.[11] Before electoral reform in 1994, three to five representatives were elected from each district. In the case of the LDP, even if challengers failed to gain party endorsement, some ran as independents and were elected (and they were "endorsed" by the LDP after election). But after the introduction of single-member districts (SMD), only one seat is assigned to every district, making it almost mandatory for candidates to obtain party endorsement for electoral victory.

Since the caucus of parties decides party endorsement, the caucus exerts stronger party discipline over ranks and files than before. Ex-bureaucrats, secretaries of lawmakers, and local politicians have no advantage in obtaining party endorsement. Dynastic candidates have decreasing advantage when compared with the prereform era. College graduates are more likely to get party endorsement, whereas old candidates are less likely to obtain it. Factions still matter. The faction of prime minister, secretary-general, PARC (Policy Affairs Research Committee) chairman, general council chairman, and the antimainstream have an effect on the endorsement process in this descending order.[12]

WHILE SERVING THE DIET

Reelection

The incumbent usually has priority in party endorsement, but the reelection rate plummeted from 81.7 percent (1983–1993) to 61.5 percent (1996–2005).[13] Only under SMD, the return rates of first- to third-term incumbents are lower than that of more senior members. This shows that the post-1996 SMD system is more competitive than the pre-1993 electoral system (see endnote 1), partly because some districts have more than one incumbent who lost the SMD election but were elected from proportional representation (PR) districts.

Promotion

Since the LDP is the major party of all cabinets, except for two since 1993, in this section I focus on LDP members. Their promotion to higher ranks is on the basis of seniority. In the United States, when Congress members lose an election and then win in the next, their seniority restarts from scratch. In Japan, their seniority resumes from where it had been the last time they were in office.

The typical path is shown in Table 3.2.[14] A legislator's career is composed of two paths: government (the executive and legislature) and party (national party and factions).[15] The column of "change" shows whether required seniority increased or decreased when compared with the prereform era. Once legislators become ministers, the career path is not institutionalized.

After 1993, many middle-rank LDP members left the LDP for other parties. Their seniority would be in line for a PARC division chairman or a vice secretary-general position. Thus, seniority required for middle-rank positions decreased by one or two electoral terms. That is, the LDP loosened the seniority rule, because so many LDP legislators left due to the strict application of the rule. In addition, the number of positions for LDP members decreases, when the LDP is in opposition or share power with other parties in a coalition government. Thus, post-1993 freshmen have fewer positions

Table 3.2　Typical Career Path of LDP Legislators

Term	Change			Post
2~3	−1		D	Director, Committee
2	−1	P		Deputy Director, PARC Division
2~3	−1	P		Director, PARC Division
3	+1	P		Vice Secretary-General or Director-General, Bureau
3~4	+1	G		Parliamentary Vice Minister
4~5	0		D	Chairman, Committee
5~6	0	G		Minister

P = Party.
G = Government.
D = Diet.
Source: Todai Ho Dai 7 Ki Kabashima Ikuo Zemi (2008, 2:218–22, 274), Ishidaka (2000).

offered to them, compared to the prereform era when they would have been assigned Diet committee director position. On the other hand, the value of high-ranking positions (such as ministers and committee chairman) did not deteriorate.

During the Koizumi prime ministership, the LDP seniority rule was in flux. Using his discretion, Koizumi did not guarantee minister positions to more-than-six-term Diet members, while he appointed less-than-six-term representatives to ministers. As a result, the average electoral terms of ministers decreased from six to five terms. For the top four positions of the LDP (president, secretary-general, PARC chairman, and general council chairman), legislators needed to have won only 8 or 9 elections, compared to 10 elections in the prereform era. Conversely, more-than-six-term-Diet members were assigned to vice minister (*fuku daijin*) positions, which were established in 2001.[16]

Policy Position

What policy would lawmakers like to promote? In the United States, by way of roll call voting, individual legislator's policy positions are known. But in parliamentary systems, including Japan, party discipline deprives us of such opportunities. Instead, scholars employ two methods: survey of the Diet members and analysis of their electoral campaign pledges.[17]

In asking about legislators' attitudes toward several issues and analyzing their responses statistically, two dimensions emerge. The first, the "security" dimension, is concerned with Self-Defense Forces (SDF) and the Japan-U.S. Security Treaty. From right wing (conservative, namely, support for SDF and the treaty) to left wing (progressive, that is, opposition to SDF and the treaty) on this dimension, the LDP, the New Komeito Party (Clean Government Party, CGP), the DPJ, the SDP, and the JCP are positioned in terms of their policy. The second is the "economy" dimension. From right wing (conservative, that is, small government, low taxes and thrift expenditure) to left wing (liberal, namely, big government, high taxes, and lavish spending) on this dimension, the LDP, the SDP, the JCP, the CGP, and the DPJ are located in terms of their policy.[18] The economy dimension is found in most developed countries, whereas the dominance of the security dimension over the economy is characteristic of postwar Japan. Actually, when directly asking representatives their position on the traditional dimension, from "conservative" to "progressive" (*kakushin*), the LDP, the CGP, the DPJ, the SDP, and the JCP are ranked.[19] Moreover, the security dimension represents the voters' ideology structure; on the economy dimension, there is consensus on improvement of welfare programs, promotion of women to higher ranks and occupation, and reform of the government.[20] The security dimension is a "position issue" (over which parties debate), while the economy dimension is a "valence issue" (on which parties agree).

The range (statistically speaking, variance) of members' positions on issues increases in the order of the JCP, the SDP, the CGP, the LDP, and the DPJ.[21] In particular, party labels do not help to predict positions on the economy dimension. On the security dimension, dynastic representatives are a little against SDF. On the economy dimension, representatives elected from urban districts are for big government.[22]

Another way to probe lawmakers' policy goals is to utilize electoral campaign pledges. We have two dimensions. On the one hand, there remains the traditional (ideological) cleavage between the "conservative" camp (distribution such as pork barrel projects) and the "progressive" camp (redistribution such as welfare programs to labor and the poor). On the other hand, new "reform" issues (of government, budget, and election) attack vested interests and create the second dimension between "national or aggregate issues" (e.g., electoral reform) versus "local or sectional issues" (e.g., pork barrel projects). Thus, we have four types of campaign pledges. To begin, the local and distribution type consists of bringing public spending projects (such as [rail]roads, bridges, and ports) to local districts. The LDP candidates emphasize these issues. Moreover, these pledges promise more votes to advocates. Senior and freshmen legislators refer to these issues more frequently than middle-rank legislators. Next, the national and redistribution type is illustrated by tax and security (SDF, Article 9 of the constitution, which prohibits an offensive military, and Japan-U.S. Security Treaty). This national and redistribution type of pledges is advocated by SDP and JCP members. The above two are standard points of contention and conflict in postwar Japan. Third, the national and distribution type is made of reform issues aimed at the postwar political economy system. These are pet issues of newly formed parties such as the DPJ and New Frontier Party (NFP). Finally, the local and redistribution type is welfare programs delivered to the more vulnerable, such as the elderly, the young, women, and workers. Note that these issues were regarded as part of the progressive camp issues a few decades ago, while they are thought to target a narrow slice of the nation and due to fiscal pressure are under threat of reduction now. These programs now receive consensus (valence issue), so that candidates of any party refers to them. Note that the above is the average trend and that individual candidates talk about issues that differ from party average. Even after the electoral reform, party cohesion has not improved. Variance of position scores increases in the order of the JCP, the LDP, and the DPJ. Variance of the LDP scores does not decrease.[23]

LIFE AFTER POLITICS

There are four reasons why lawmakers cease to serve: electoral defeat (71.0 percent, the average age is 56.8 years), retirement (16.0 percent, average age is 66.0 years), death (9.1 percent, average age is 64.9 years), and other (3.9 percent, average age is 55.8 years).[24] Note that some may strategically retire when they expect to lose if they dare to run.[25] The average retirement age of the CGP is 61.8 years and that of the JCP is 62.1 years, younger than their peers in other parties. The CGP is said to have an age limit of 65 years.[26] The JCP officially denies an age limit.[27]

DISCUSSION

I anatomize political life into several separate aspects, although some overlap exists among them.

Rural (agricultural) districts return to the Diet more LDP members than urban (industrial) districts (because of stable organized support as campaign clubs). Thus, rural members are more likely to be reelected and, due to the seniority rule, be promoted to higher ranks, such as ministers and PARC division chairpersons. As a result, policy that high rank members make is favorable to agricultural interests. In return, this policy facilitates rural members' electoral victory, the starting point of this paragraph; here is a circle.[28] Through the 1990s, however, this agricultural bias disappeared.

As a result of electoral strength, dynastic lawmakers can afford to spend their time on policymaking and power struggles in Tokyo rather than electioneering in districts. In addition, since they start their political career at a younger age, they are more likely to cumulate seniority and be promoted to higher ranks. This is beneficial for supporters as well. Therefore, when an old legislator retires, the campaign club fields a (young) relative of his (usually, son).[29]

By contrast, former bureaucrats enter the world of politics at an older age, and are, therefore, less likely to reach powerful positions. If they retire at a younger age, they may be on par with their colleague politicians in terms of seniority, but they fail to bring as much bureaucratic expertise, which is their advantage in the first place.[30]

SHORT-TERM VIEW: IN DISTRICTS OR IN TOKYO
"Go Home Friday, Come Back Tuesday"

So far, in this chapter I approach legislators from a long-term perspective. How about the short term? To start with, I examine legislator's time budget. Below is an example week of a LDP Representative, Katsuhiko Shirakawa.[31]

Tuesday (in Tokyo)

8:00. Study group[32]

8:30. Agriculture Division, PARC, LDP

9:00. Communication Division, PARC, LDP

9:30. Lobbyists come

10:00. Directorate meeting, Audit Committee, House of Representatives (HR)

10:30. Audit Committee, HR, during which two visitor parties come

12:00. Caucus meeting

12:30. Policy study group

13:00. Plenary meeting, HR

15:00. Bureaucrats of Ministry of Agriculture and those of Ministry of Posts and Telecommunications come to explain their bills, three visitor parties come

16:00. Visit Ministry of Construction and Ministry of Agriculture to ask a favor

17:00. Caucus party

18:00. Representative's party

18:30. Reception of Communication Division, PARC, LDP

20:00. Meet with campaign club officers in Tokyo

22:00. Home

Saturday (in Niigata, 4th District)

8:00. Staff meeting

8:30. Five visitor parties come

10:00. Visit five companies

12:00. Rotary Club

14:00. Small group meetings (30 people)

16:00. Dinner with campaign club officers in the district

18:00. Conference to report Diet activities (100 people)

20:00. Conference reception

22:00. After-reception with campaign club officers

24:00. Home

Lawmakers usually go to their districts on Friday and come back to Tokyo on Tuesday ("Go Home Friday, Come Back Tuesday" [*Kinki Karai*]).[33]

Over the weekend, they are engaged in de facto electoral campaigning and asking for requests from their supporters. On weekdays, they are engaged in policy affairs at the Diet, ministries, and party. In the first place, the regular meeting days of Diet committees are set between Tuesday and Friday exactly for this purpose. This is helpful, especially for members from rural districts, which are usually LDP dominant areas.[34]

In detail, 16.8 percent, 21.0 percent, and 57.8 percent of representatives go to their districts every day, once every few days, once a week, respectively.[35] They return to their home, especially when their districts are close to Tokyo, and they have many voters, their previous vote margins were small, they have not served many terms, and they are elected from SMD, not PR. It is often said that, just after the election is over, the next election campaign begins. In particular, members of the House of Representatives do not know when the House will be resolved. Thus, they say "we are always on the battle field" (*Jozai Senjo*). The elected members visit their districts in the first year after election as often as in the third and fourth year. Conversely, this is not the case for members of the House of Councilors. Their return visits to the districts are more frequent prior to the election than postelection because their term is fixed at six years.[36] In fact, the one-half of the councilors who run for the next election (in particular, just before the election) are less likely to attend the plenary session than the other half.[37]

District activities were expected to increase after the introduction of SMD, but in reality they decreased. One of the reasons is that many districts become safe for incumbents and, therefore, do not have to campaign very hard.[38]

IN DISTRICTS: CAMPAIGN AND CONSTITUENCY SERVICE

Contact TargetsWhom and how often do legislators meet in districts? 48.5 percent, 30.9 percent, and 20.6 percent of representatives have contact with voters every day, once every few days, and once a week, respectively.[39]

Of the representatives, 11.8 percent, 26.5 percent, and 43.4 percent answer that they have contact with interest groups every day, once every few days, once a week, respectively.[40] Contact with interest groups increases; for 36.0 percent of representatives, more than 10.0 percent of their contact targets are interest groups.[41] This is partly because representatives have contact with much more various kinds of interest groups than the prereform era when the division of labor was established among LDP members of the same districts. For example, LDP members rarely meet with labor union members and organizations, while LDP members now tend to meet with labor union members and organizations.

Of the representatives, 3.7 percent, 28.7 percent, and 40.4 percent have contact with prefectural assembly members every day, once every few days, once a week, respectively. This frequency, for both the LDP and opposition members, is lower than before. Representatives' contact with governors, mayors, and top bureaucrats of local governments are less frequent, whereas contact with municipal assembly members is more frequent. LDP members meet local politicians more frequently than opposition party members.[42] Both the LDP and opposition members rarely engage in party branch activities; for 99.2 percent of them, less than 6 percent of their contact target is the party branch.[43]

Communication Topics

What do representatives talk about in districts? The most popular topic with voters and local organizations is personal affairs (e.g., placement, finance, family trouble) for 31.6 percent of legislators; public works (e.g., roads and bridges) for 22.1 percent; policies that affect the related group's interests (the making and implementation of laws, plans, and outlines and getting subsidies) for 19.9 percent; national policy for 17.6 percent; and coordination of local interests for 6.6 percent.

The most popular topic with governors and mayors for 36.0 percent of legislators is local policy, followed by national policy for 35.3 percent, and public works for 25.3 percent. The corresponding numbers for local assembly members are 24.3 percent, 47.1 percent, and 17.6 percent. The frequency of reference to public works decreased and the reference to policy increased . But still, LDP members are more likely to mention public works than opposition members.[44]

Money

The laws distinguish electoral campaigns and other (usual) political activities in terms of contents, period, and funds.[45] "Electoral Campaign Fund" is supposed to be used only for the purpose of electoral campaigns during the "Electoral Campaign Period" (12 days before the election). Otherwise, politicians are only supposed to use "Political Funds." In reality though, politicians are engaged in *de facto* electoral campaign well in advance of the election, using political funds. Thus, I describe political funds below, unless otherwise noted.

Legislators have the three "wallets." The first is party branch, whose head is usually legislators or candidates. The second is "Fund Management Organization (FMO)." Each politician can have only one FMO. The third is other political organizations, which are usually campaign clubs. Companies and interest groups, such as labor unions, can contribute to party branches but not to the other two. The cap of the annual total amount of contribution per organization ranges from 7.5 to 100 million yen, depending on its size. An individual can contribute up to 20 million yen to party branches and other political organizations (including FMOs) and politicians up to 10 million yen; the maximum one citizen can contribute to one political organization or one politician is 1.5 million yen.

One of the aims of the Political Fund Regulation Law is to reduce the amount of political funds, although loopholes exist. First, there is no limitation over how many party branches a politician (establishes and) presides.

Politicians can collect as much money as they wish by making a lot of (regional and functional) party branches. Second, the regulations above are not applied to fundraising party tickets. Individuals can pay up to 1.5 million yen per fundraising party.

In the case of LDP members, on average, they earned 144 million yen in political funds in 1996, an election year. This is much more expensive than U.S. House members, whose average expenditure was 0.67 million dollar (about 67 million yen) in the same year. Party branches received 75 million yen (52 percent of the total revenue of a legislator), a FMO received 44 million yen (31 percent), and campaign clubs received 13 million yen (9 percent). Of this revenue, 53 percent comes from contributions; 23 percent of it originates in fundraising functions; and party branches obtained transfer money from the national party, representing 11 percent of incoming revenue.[46] The more terms LDP members serve, the more money they acquire. If a legislator is from a dynastic line, a former bureaucrat, or a member of a large party, he or she obtains more funds.[47]

These organizations spend political funds three ways: ordinary expenditure (personnel expenses, office rent, 57 million yen or 40 percent of the total expenditure), political activities (organizational activity, newsletter issuance, 66 million yen or 46 percent of the total expenditure), and transfer to other organizations (21 million yen or 15 percent of the total expenditure). The laws allow candidates to spend Electoral Campaign Funds for the following expenses: personnel, office rent, rally place rent, correspondence expenses, transportation expenses, printing, advertising, stationeries, food and drink, hotel, electricity, and heating expenses. There is an upper limit that depends on the number of voters in the districts.

The laws regulating political money play some roles of transparency in spite of some flaws. For example, if politicians report false records or fail to report their transactions of political funds, they are suspected of illegal fundraising and, politically, have to account their financial activities. Due to the mishandling of political money scandals, numerous politicians have lost their political (and sometimes biological) life.

The more money you spend, the more votes you get and the fewer votes your opponents get.[48] For example, if you spend 500 yen more per voter, you will receive three percentage points more votes. The way you spend money also affects the election. Printing expenses (for posters, fliers, and postcards) boosts turnout of the whole district. Correspondence expenses (for get-out-the-vote call) are target specific and increase the variance of vote rates of the candidates.[49]

IN TOKYO: POLICYMAKING

Diet

The source of legislators' power lies in that they are Diet members. But this does not mean that their main arena is the Diet. Actually, they are often absent from Diet meetings, mainly for electoral campaigning and other (more important) appointments with bureaucrats, interest groups, and fellow Diet members. Committee members are substituted every day, especially with freshmen.[50] The older members (those over 70 years) are less likely to attend the plenary session, not because their posts are derived from seniority but because of physical reasons. The younger members (those under 40 years) are more likely to attend the plenary session.[51]

Opposition party members propose bills. Former bureaucrats and non-LDP and former lawyers are more likely to submit bills taking advantage of their policy expertise. Those who have local political experience are less likely to legislate. Most junior members are engaged in a few legislative initiatives, whereas specific senior members sponsor most members' bill, probably because they are in charge of policy matters in their parties.[52]

Opposition party members, junior lawmakers, and legislators who have small vote margins are more likely to ask questions in the Diet.[53]

Party

Before the Diet, there are substantial policymaking stages in the LDP and ministries. Among them, divisions of LDP's PARC are main arenas. LDP politicians can join as many divisions as they want. Under SMD, lawmakers must deal in every policy area. In the first place, division membership is abolished; actually, the list of division members does not exist anymore. Only chairpersons and vice chairpersons are specified. Since the caucus of the LDP has strong powers of control (thanks to the power of endorsement and public fund allocation), it becomes easier for the caucus to assign unwilling members to an unpopular division. In particular, unpopular divisions' posts consist of legislators from PR districts who are more sensitive to caucus pressure.[54] In addition, junior (and, therefore, not powerful) members obtain chair positions of unpopular PARC divisions, such as Diplomacy, Education, Environment, and Defense, because these policy areas are not related to pork barrel projects.[55] Attendance at PARC divisions increases by 5 percent to 10 percent in the postreform era than in the prereform era. Junior members and those whose vote margins are small attend PARC divisions more frequently.[56]

Legislators, both the LDP and oppositions, are in contact with PARC leaders about policy matters in which they are interested. They have consultation on bills and budgets, prior to being tabled in the Diet, with LDP leaders and bureaucrats. But frequency of consultation is lower now than in the 1980s.[57]

Ministries

Bureaucrats consult 60.0 percent of the LDP members and 12.2 percent of opposition party members on policy decision and implementation "very often" and "fairly." Of bureaucrats, 18.4 percent contact LDP members every day, 30.2 percent once every few days, and 20.1 percent once a week.

Of bureaucrats, 4.8 percent contact opposition party members every day, 15.6 percent once every few days, and 27.0 percent once a week. In addition, bureaucrats initiate 43.6 percent of contact with LDP legislators and 27.3 percent of contact with opposition legislators.[58]

Interest Groups

Of representatives in 2002, 11.8 percent get in touch with interest groups every day, 26.5 percent once every few days, and 43.4 percent once a week. The corresponding numbers in 1987 are 28.1 percent, 32.2 percent, and 33.1 percent. Therefore, we can conclude that lawmakers meet pressure groups less often than before.[59]

Public Relations

Of legislators, 70 percent think that TV and 47 percent think that newspapers have an effect on voters' political opinion. TV appearance is a good way to increase lawmakers' presence in voters' mind. Of legislators, 53 percent have appeared in TV programs, 37 percent of them appeared just once on TV, and 41 percent of them appeared two to four times. But their evaluation of TV is mixed. One-half of legislators want to appear more, whereas the other one-half have no such wish. Opposition party members and urban representatives are inclined to want to appear on the TV programs. Electoral support of urban representatives is unstable, partly due to the presence of many independent voters. Thus, this group hopes to appear on TV to appeal to these voters.[60]

In 2000, 28.4 percent of candidates had homepages. In 2003, the corresponding value rose to 63.5 percent. The JCP is negative toward its members' individual websites and prefers that voters rely on the party homepage. The laws prohibit candidates from updating their homepages during electoral campaigns, although many candidates challenge them without penalty. There are two hypotheses about the effects of websites. On the one hand, according to the equalization hypothesis, since it does not take much money to make homepages, less resourceful candidates take advantage of their own websites as much as advantageous politicians. On the other hand, the normalization hypothesis predicts that strong lawmakers are better at producing more attractive homepages than weak ones. The literature finds evidences to support the latter. Incumbents (in particular, senior members), college graduates, and those candidates who run both SMD and PR are more likely to have their homepages than others.[61]

Notes

1. From 1947 to 1993, three to five representatives were elected from each district. After 1996 general elections, 300 lawmakers are elected from single-member

districts and 200 lawmakers (after 2000, 180) are elected from proportional representation districts. In the course of this electoral reform in 1993–1994, the Liberal Democratic Party (LDP) split and lost power for the first time in 38 years. The LDP regained power from 1994 to 2009 with various coalition partners.

2. Todai Ho Kabashima Ikuo Zemi (2000).

3. Fukumoto (2007b, Appendix 3). The averages are weighted by the number of months they serve in the Diet.

4. Aoki (1980, p. 88) also claims that 30 percent to 40 percent of legislators who were secretaries of legislators are dynastic ones.

5. Fukumoto (2007b, p. 202).

6. Explanation of dynastic legislators is largely based on Taniguchi (2008), which utilizes data of the general elections between 1996 and 2003. Operational definition of dynastic legislator depends on answers to the following questions: How large is the family umbrella when counting family members? Are spouse's families considered? Do we not only count representatives but also councilors and local politicians? What if a son runs in a district different from his father's? Scholars do not agree with these issues.

7. Fukumoto and Nakagawa (Nd).

8. Fukumoto (1999).

9. Iida, Ueda, and Matsubayashi (2010).

10. Data source is Mizusaki (2000), Asahi Shimbun Sha (2003), and Asahi Shimbun Sha (2005). I appreciate Jun Saito for his help in data formatting.

11. Kohno (2000).

12. Asano (2006).

13. Dataset is the same as endnote 10. If an incumbent loses in SMD but is saved by PR, this incumbent is regarded as losing.

14. Ishidaka (2000) and Todai Ho Dai 7 Ki Kabashima Ikuo Zemi (2008, 2:218–222, 274).

15. Epstein et al. (1997).

16. Hiwatari (2006, p. 126, Figure 2a) and Shiraito (2008).

17. Taniguchi (2005) and Uekami and Sato (2009) discuss merits and demerits of various methods to estimate legislators' policy position.

18. Taniguchi (2006). The data is as of 2003.

19. Kabashima (2004, Chapter 12). The data is as of 1998.

20. Kabashima and Takenaka (1996).

21. Kabashima (2004, Chapter 12).

22. Taniguchi (2008).

23. Shinada (2001, 2002) are based on the 1990 through 1996 general elections. Tsutsumi and Uekami (2007), with another content analysis coding, basically confirm Shinada's findings for the 1990 through 2003 general elections. Tsutsumi (1998, 2002, 2005) argues that reform issues increases the number of votes; the local and distribution type pledges are more likely to be advocated in local districts; welfare issues are the issue most frequently mentioned. Using the 2003 and 2005 general elections and the 2001 and 2004 elections of House of Councilors, Kobayashi (2008, Chapter 2) classifies electoral pledges on the basis of whether they increase, decrease, or maintain expenditure level for which policy area. His first dimension looks like the same as that of other scholars, while his second dimension is conflict between fiscal liberal versus conservative.

24. Fukumoto (2004). The data is from 1947 to 1990.
25. Fukumoto (2007a).
26. *Sankei News*, December 21, 2007.
27. *Shimbun Akahata* (the JCP official newspaper), October 18, 2001.
28. This reminds us of American Southern Democrats in the mid-twentieth century, who were easily reelected many times, piled up seniorities and obtained powerful positions in the U.S. Congress. Hiwatari (2006, esp. Figure 2b and p. 126).
29. Fukumoto (2007b, pp. 101, 199, 202) and North (2005).
30. North (2005).
31. *Jurisuto*, Special Issue, no. 35 (1984): 103. Though this example is a bit old, it is still typical and most detailed. For a newer example, see *Shukan Toyo Keizai*, December 22, 2007, 59 (Tsutomu Okubo, DPJ, House of Councilors, Fukuoka District).
32. Lawmakers gather policy information, usually from bureaucrats, at breakfast.
33. This reminds us of "Home Style" and "Hill Style" for the U.S. Congress.
34. Sugawara (2005).
35. As for data as of 1985, see Inoguchi and Iwai (1987, Chapter 2, Sections 2–4).
36. Hamamoto (2008).
37. Yamauchi and Sugawara (2005).
38. Hamamoto (2007, 2008).
39. Data source is *Policy Actor Survey*, the Third Survey of Representatives in 2002 (hereafter "PA Survey 3"), Q26, SQ5. This survey was conducted by Michio Muramatsu's group, which I also joined. For the details, see Muramatsu and Kume (2006). I appreciate Michio Muramatsu for sharing this data.
40. PA Survey 3, Q26, SQ6 and Kume (2006, p. 261).
41. Hamamoto (2005, 2007, 2008, Figure 5).
42. PA Survey 3, Q26, SQ1-4 and Shinada (2006).
43. Hamamoto (2005, 2007, 2008, Figure 6).
44. PA Survey 3, Q31 and 32 and Shinada (2006).
45. Regulations described here are as of 2009. As for English explanation of the electoral regulation, see McElwain (2008).
46. Sasaki et al. (1999, esp. pp. 19, 21, 89).
47. Umeda (2000).
48. Kawato (2004, Chapters 8 and 9, esp. p. 239).
49. Endo (2007).
50. Fukumoto (2007b, Chapter 3).
51. Yamauchi and Sugawara (2005).
52. Ono (2000).
53. Matsumoto and Matsuo (2008).
54. Tatebayashi (2004, Chapter 6).
55. Ishidaka (2000).
56. Hamamoto (2005).
57. Ito (2006, pp. 44–45) and Kume (2006, p. 261).
58. Ito (2006, pp. 40–41) and Kume (2006).
59. The Second Survey to Representatives in 1987, Q29, SQ13, PA Survey 3, Q26, SQ6 and Kume (2006, p. 261).
60. Hoshi and Osaka (2006, pp. 104–106) and Osaka (2004, pp. 106–110).
61. Okamoto (2001, 2005) and Yamamoto (2005).

BIBLIOGRAPHY

Aoki, Yasuhiro, "Gikai heno Michi: Shinjin Giin to Seshu Giin" (The Passage to the Diet: Freshmen and Dynastic Legislators), in H. Naka, ed., *Kokkai Giin no Kosei to Henka* (Composition and Change of the Diet Members) (Tokyo: Seiji Koho Senta, 1980).

Asahi Shimbun Sha, *Asahi.com de Miru 2003 Sosenkyo no Subete CD-ROM* (All about the 2003 General Election) (Tokyo: Asahi Shimbun Sha, 2003).

———, *Asahi.com de Miru 2005 Sosenkyo no Subete CD-ROM* (All about the 2005 General Election) (Tokyo: Asahi Shimbun Sha, 2005).

Asano, Masahiko, *Shimin Shakai niokeru Seido Kaikaku: Senkyo Seido to Kohosha Rikuruto* (Institutional Reform in Civil Society: Electoral System and Candidate Recruiting) (Tokyo: Keio Gijuku Daigaku Shuppan Kai, 2006).

Endo, Naka, "Senkyo Undo to Tohyo Sanka" (Electoral Campaigns and Voter's Participation: The Effect of Electoral Campaigns on Turnout and Voters' Regional Bias) *Leviathan* 41 (2007): 97–116.

Epstein, David, David Brady, Sadafumi Kawato, and Sharyn O'Halloran, "A Comparative Approach to Legislative Organization: Careerism and Seniority in the United States and Japan," *American Journal of Political Science* 41, no. 3 (1997): 965–988.

Fukumoto, Kentaro, "Shikin kara Mita Seijiteki Kiban no Keisho: Watanabe Michio kara Yoshimi he" (Succession of Political Resources in Terms of Fund: From Michio Watanabe to Yoshimi Watanabe), in T. Sasaki, M. Taniguchi, S. Yoshida, and S. Yamamoto, eds., *Daigishi to Kane: Seiji Shikin Zenkoku Chousa Houkoku* (Representatives and Money: A Report of National Research on Political Fund) (Tokyo: Asahi Shimbun Sha, 1999).

———, "Kokkai Giin no Nyujo to Taijo: 1947–1990" (Entrance and Exit of the Diet Members), *Senkyo Kenkyu* 19 (2004): 101–110.

———, "Nihon niokeru Seijigaku Hohoron ni Mukete" (For Political Methodology in Japan) *Leviathan* 40 (2007a): 173–179.

———, *Rippo no Seido to Katei* (Legislative Institutions and Process) (Tokyo: Bokutaku Sha, 2007b).

Fukumoto, Kentaro and Kaoru Nakagawa, Nd, "Jiban Keisho no Koritsusei to Seshu: Seito Hyo, Koenkai Hyo, Kohosha Hyo" (Sons Inherits Their Dads' Votes Efficiently: Party Vote, Supporters' Vote, and Personal Vote) mimeo.

Hamamoto, Shinsuke, "Senkyo Seido Kaikaku to Giin Kodo" (Electoral Reform and Legislators' Activities) *Tsukuba Hosei* 38 (2005): 435–458.

———, "Senkyo Seido Kaikaku to Jiminto Giin no Seisaku Senko: Seisaku Kettei Katei Henyo no Haikei" (Electoral Reform and Liberal Democratic Party Legislators' Policy Preference) *Leviathan* 41 (2007): 74–96.

———, "Senkyo Seido to Giin no Senkyoku Katsudo: Senkyo Seido no Hikaku kara" (How Legislators' Incentives to Cultivate the Personal Vote Differ Across Electoral Systems? According to Constituency Size, Magnitude and Term) *Nihon Seiji Kenkyu* 5, nos. 1 and 2 (2008): 124–148.

Hiwatari, Nobuhiro, "Koizumi Kaikaku no Joken: Seisaku Rengo no Shikan to Seisaku Katei no Henyo" (How the Mold Was Broken: The Determinants of Deficit Spending and Fiscal Reform in Japan) *Leviathan* 39 (2006): 100–144.

Hoshi, Hiroshi and Iwao Osaka, *Terebi Seiji: Kokkai Hodo kara TV Takkuru made* (TV Politics: From Diet Broadcasting to "TV Tackle") (Tokyo: Asahi Shimbun Sha, 2006).

Iida, Takeshi, Michiko Ueda, and Tetsuya Matsubayashi, "Seshu Giin to Minshu Seiji" (The Dynastic Politicians in Japan) *Senkyo Kenkyu* 26–22 (2010): 139–153.

Inoguchi, Takashi and Tomoaki Iwai, *Zoku Giin no Kenkyu* (A Study on Tribe Politicians) (Tokyo: Toyo Keizai Shimpo Sha, 1987).

Ishidaka, Haruna, "Jiminto no Yakushoku Jinji to Seisaku Kettei" (Posts and Policy Decision of the Liberal Democratic Party), in Todai Ho Kabashima Ikuo Zemi, eds., *Gendai Nihon no Seijika Zo* (Members of the Japanese Diet: An Analysis of Their Political Activities, 1990–1998, Vol. 1) (Tokyo: Bokutaku Sha, 2000).

Ito, Mitsutoshi, "Kokkai 'Shugo Zai' Moderu" (A "Collective Goods" Model of the Diet), in M. Muramatsu and I. Kume, eds., *Nihon Seiji Hendo no 30 Nen: Seijika Kanryo Dantai Chosa ni Miru Kozo Henyo* (30 Years of Political Change in Japan: Structural Change Reflected in Survey for Politicians, Bureaucrats and Pressure Groups) (Tokyo: Toyo Keizai, 2006).

Kabashima, Ikuo, *Sengo Seiji no Kiseki: Jiminto Shisutemu no Keisei to Henyo* (Development of Postwar Politics: Formation and Change of the Liberal Democratic Party System) (Tokyo: Iwanami Shoten, 2004).

Kabashima, Ikuo and Yoshihiko Takenaka, *Gendai Nihonjin no Ideorogi* (Political Ideology in Japan) (Tokyo: Tokyo Daigaku Shuppan Kai, 1996).

Kawato, Sadafumi, *Senkyo Seido to Seito Shisutemu* (Electoral Systems and Party Systems) (Tokyo: Bokutaku Sha, 2004).

Kobayashi, Yoshiaki, *Seido Kaikaku Iko no Nihon Gata Minshu Shugi* (Is Democracy Working in Japan after the Political Reform?) (Tokyo: Bokutaku Sha, 2008).

Kohno, Masaru, "Nihon no Chusenkyoku Tanki Hiijoshiki Tohyo Seido to Senryakuteki Tohyo" (Japan's Multimember SNTV System and Strategic Voting: The "M+1 Rule" and Beyond), *Senkyo Kenkyu* 15 (2000): 42–55.

Kume, Ikuo, "Rieki Dantai Seiji no Henyo" (Change of Pressure Group Politics), in M. Muramatsu and I. Kume, eds., *Nihon Seiji Hendo no 30 Nen: Seijika Kanryo Dantai Chosa ni Miru Kozo Henyo* (30 Years of Political Change in Japan: Structural Change Reflected in Survey for Politicians, Bureaucrats and Pressure Groups) (Tokyo: Toyo Keizai, 2006).

Matsumoto, Shunta and Akitaka Matsuo, "Kokkai Giin wa Naze Iinkai de Hatsugen Suru noka? Seito, Giin, Senkyo Seido" (Why Japan's Lower House Members Speak in Committees? Political Parties, Legislators, and electoral Systems) *Senkyo Kenkyu* 26–22 (2010): 84–103.

McElwain, Kenneth Mori, "Manipulating Electoral Rules to Manufacture Single-Party Dominance," *American Journal of Political Science* 52, no. 1 (2008): 32–47.

Mizusaki, Setsufumi, *Sosenkyo Deta Besu (JED-M): 1958–2000* (General Election Database) (Tokyo: Leviathan Data Bank, 2000).

Muramatsu, Michio and Ikuo Kume, *Nihon Seiji Hendo no 30 Nen: Seijika Kanryo Dantai Chosa ni Miru Kozo Henyo* (30 Years of Political Change in Japan: Structural Change Reflected in Survey for Politicians, Bureaucrats and Pressure Groups) (Tokyo: Toyo Keizai, 2006).

North, Christopher Titus, "From Technocracy to Aristocracy: The Changing Career Paths of Japanese Politicians," *Journal of East Asian Studies* 5 (2005): 239–272.

Okamoto, Tetsukazu, "2000 Nen Shugiin Sosenkyo niokeru Kohosha Homu Peji no Bunseki" (A Study on the Use of Internet Homepage in the 2000 House of Representative Election), *Leviathan* 29: (2001): 141–154.

LEGISLATORS 69

———, "Shimin Shakai niokeru Intanetto to Senkyo" (The Internet and Election in Civil Society: An Analysis on Candidates' Websites of the 2004 Upper House Election in Japan) *Nempo Seijigaku,* 2005 no. 2 (2005): 87–104.
Ono, Yoshikuni, "Seiji Hendo Ki niokeru Giin Rippo" (Member's Bills in an Era of Political Change), in Todai Ho Kabashima Ikuo Zemi, ed., *Gendai Nihon no Seijika Zo* (Members of the Japanese Diet: An Analysis of Their Political Activities, 1990–1998), Vol. 1 (Tokyo: Bokutaku Sha, 2000).
Osaka, Iwao, "Nihon niokeru Seijika no Masumedia Kan" (Politicians' View of Mass Media in Japan), *Nihon Seiji Kenkyu* 1, no. 1 (2004): 87–130.
Sasaki, Takeshi, Shin'ichi Yoshida, Masaki Taniguchi, and Shuji Yamamoto, *Daigishi to Kane: Seiji Shikin Zenkoku Chousa Houkoku* (Representatives and Money: A Report of National Research on Political Funds) (Tokyo: Asahi Shimbun Sha, 1999).
Shinada, Yutaka, "Jimoto Rieki Shiko no Senkyo Koyaku" (The Pledges of the Parochial Pork Barrels in the Japanese 1990s General Elections), *Senkyo Kenkyu* 16 (2001): 39–54.
———, "Seito Haichi" (Party Position), in N. Hiwatari and M. Miura, eds., *Ryudo Ki no Nihon Seiji "Ushinawareta 10 Nen" no Seiji Gakuteki Kensho* (The Lost Decade and Beyond: Japanese Politics in the 1990s) (Tokyo: Tokyo Daigaku Shuppan Kai, 2002).
———, "Kokkai Giin no Shakaiteki Shiji Kiban tono Tsunagari" (Dietmen's Tie with Supprters' Social Group), in M. Muramatsu and I. Kume, eds., *Nihon Seiji Hendo no 30 Nen: Seijika Kanryo Dantai Chosa ni Miru Kozo Henyo* (30 Years of Political Change in Japan: Structural Change Reflected in Survey for Politicians, Bureaucrats and Pressure Groups) (Tokyo: Toyo Keizai, 2006).
Shiraito, Yuki, "Koizumi Seiken Ki no Shinioriti Ruru to Habatasu" (Seniority Rule and Factions in Koizumi Administration), in Todai Ho Dai 7 Ki Kabashima Ikuo Zemi, ed., *Koizumi Seiken no Kenkyu* (The Koizumi Regime) (Tokyo: Bokutaku Sha, 2008).
Sugawara, Taku, "Kokkai Katsudo Ryo no Kenkyu" (A Study on the Amount of Legislative Activity), in Todaiho Dai 5 Ki Kabashima Ikuo Zemi, ed., *Sangiin no Kenkyu* (Japan's Upper House: Members and Their Activities, 1947–2002), Vol. 2 (Tokyo: Bokutaku Sha, 2005).
Taniguchi, Masaki, "Shugiin Sosenkyo Kohosha no Seisaku Ichi" (Candidate Positions in Japanese General Elections), *Nempo Seijigaku,* 2005, no. 2 (2005): 11–24.
———, "Shugiin Giin no Seisaku Ichi" (Policy Positioning of Japanese Representatives), *Nihon Seiji Kenkyu* 3, no. 1 (2006): 90–108.
Taniguchi, Naoko, "Diet Members and Seat Inheritance: Keeping It the Family," in S. L. Martin and G. Steel, eds., *Democratic Reform in Japan* (Boulder, CO: Lynne Rienner, 2008).
Tatebayashi, Masahiko, *Giin Kodo no Seiji Keizai Gaku: Jiminto Shihai no Seido Bunseki* (The Logic of Legislators' Aciivities) (Tokyo: Yuhikaku, 2004).
Todai Ho Dai 7 Ki Kabashima Ikuo Zemi, *Koizumi Seiken no Kenkyu* (The Koizumi Regime) (Tokyo: Bokutaku Sha, 2008).
Todai Ho Kabashima Ikuo Zemi, *Gendai Nihon no Seijika Zo* (Members of the Japanese Diet: An Analysis of Their Political Activities, 1990–1998) (Tokyo: Bokutaku Sha, 2000).
Tsutsumi, Hidenori, "1996 nen Shugiin Senkyo niokeru Kohosha no Koyaku to Tohyo Kodo" (The Characteristics of Campaign Pledges and Voting Behavior in the 1996 General Election), *Senkyo Kenkyu* 13 (1998): 89–98.

————, "Senkyo Seido Kaikaku to Kohosha no Seisaku Koyaku: Shosenkyoku Hireidaihyo Heiritsu Seido Donyu to Kohosha no Senkyo Senryaku" (The Effect of the Electoral Reform on the Pledge in Japan), *Kagawa Hogaku* 22, no. 2 (2002): 90–120.

————, "Nihon niokeru Seisaku Soten to Sono Henyo" (Policy Issues in Japan and Their Change), in Y. Kobayashi, ed., *Nihon niokeru Yukensha Ishiki no Dotai (Dynamics of Citizens' Mind in Japan)* (Tokyo: Keio Gijuku Daigaku Shuppan Kai, 2005).

Tsutsumi, Hidenori and Takayoshi Uekami, "2003 nen Sosenkyo niokeru Kohosha Reberu Koyaku to Seito no Rieki Shuyaku Kino" (Party Policy Coherence in Japan: Evidence from 2003 Candidate-Level Electoral Platforms), *Shakai Kagaku Kenkyu* 58, nos. 5 and 6 (2007): 33–48.

Uekami, Takayoshi and Tetsuya Sato, "Seito ya Seijika no Seisakutekina Tachiba wo Suiteisuru: Konputa niyoru Jido Kodingu no Kokoromi" (Estimating the Policy Positions of Political Actors: An Application of Computerized Coding to the Japanese Policy Documents), *Senkyo Kenkyu* 25, no. 1 (2009): 61–73.

Umeda, Michio, "Seiji Shikin no Kenkyu" (Study on Political Funds), in *Gendai Nihon no Seijika Zo* (Members of the Japanese Diet: An Analysis of Their Political Activities, 1990–1998), Vol. 1, ed. Todai Ho Kabashima Ikuo Zemi (Tokyo: Bokutaku Sha, 2000).

Yamamoto, Tatsuhiro, "2003 nen Shugiin Senkyo niokeru Kohosha Homupeji to Sono Seisaku to Koyaku nikansuru Bunseki" (The Analyses of Japanese Candidates' Homepages and Their Pledges in 2003 General Election), *Senkyo Gakkai Kiyo* 5 (2005): 79–95.

Yamauchi, Yurika and Taku Sugawara, "Honkaigi" (Plenary Session), in *Sangiin no Kenkyu* (Japan's Upper House: Members and Their Activities, 1947–2002), Vol. 2, ed. Todaiho Dai 5 Ki Kabashima Ikuo Zemi (Tokyo: Bokutaku Sya. 2005)

4

WINNING ELECTIONS IN JAPAN'S NEW ELECTORAL ENVIRONMENT

Steven R. Reed

The Japanese electoral environment has changed. The campaign strategies that proved effective in the past are producing fewer votes now. Parties and candidates are being forced to search for new strategies to win elections. An evolutionary struggle is going on, each party and every candidate is trying to discover and implement the most effective strategy for the new environment, constantly checking out the competition for any clue as to what those strategies might be.

The most fundamental change is the decline of the "organized vote" (*soshiki-hyo*),[1] the rise of the "floating vote" (*fudo-hyo*), and the increasing number of voters not affiliated with any party (*mutohaso*, Tanaka 1997). A steady decline in the ability of organizations to deliver the vote of their members to particular candidates or particular political parties and a corresponding need to appeal to voters through the mass media is apparent. Variations of this phenomenon have occurred in most industrial democracies, though labeled differently in different countries, from "dealignment" through the decline of "machine politics" to the weakening of party identification.[2] In consociational democracies, it is known as "dipillarization."[3] In the context of discussing religious parties, it is often called "secularization." The most theoretically useful way of approaching the phenomenon may well be a shift in the mode of linking voters to parties from clientelistic to policy linkages.[4] In this chapter, however, I use the Japanese terms "organized vote" and "floating vote."

The second major change is the new electoral system that combines single-member districts (SMDs) and proportional representation (PR).[5] The optimal strategy for winning SMDs is well understood: run one and only one candidate per district. This principle not only applies to political parties but also to coalitions of parties. The party best able to withdraw from some SMDs and support a (potential) coalition partner in order to receive support in other districts will have an advantage in the SMDs. The PR tier poses novel strategic challenges and opportunities that are not well understood.

The party that first discovers and implements the optimal strategy for using the PR tier will have the advantage.

The third change is largely the result of the previous two: the availability of an alternative government to that offered by the Liberal Democratic Party (LDP). The LDP ruled in a predominant party system from its founding in 1955 until 1993 and then again in coalition until 2009. One secret to LDP longevity was the assumption that, no matter what else happens, the LDP would control the government after the next election. The Democratic Party of Japan (DPJ) has been chipping away at that assumption. In the 2000 general election the DPJ became the leading opposition party. In the 2003 general and 2004 upper house elections it won more PR votes than did the LDP, although this did not translate into a majority of seats because the DPJ was unable to match this performance in the SMD tier. After a serious setback in the 2005 general election, the DPJ got back on track in the 2007 upper house election, actually winning more seats than the LDP. Finally, in the 2009 general election the DPJ won a landslide victory, destroying the assumption that the LDP would always control the government and changing Japanese democracy fundamentally and irreversibly.

These changes in the political environment pose particularly difficult problems for the LDP as it was almost perfectly adapted to the previous electoral environment. The LDP was not a particularly popular party, at least as reflected by support in opinion polls, but won elections by using the personal support organizations (*koenkai*) of their candidates and interest groups and other organizations to run their election campaigns. The decline of the organized vote thus hit the LDP square in the middle of their primary election strategy. Second, under the previous electoral system, the LDP had developed a simple but effective candidate nomination strategy: "if you win, you are LDP."[6] Because the party had little organization of its own and was thus forced to rely on candidate *koenkai*, the party nomination was not a necessary condition of victory. A candidate who was refused the nomination could run as an independent and, if he won, the party had little choice but to welcome him into the party and nominate him at the next election. Faced with the need to nominate only one candidate in each SMD, the party found it difficult to keep independents from running and impossible to deny them reentry into the party if they won. Even more difficult was convincing LDP candidates to stand down in favor of candidates from their coalition partner, the New Komeito Party (hereafter referred to as Komei).

The challenges for the DPJ were, in many ways, a mirror image of the LDPs. As a new party, the DPJ was dependent on the floating vote. It needed to develop more dependable support and that meant developing stable supporters among the voting public and stable relationships with interest groups and other politically relevant organizations. Since its founding in 1996, the pattern has been that, as an election approached, floating voters would choose sides and most would choose the DPJ. Support would thus rise during elections but would fall back soon after the election was over. Floating voters would become Democrats during an election but revert to an independent position after the election. Because the LDP had a stable, albeit declining, base, the DPJ needed to win many more floating voters than did the LDP. For example, the LDP might have 30 percent support in the opinion polls, whereas the DPJ had only 10 percent, with 50 percent supporting no party. If the two parties split the uncommitted vote evenly, 25 percent to each party, the LDP would finish first with 55 percent to the DPJ's 35 percent.

The DPJ's problem with running a single candidate in every district was also the mirror image of the LDP's problem. The LDP had a surfeit of candidates wanting an SMD nomination; the DPJ had trouble finding qualified candidates, especially in rural areas.[7] The DPJ also had to negotiate stand-down agreements with potential coalitions partners, most notable the Social Democratic Party of Japan (SDP). Yet the problem was much less one of getting a DPJ candidate to stand down in favor of a coalition partner than of getting the potential coalition partner to stand down in favor of the DPJ, thereby increasing the chances of defeating the LDP (or Komei) candidate in the district. Whereas the LDP was in desperate need of Komei votes, the DPJ was less interested in socialist votes than in presenting a united front (ideally in the long run, a single party) against the LDP.

The LDP started with a tremendous lead over the DPJ in all of the resources necessary to win elections, voter and organizational support, financial backing, and quality candidates. However, the DPJ had two advantages over the LDP. First, as a new party, founded in 1996 right before the first election under the new electoral system, it had little baggage to discard before it could learn how to deal with the new electoral environment. Second, as an opposition party, it had both the time and a powerful incentive to focus attention on internal party affairs. As I outline below, the DPJ adjusted to the new electoral environment more rapidly than did the LDP and, finally in 2009, overcame the LDP's original advantage in political resources.

In this chapter I trace the evolutionary competition between the LDP and the DPJ from 1996, the first election under the new system, through the 2009 election. I first document the decline of the organized vote and its implications for this competition. Next I turn to the competition between these two parties to learn how each party uses the new electoral system, first the SMD tier and then the PR tier. Finally, I turn to both parties' efforts to produce attractive policy manifestoes, send clear messages to the voters, and keep all of their candidates "on message" throughout the campaign, paying particular attention to Junichiro Koizumi's success to do so and the failure of his successors to learn the lesson. I conclude with some thoughts on the future of Japanese democracy.

THE ORGANIZED VOTE

Since the 1980s, one of the staple story lines of campaign reporting has been the decline of the organized vote. For example, in the 1980 House of Councillors election, the construction industry elected two candidates with

1,749,944 votes, but in 2001 the group produced only 278,521 votes and elected only one candidate. Similarly, the union representing local government officials elected two candidates with 1,411,363, but produced only 216,911 votes and one winner in 2001.[8] The electoral system had changed between these two elections so the vote totals are not directly comparable, but the decline is so large and the trend so consistent across groups as to leave little doubt about the decline. More important than the number of votes is the reality that groups that used to be able to elect two candidates now elect only one and groups that used to be able to guarantee victory can no longer do so. An electoral strategy based on getting organizational backing no longer works as well as it once did.

The most dramatic evidence of the decline of the organized vote has come in gubernatorial elections. Under LDP rule, governors had become a pivot of clientelistic politics and a paradigm of the organized vote. The standard pattern was for the incumbent or his designated successor to collect the recommendations of almost every politically relevant organization in the prefecture before declaring his intention to run. At this point the election was effectively over and all parties except the communists would support the anointed candidate. The election itself was merely a formality. Noncompetitive elections allowed corruption to get out of control. For example, several scandals revealed that bid-rigging (*dango*) had become standard practice in many prefectures. A candidate could win elections running against corruption, but found it difficult to govern or to win reelection without the support of the construction industry. Thus, reform governors who had originally run against bid-rigging were themselves arrested for bid-rigging in Fukushima in 2006 and Miyazaki in 2007. However, recently several candidates backed by the organized vote, precisely the type of candidate who would have once been seen as invincible, have lost to a candidate with little or no organizational backing, the kind of candidate who would have been seen as no more than a token candidate in the past.

The first governor to attract nationwide attention for breaking the mold of gubernatorial elections was Yasuo Tanaka in Nagano prefecture. When the incumbent governor retired in 2000, a powerful political machine had governed Nagano prefecture for 40 years. Retiring governors were succeeded by their vice governors and were normally supported by all the major political parties. No party wished to risk supporting the losing candidate because opposition parties were effectively excluded from the policymaking process, most notably the allocation of construction projects. Yet in 2000, Tanaka, a well-known author decided to challenge the vice governor and designated successor to the retiring governor. Tanaka was supported by the prefectural labor federation though not the union of local government employees, and he refused formal support from any political party. He ran as an outsider, appealing to anyone frustrated with the status quo and, according to a poll by the *Shinano Mainichi Shimbun* (September 30, 2000), 40 percent of voters wanted major changes and 49 percent more wanted some change in prefectural politics. The voters wanted change and Tanaka promised to deliver.

The DPJ declared its neutrality. Although the national party headquarters showed an interest in supporting Tanaka, the local party did not want to risk being on the losing side and becoming a prefectural opposition party. The political establishment resorted to dirty tricks. The local government employees' union distributed a false report that Tanaka planned to cut the salaries of civil servants across the board. Prefectural bureaucrats centered on the construction bureau, illegally mobilized to defeat the challenger. Several faced criminal prosecution after the election. Despite these antics from the political establishment, Tanaka won a comfortable victory.

As governor, he attracted media criticism for his "dictatorial" methods, but his popular support remained high. The Nagano prefectural assembly was dominated by conservatives linked to the LDP, many of whom not only depended on the construction industry and other interest groups to win their election campaigns but also sincerely believed pork barrel projects to be the essence of democracy. Governor Tanaka's declaration of a moratorium on dam construction struck at the heart of their electoral base and their conception of democracy. The assembly passed a motion of no confidence in the governor, forcing the governor to resign and a new election to be held. Not only did Tanaka win reelection but the LDP could not even agree on a single candidate to oppose him. The clientelistic political machine had been thoroughly defeated and Tanaka became a symbol of change, campaigning for candidates in various elections around the country.

Tanaka was not an effective administrator and proved much more adept at making new enemies than winning new friends, even among voters. His popular support waned and he was defeated in the 2006 gubernatorial election. Yet his success encouraged others to challenge and defeat the political machines in other gubernatorial elections around the country. Today, he continues to serve as a (somewhat controversial) symbol of change, as leader of a one-seat party allied with the DPJ.

These gubernatorial elections demonstrate that candidates with no organizational or party support can beat candidates backed by the organized vote but do not indicate that it is easy to do so. Successful candidates tend to be outsiders, this largely is because insiders "know" that the incumbent is invulnerable. The DPJ has repeatedly failed to back candidates who espouse policies that resonant with their own policies because the local DPJ wants to back the "winner." Conversely, DPJ candidates who win gubernatorial elections have not necessarily been at the forefront of reform and have not even remained active in the party. The DPJ has learned the lesson, at least, in theory, if not yet always in practice. The stated policy is never to back a gubernatorial candidate who is also backed by the LDP.

More generally, candidates and parties have been searching for ways to attract the floating vote. Many of their answers have focused on changing window dressings, without changing substance. One of the first responses was to nominate "talent" candidates, people who had won widespread name recognition in other career fields, the mass media (newscasters and commentators), entertainment, and sports. Talent candidates like Tanaka experienced some success in gubernatorial elections and the House of Councillors, but were much less successful in the all-important House of Representatives. It took the parties much longer to realize that strong leadership and the promise of reform were the keys to winning the floating vote. Both violated LDP tradition. LDP tradition dictated a careful balance of power within the party, a quality incompatible with strong leadership. The LDP policymaking process was based on "consensus decision making,"[9] which meant spending a long time before reaching a decision and made bold policy initiatives difficult.

LEARNING TO USE SINGLE-MEMBER DISTRICTS

The fundamental secret to winning single-member districts (SMDs) is simple: run one and only one candidate per district. The DPJ has managed this task much better than has the LDP. DPJ candidates faced intraparty competition in a maximum of 3.3 percent of the SMDs while LDP candidates faced intraparty competition in 7–15 percent of the SMDs.

The DPJ's tactical success is due primarily to it being a new party. It has had trouble finding enough candidates to run in all of the SMDs, but it has seldom been troubled by the need to choose from among more than one potential candidate. In contrast, the LDP often faced the problem of choosing between two candidates, both with significant personal support in the district and both wanting the same SMD nomination. Moreover, the LDP nomination was considered so valuable that potential candidates were always waiting in the wings and not necessarily waiting patiently. LDP tradition dictated that a candidate who ran as an independent and defeated the nominee would join the LDP and be nominated at the next election. Because the LDP depended on candidates' personal support organizations, party headquarters had little bargaining power that it could use to force these independents to withdraw. Table 4.1 underestimates the LDP's problem because, as I show below, the party was often forced to buy off potential candidates with winnable PR nominations in order to prevent them from running and splitting the LDP vote in the SMD.

The case of Tochigi third district neatly illustrates the problem for the LDP leadership. Michio Watanabe had a powerful *koenkai* in the district, but died before the 1996 election. Another incumbent from the old system looking for an SMD nomination, Susumu Hasumi, claimed Tochigi third district. Not only was party policy to give preference to incumbents but Hasumi also produced a document showing that Watanabe had promised him the nomination after Watanabe retired. However, Watanabe had a son who decided to run, with or without the nomination. It was obvious to all concerned that the Watanabe *koenkai* was strong enough to elect the younger Watanabe against any and all challengers, so Hasumi and the LDP bowed to the inevitable, nominating Watanabe and compensating Hasumi with a PR seat. Both won their respective elections.

Negotiations were repeated in 2000 and 2003 with the same results, but in 2005 the party decided that Hasumi did not deserve a PR nomination and should find his own SMD. He ran in Fukushima third district but lost. Hasumi's career inside the LDP was over. Meanwhile, the DPJ has been unable to field a credible candidate back in Tochigi third district. The Watanabe *koenkai* was simply too strong. Hasumi thus applied for the DPJ nomination. He offered the DPJ a candidate with a *koenkai* of his own in the district in return for the chance to win a seat on the DPJ PR list but, as explained below, the DPJ decided not to run anyone against Watanabe.

Watanabe is a reformer inside the LDP and, leading up to the 2009 election, he was so disgusted with the LDP government's failure to enact reforms that he decided to leave and form his own party, Minna-no-to (Your Party). Because Watanabe's policy positions are close to those of the DPJ, the Democrats did not nominate anyone in the district, hoping that Watanabe would join them after the election. LDP party headquarters declared their firm intention to run a nominee against the turncoat Watanabe. Hasumi applied for the job. The local LDP, however, was much more afraid of Watanabe's *koenkai* than they were of national party headquarters and opposed any attempt to run a nominee against Watanabe. In the end, Watanabe ran opposed only by a token candidate from a fringe religious party. Not only did he win the SMD but his party finished first in the PR voting in his district, driving the LDP into third place, winning more than twice the LDP PR vote.

The Watanabe *koenkai* is strong enough to elect him without support from a political party and with no need to attract floating voters. No more than 10 politicians around the country find themselves in such a strong position. But consider Hasumi, a much more typical case. He managed to parlay a weak *koenkai*, even though he had no chance of winning his SMD, into a PR seat in three consecutive elections. The LDP was unable to just say "no" because they were afraid Hasumi would run as an independent or, worse yet, for the DPJ. Indeed, he tried to do just that when the party finally worked up the courage to refuse him a nomination. A party that cannot simply deny a nomination to a candidate like Hasumi is too decentralized to consistently win elections in the new political environment. Indeed, the party found it extremely difficult to get candidates to move to open districts where the candidates had no *koenkai* and proved even less capable of getting candidates to stand down in favor of Komei, its coalition partner, even in return for a guaranteed PR seat.[10] The LDP has yet to master the basic task of SMD election strategy.

LEARNING TO USE PROPORTIONAL REPRESENTATION

The proportional representation (PR) tier of the new electoral system is a closed-list system, unlike the open-list system used to elect the House of Councillors. In the latter, voters can write either the name of the party or a candidate on their ballots. Seats are awarded to parties based on the sum of votes received by the party and the votes received by the party's nominees. The candidates to fill those seats are then determined by the number of votes gained by the nominees. However, in the closed-list PR tier used to elect the lower house, voters write only the name of the party on their ballots. The allocation of seats is proportional to the number of votes received, but the allocation of those seats to candidates is determined before the election by the party.

Under most closed-list PR systems, the party simply ranks its candidates from first through the total number of candidates nominated. The Japanese combination of PR with SMDs, however, produced a novel variation on this theme. As in most mixed-member systems, SMD candidates may also be nominated on the PR list. The "dual listed" candidates who win their SMDs are deleted from the PR list before the PR seats are allocated. The Japanese twist is that parties may give dual listed candidates the same rank, ties to be broken by how close the candidate comes to winning her SMD. The decision to list SMD candidates at the same rank is made by the party, but doing so adds an open-list flavor to the system, allowing voters a say not only in how many seats a party receives, but which candidates will fill those seats.

Soon after their first experience with the new electoral system, both major parties came to the conclusion that the optimal strategy was to rank all SMD candidates tied in first place. From the party's point of view, SMD seats are earned by the candidate and given to the party, whereas PR seats are earned by the party and given to the candidate. The party should thus award its PR seats to those candidates who provided the most votes to the party by campaigning hard in their SMDs. In principle, every candidate should earn a PR seat by competing in an SMD. No candidate should get a free ride at the top of the list. However, both parties have made exceptions.

In practice, both major parties nominate most of their SMD candidates in a single large tied clump in the middle of the PR list. We may call these "competitive nominations" because the SMD candidates were forced to compete for a PR seat. Those nominations above the clump may be called "negotiated nominations." These are presumably "winnable PR list positions" that represent a bargain struck between the candidate and the party. The candidate has to offer the party something to get a negotiated PR nomination. Those below the clump are "token nominations" because they are normally given with no expectation that the candidate might actually win a seat.

Both major parties aim at zero negotiated nominations on the principle that all candidates should have to compete in an SMD to win a PR seat. The DPJ approached this goal rapidly, but the LDP has been slow to adapt. If one takes the percentage of PR seats won by candidates with a negotiated nomination, one finds that the LDP allocated over one-half of its PR seats in negotiated nominations through 2003, dropping to 46 percent in 2005, and finally falling to 20 percent in 2009. The DPJ allocated over 60 percent of its PR seats to negotiated nominees in 1996 and 2000, but that percentage dropped to below 10 percent in 2003, below 5 percent in 2005, and to zero in 2009.

Token candidates win when, after subtracting SMD winners, the party still has some PR seats to allocate. For example, the Hokkaido PR bloc contains 8 PR seats and 12 SMD seats. A party might nominate all 12 SMD candidates tied at the top of the list. If all of the party's SMD candidates each win their SMD, all of their PR seats go to pure PR candidates (those not running in an SMD) ranked thirteenth and higher. The 2005 and 2009 elections were landslide victories, 2005 for the LDP and 2009 for the DPJ. In both elections, the winning party not only elected several token candidates but also failed to nominate enough token candidates to fill all of the seats they had won. The question of who should get token nominations was not considered a problem until after the 2005 election, the first time a significant number of token nominees won seats. The LDP had not paid much attention to these nominations, giving many of them to young party employees. In 2009 the DPJ put their token PR nominations to better use, and given the experience of 2005 and the polls leading up to the election, token DPJ nominations were seen as potential seats. Many of the DPJ's token PR nominees were potential SMD nominees, candidates who had lost in some previous election, local assembly members, and political secretaries. The DPJ has had such trouble developing a pool of potential candidates that they are careful to take good care of the candidates they have.

The DPJ also used token nominations to split the LDP vote. In Tokyo they nominated Koki Kobayashi at twenty-fifth on the PR list. Kobayashi had been a LDP member of the Diet elected from Tokyo tenth district, but had voted against Koizumi's postal reform and was thus denied the nomination in 2005. He was defeated by one of Koizumi's "assassins" (see below). Kobayashi still had some personal support in the district but not enough to negotiate a safe PR nomination with any party. He also had good reason to believe that a token DPJ nomination in 2009 might win a seat. The DPJ also nominated a LDP member of the upper house who had retired at the age of 77, but still had significant support. A PR nomination allowed the elderly candidate to avoid the rigors of a district campaign and presumably attracted LDP supporters to the DPJ. Finally, the party nominated Hirohisa Fujii, a DPJ member of the Diet who had retired from Kanagawa fourteenth district. In this case the point was Fujii's expertise in financial affairs and the internal workings of the Ministry of Finance. He became minister of finance in the new Hatoyama cabinet. In each of these cases, the nomination cost the party nothing and in each case the candidate won a seat in the DPJ landslide.

LEARNING TO CAPTURE THE FLOATING VOTE

As illustrated in Figure 4.1, with two important exceptions (both to be discussed below), the DPJ has been gaining on the LDP every since it was founded in 1996. Figure 4.1 presents the difference in the PR vote as the best indicator of relative preferences between the two parties among the voting public. Because of the LDP advantage in quality candidates, both the SMD vote and the total number of seats favor the LDP much more than does

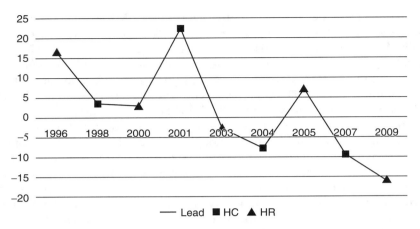

Figure 4.1   The LDP Lead over the DPJ in PR.

the PR vote. The PR vote is thus an estimate of how well the parties would fare if the LDP had no resource advantage.

The LDP has been in electoral decline since at least 1989 when the Recruit Scandal and new leadership in the Japan Socialist Party (JSP) defeated the LDP in the upper house of election of that year. The LDP used all of the tactics in its traditional playbook to maintain power. When in trouble, the LDP has found that changing leadership to be an effective tactic since Hayato Ikeda replaced Nobusuke Kishi in 1960. Between its landslide victory in 2005 and its landslide defeat in 2009, the LDP changed leaders four times, but experienced only temporary reprieves in the opinion polls, never enough to be confident of winning the election. Since Kakuei Tanaka, the LDP has incorporated new organizations into its clientelistic networks whenever it faced defeat. This tactic proved successful in 1999 when the party incorporated the Soka Gakkai religious group, the best organized vote in Japan today, by talking Komei into joining the LDP in coalition. However, the effectiveness of this coalition began to fade, especially in the 2007 House of Councillors election.[11] According to exit polls, Komei supporters voted for LDP candidates in increasing numbers, rising from 61 percent in 2000 to 72 percent in 2003 and 78 percent in 2005,[12] but that percentage fell to 73 percent in 2009.[13] Although this percentage made Komei the most loyal supporters of the LDP, more loyal than LDP supporters, the effectiveness of electoral cooperation was clearly in decline. The pattern among LDP supporters is similar. Only 38 percent of LDP supporters voted for Komei candidates in 2000, but that percentage rose to 56 percent in 2003 and to 68 percent in 2005, before dropping back to 54 percent in 2009. Prior to the 2009 election, the LDP also tried to incorporate the National Association of Prefectural Governors, especially two popular reform governors who had been supported by the LDP in their respective elections. Not only did the governors' demands exceed what the LDP was willing to offer but the DPJ matched the offer they did make. None of the old tricks was working, but Koizumi showed the party a few new tricks that worked remarkably well.

In 2001 the party chose Koizumi, a party maverick who had lost two previous leadership elections, to lead the party out of its doldrums.[14] Koizumi's campaign theme was the promise to "change Japan by changing the LDP." Interestingly, he ran against his own party promising that, if the LDP would not change, he would "break it apart" (*butsukowasu*). His campaign partner was Makiko Tanaka, daughter of Kakuei Tanaka, who used her inimitable aggressive style to reinforce the message of change. He followed up his selection as leader with a cabinet that violated LDP tradition. Factional balance and faction leaders played no role in the selection of ministers, although he allowed factions to influence the selection of vice ministers. He appointed Tanaka as minister of foreign affairs and an economics professor minister in charge of finance and the economy. Koizumi's first electoral test came in the 2001 House of Councillors election (which is shown through the first peak in Figure 4.1) and the first clear electoral victory for the LDP since 1986.

Koizumi seemed poised to deliver on his promise of reform, but standard LDP consensus decision-making procedures prevented him from making much progress. Tanaka fought with the bureaucrats in her ministry and members of her own party undermined her. Koizumi let her go and his poll ratings fell dramatically. A trip to North Korea raised his support ratings temporarily, but he began to look more and more like an ordinary LDP prime minister and his support dwindled. Koizumi's second and third electoral tests were the 2003 general and 2004 upper house elections. Not only did the LDP lose ground in both but the DPJ received more PR votes than the LDP did for the first time, falling below zero as shown in Figure 4.1. Finally, in 2005 he railroaded his pet project—privatization of the post office through the LDP. The bill passed the lower house of the Diet with 37 defections from the ranks of the LDP, only to be defeated by LDP defections in the House of Councillors.[15] At this point the LDP seemed doomed to defeat. Tradition dictated that Koizumi resign and let a new leader restore the party's popularity but instead he dissolved the Diet and called an election. The move looked like political suicide until Koizumi gave his dissolution speech that evening.

Koizumi said he had promised to dissolve the Diet if his postal privatization bill was not passed, and so that is just what he did; he was just keeping his promise. Koizumi went on to say that no member of the Diet who had voted against postal privatization would get a LDP nomination. In addition, every district would have a LDP nominee who favored postal privatization. This election would be a referendum on postal privatization and every single Japanese voter would have the choice of voting for or against reform. After four years of dawdling, Koizumi again appeared to be fulfilling his promise to change Japan by changing the LDP. The LDP nominees who ran against the postal rebels were promptly dubbed assassins. Koizumi managed to come up with an attention-grabbing assassin at regular intervals, leaving the media with little else to talk about. He won an overwhelming victory for the LDP (which is shown through the second peak in Figure 4.1).

Note that neither of Koizumi's victories was about policy. Most of Koizumi's reform program put him closer to the DPJ proposals than to the other members of his own party. Moreover, although his policy stance did not change during his administration, he won two elections and lost two. Nor was postal privatization a particularly popular policy. Voters rallied behind postal reform only because Koizumi's dissolution speech had managed to make this issue the symbol of reform in general. Koizumi won when he fought with the old guard of the LDP and lost when he acted like an ordinary LDP prime minister. Voters liked Koizumi's "New LDP," but continued to dislike the old LDP.

Soon after his resounding victory in 2005, Koizumi retired as party leader and prime minister. He has not played an active role in LDP politics since, and in 2009, he passed his seat in the Diet onto his son. His successors refused to learn the lessons of Koizumi's success, returning to LDP politics as usual. The postal rebels who had won seats in the Diet were allowed back into the party, after they had promised to support postal reform in the newly elected Diet. The tradition of "if you win, you are LDP" remained in full force. The LDP did not change and resumed its downward trend against the DPJ, losing the 2007 House of Councillors election, thereby making the DPJ the largest party in the upper house, and the first time the LDP had ever been relegated to second place in either house.

In 2009 the DPJ campaigned on *seiken kotai* (literally "alternation in power" but probably best translated as "time for a change"). Prime Minister Taro Aso adopted as many of the trappings of the Koizumi campaign style as he could manage, but none was of substance. The election was a landslide defeat because the old LDP was and, in many ways, a mirror image of the 2005 landslide win. Polls indicated that floating voters moved from the LDP to the DPJ in 2009,[16] reversing the flow of votes to the DPJ in 2005. In the 2005 election, the Koizumi LDP took back floating voters from the DPJ, especially in rural areas. However, the reverse flow in 2009 was more complex due to the presence of Watanabe's party, *Minna-no-to*.

I decided to analyze the PR vote by SMD because it provides evidence of major party support in each of the 300 districts, even if the party did not run a candidate in the SMD. In 2005 the PR swing to the LDP and the swing away from the DPJ were highly correlated (−0.589). The basic story of 2005 was simply that the LDP won back urban districts from the DPJ. By contrast, in 2009 the correlation had dropped to −0.247 and was not highly correlated with the urban-rural dimension. The confusing factor was Watanabe's party. If we analyze only those districts in which Watanabe had no SMD candidate, the correlation rises to −0.329, and if we limit ourselves to those districts in which his party did not run in the PR tier (65 SMDs),

Table 4.1   Determinants of the Swing Away from the LDP in 2009

Dependent Variable = Change in the percentage of the electorate voting for the LDP between 2005 and 2009.

LDP candidate	0.644 (0.753)
DPJ candidate	0.124 (0.505)
Minna candidate	–2.477 (0.639)*
Minna PR	–3.454 (0.347)*
Percent DID	–4.637 (0.506)*
Constant	–1.760 (0.900)
n	300
R-squared	0.5017

* = significant at the .001 level.
Standard errors in parentheses.

the correlation rises to –0.557. When offered a choice between the LDP and the DPJ, voters chose the DPJ, but when offered a choice between the LDP, the DPJ, and *Minna-no-to*, LDP voters were more likely to move to Watanabe's party than to the DPJ, as illustrated in Table 4.1.

The swing away from the LDP was not affected by the presence (or absence) of either a LDP or a DPJ candidate. There was a clear tendency for LDP candidates who faced either a SDP opponent or a *Kokumin Shinto* candidate to do better than those who faced a DPJ candidate, but this relationship disappears when a control for urban-rural voters is entered into the equation. The DPJ withdrew in favor of one of its potential coalition partners only in rural districts with strong LDP incumbents. In 2009 the LDP lost the urban votes it had gained in 2005, but those votes did not necessarily go to the DPJ. The LDP lost to the DPJ, but lost more when voters were offered the option of voting for Watanabe's party. In those blocs where *Minna-no-to* ran a PR slate, the LDP lost 3.5 percentage points more than in those blocs where Watanabe's party did not run. In those districts in which *Minna-no-to* fielded a candidate in the SMD, the LDP lost an additional 2.5 percentage points.

THE CULMINATION: A TWO-PARTY SYSTEM

When electoral reform was enacted in 1994, many of the reformers hoped that the SMD tier would move Japan toward a two-party system. This hope was based on Duverger's Law, among the reliable generalizations in political science.[17] Many were disappointed that Japan was not magically transformed into a two-party system within minutes after the reform was passed, but a more realistic evaluation indicates that Duverger's Law has indeed been working in Japan.[18] After each election since the reform, Japan has moved closer to a two-party system.

Duverger's Law is working in the following ways. Most Japanese voters have an effective choice between two and only two candidates in the SMDs and that choice has been increasing between one and only one representative of the government and one and only one representative of the opposition. The effective number of parties per SMD has fallen at each election and has now reached 2.26, one of the lowest figures found in SMD systems. If we add the LDP vote to the DPJ vote and divide by the total number of eligible voters, we get the two-party percentage of the electorate. In both the SMD and PR tiers, this percentage has risen at each successive election. The 58 percent figure for SMDs in 2009 is also high by international standards. Even in the PR tier, the two-party percentage of the electorate is approaching 50 percent. Finally, in 2009 Japan experienced its first party shift in power since electoral reform, the hallmark of a two-party system.

Japanese commentators complain that Japan's two-party system is unbalanced and may be subject to wild swings between large LDP majorities and large DPJ majorities. This worry is real, but applies equally to Great Britain, the archetype of two-party systems. After the 1983 election, British commentators worried that the Labour Party would never recover, and after the 1997 election they worried that the the Conservative Party would never recover. Both worries proved unfounded.

Japanese commentators also complain that there are few if any policy differences between the LDP and the DPJ, yet policy convergence is the hallmark of a two-party system. One might well wish for clear policy differences, but this is not the nature of the system. The group that best understands how a two-party system works is the National Conference of Prefectural Governors. They produced a specific list of demands and several prominent governors pledged to evaluate and grade the two parties' manifestoes, giving their public support to one or the other party. In the end Governor Toru Hashimoto of Osaka was the only governor to publicly announce his choice (the DPJ), although the question had become almost moot as both parties had promised so much of what the governors had demanded. The governors would get what they wanted, regardless of who won. In the next several years interest groups will come to understand that, if they support only one party, they will periodically find themselves with no voice in government. All groups will need a foot in both camps. That is how a two-party system operates.

If Japan is not a two-party system then neither is Great Britain. Indeed, if Japan is not a two-party system, then the two-party system can be found only in utopia. That Japan is now a two-party system tells us a lot about the future of Japanese democracy, but does not indicate that nirvana has been achieved or that Japan has no more problems. Great Britain is a two-party system and it has many problems. I now offer a few thoughts about the future of Japanese democracy.

THE PROSPECTS FOR JAPANESE DEMOCRACY

The positions of the two major parties have been reversed by the results of the 2009 election. The DPJ is now in government, backed by a large majority. The LDP is in the opposition, having suffered the worst defeat in its history. The DPJ now has the resource advantage and the LDP now has the time to focus on reforming the party organization. How each responds to their new challenges will determine the future of Japanese democracy.

Can the DPJ govern? Will the DPJ become more like the old LDP in order to govern effectively? The latter question has a clear answer: no. To suggest that the DPJ will have to develop factions, policy tribes, and consensus decision making like the old LDP is to suggest that, in order to succeed, the DPJ will have to copy those aspects of the LDP that have just failed. The LDP was perfectly adapted to the old electoral environment, but adapted poorly to the new electoral environment. If the DPJ wishes to govern effectively, they will have to develop new techniques, appropriate to the new electoral environment.

Can the DPJ develop new modes of governance that work in the new electoral environment? On the one hand, the DPJ has the advantage of having little or no baggage to discard before they can search for new modes of governance. In addition, not only has the DPJ been thinking about how to govern effectively in the new environment since the party was founded in 1996, reformers inside the LDP have been contemplating the same issue for much longer. There is no shortage of ideas about what was wrong with the old LDP mode of governance and of reform proposals for how to fix those problems. On the other hand, none of those ideas is guaranteed to work. It will take years of trial-and-error experimentation to determine which of the reform ideas work and which do not. The DPJ government will make mistakes. We can be reasonably certain that the DPJ mode of governance will be better adapted to the new environment than the LDP's traditional mode of governance. We can also be certain that the DPJ will not get it right on its first attempt. The evolutionary struggle to find the optimal mode of governance will continue.

Now that the LDP is in opposition, it will have time to focus on reforming the party organization. Will it be able to do so? The party has two models for reforms that work, the Koizumi cabinet and the DPJ. The LDP needs to jettison many of its traditions and adopt many of the practices of its rival. The evidence provided by recent election results is overwhelming and would seem clear to even the most obtuse observer, but it is hard to give up traditions that worked perfectly well for over 40 years simply because they are not working any more. For example, is seems clear that the party should abolish factions, an issue that has been on the LDP agenda since the 1970s. Yet, when the younger members of the LDP Diet delegation, notably those who have never experienced an election under the old system, proposed the idea, the older generation quickly took the idea off the agenda. The comparative evidence suggests that governing parties seldom reform after a single election defeat. It usually takes two consecutive defeats to drive the need for serious reform home. However, the same evidence indicates that a reformed LDP will be back in power within three or four elections.

NOTES

1. Kollner, "Upper House Elections in Japan and the Power of the 'Organized Vote.'"
2. Mair, Muller, and Plasser, *Political Parties and Electoral Change.*
3. Luther and Deschouwer, *Party Elites in Divided Societies.*
4. Kitschelt, "Linkages between Citizens and Politicians in Democratic Polities."
5. Christensen, "Electoral Reform in Japan"; McKean and Scheiner, "Japan's New Electoral System: la plus ca change"; Reed and Thies, "The Causes of Political Reform in Japan" and "The Consequences of Electoral Reform in Japan."
6. Reed, "Party Strategy or Candidate Strategy."
7. Scheiner, *Democracy without Competition in Japan.*
8. *Yomiuri Shimbun,* "*Hirei: Kakuto tekoire Soshihyo ni Kageri?*" (PR: Is the Organized Vote Fading?) July 8, 2004.
9. Campbell, "Policy Conflict and Its Resolution within the Governmental System."
10. See Reed and Shimizu, "Avoiding a Two-Party System."
11. Reed and Shimizu, "Avoiding a Two-Party System."
12. *Yomiuri Shimbun,* "Mutohaso no hyo, tairyo ni Jiminn he: Jiko kyoryoku ha isso shinten" (Independent Voters Go to the LDP: LDP-Koumeito Cooperation Advances) September 12, 2005.
13. *Yomiuri Shimbun,* "Seiken Kotai: Shuinsen no bunseki" (Alternation in Power: Analyzing the Election) September 14, 2009.
14. Lin, "How Koizumi Won."
15. Maclachlan, "Two Steps Forward, One Step Back."
16. *Yomiuri Shimbun,* "Seiken Kotai: Shuinsen no bunseki" (Alternation in Power: Analyzing the Election) September 14, 2009.
17. Duverger's Law is the generalization that the single-member district electoral system promotes a two-party system.
18. Reed, "Duverger's Law Is Working in Japan."

BIBLIOGRAPHY

Campbell, John Creighton, "Policy Conflict and Its Resolution within the Governmental System," in Thomas Rohlen, Ellis S. Krauss, and Patricia Steinhoff, eds., *Conflict in Japan* (Honolulu: University of Hawaii Press, 1984).
Christensen, Raymond V., "Electoral Reform in Japan," *Asian Survey* 34 (1994): 589–605.
Epstein, Daniel J., "Clientelism versus Ideology: Problems of Party Development in Brazil," *Party Politics* 15 (2009): 335–355.
Kitschelt, Herbert, "Linkages between Citizens and Politicians in Democratic Polities," *Comparative Political Studies* 33 (2000): 845–879.
Kollner, Patrick, "Upper House Elections in Japan and the Power of the 'Organized Vote,'" *Japanese Journal of Political Science* 3 (2002): 113–137.
Lin, Chao-chi, "How Koizumi Won," in Steven R. Reed, Kenneth Mori McElwain, and Kay Shimizu, eds., *Political Change in Japan* (Washington, DC.: Brookings, 2009).
Luther, Kurt Richard and Kris Deschouwer, eds., *Party Elites in Divided Societies: Political Parties in Consociational Democracy* (London: Routledge, 1999).

Maclachlan, Patricia L., "Two Steps Forward, One Step Back: Japanese Postal Privatization as a Window on Political and Policymaking Change," in Steven R. Reed, Kenneth Mori McElwain, and Kay Shimizu, eds., *Political Change in Japan* (Washington, DC.: Brookings, 2009).

McKean, Magaret and Ethan Scheiner. "Japan's New Electoral System: la plus ca change," *Electoral Studies* 19 (2000): 447–477.

Mair, Peter, Wolfgang C. Muller, and Fritz Plasser, eds., *Political Parties and Electoral Change* (London: Sage, 2004).

Reed, Steven R., "Duverger's Law Is Working in Japan," *Senkyo Kenkyu (Electoral Studies)* 22 (2007): 96–106.

———, "Party Strategy or Candidate Strategy: How Did the LDP Run the Right Number of Candidates in Japan's Multi-Member Districts?" *Party Politics* 15 (2009): 295–314.

Reed, Steven R. and Michael F. Thies, "'The Causes of Political Reform in Japan' and 'The Consequences of Electoral Reform in Japan,'" in Matthew Soberg Shugart and Martin P. Wattenberg, eds., *Mixed-Member Electoral Systems* (Oxford: Oxford University Press, 2001).

Reed, Steven R. and Kay Shimizu, "Avoiding a Two-Party System: The LDP versus Duverger's Law," in Steven R. Reed, Kenneth Mori McElwain, and Kay Shimizu, eds., *Political Change in Japan* (Washington, DC: Brookings, 2009).

Scheiner, Ethan, *Democracy without Competition in Japan* (Cambridge: Cambridge University Press, 2006).

Shinano Mainichi Shimbun,"Chijisen 'Kanshin aru' 84%" (The Gubernatorial Election: 84% Are Interested"), September 30, 2000.

Tanaka, Aji, "Seito Shiji Nashiso no Ishiki Kozo" (Understanding Voters with No Party Identification), *Leviathan* 20 (1997): 101–129.

Yomiuri Shimbun, "Hirei: Kakuto tekoire Soshihyo ni Kageri?" (PR: Is the Organized Vote Fading?), July 8, 2004.

———, "Mutohaso no hyo, tairyo ni Jiminn he: Jiko kyoryoku ha isso shinten" (Independent Voters Go to the LDP: LDP-Koumeitou Cooperation Advances), September 12, 2005.

———, "Seiken Kotai: Shuinsen no bunseki" (Alternation in Power: Analyzing the Election), September 14, 2009.

Party Politics in Japan

J. A. A. Stockwin

Introduction

Japan stands at a momentous and critical point in its political history. Having passed through terrible economic times in 2008–2009 with the global recession, the Japanese economy has resumed modest economic growth, but has to manage the largest national debt of any advanced country.

During the recession the political system has also faced a severe crisis, linked in part to economic problems. As a direct result of the politico-economic turmoil, the long rule of the Liberal Democratic Party (LDP) was decisively ended in general elections for the House of Representatives held on August 30, 2009. Its principal rival, the Democratic Party of Japan (DPJ), won a convincing victory and was able to form a new government in coalition with two minor parties on September 16.[1] Quite apart from the economic crisis, much concern was felt about the succession of short-term prime ministers since the relatively popular Koizumi stepped down in September 2006 after five and a half years in the post, and the presence of right-wing ideologues in post since the turn of the millennium. This was compounded by frustration with bureaucratic inefficiencies,[2] concern about growing social and economic inequalities and the increasing precariousness of labor, anxieties about the declining international status of Japan with the rapid rise of China, concern about a perceived nuclear threat from North Korea, and worries about the long-term prospects for a rapidly aging society.

The decisive change of government from the LDP (in coalition with the Komeito) to the DPJ (in coalition with the SDP and PNP) gave rise to hopes of new politics, breaking with the discredited politics of the past. Unfortunately, however, these hopes are far from fulfillment, and the Hatoyama government saw its popularity as reflected in public opinion fall from 71 percent approval in September 2009 to 21 percent approval in May 2010.[3] The reasons for this are complex, and the new government has some real achievements to its credit, but I reserve an assessment of it to the final section of the chapter.

The main task of this chapter is to seek understanding of the long politi-cal dominance of the LDP and the effects that this has had upon the deep structure of the politicoeconomic system. I believe that only through such an understanding may we evaluate the prospects for future political development.

In most democracies the prospect of a change of government following general elections is seen as part of the normal political process, but in Japan this has not been the case. Elections are not rigged in Japan. Procedures for voting and for counting votes are meticulous. There have been problems of malapportionment between different electoral districts, but this has hardly been the principal cause of long-term LDP rule since the 1980s. Japan is unusual in combining a democratic and reasonably fair electoral system with the political dominance of a single party for a longer period than in any other modern democracy.[4]

Since the 1990s, however, LDP dominance has not been absolute. Between August 1993 and June 1994 the LDP was out of power, replaced by a fragile coalition of several other parties. That it was able, Houdini-like, to claw its way back to power by offering the post of prime minister to the leader of the Japan Socialist Party (JSP), which had been the largest party in the Hosokawa coalition government of 1993–1994, testifies to its strategic abilities and its thirst for power. Thereafter the LDP gradually consolidated its grip on power, but till defeat in 2009 it nearly always governed in a coali-tion with minor parties. From 1998 to 2009 its coalition partner was the Komeito, whose adherence was needed for a "stable majority," giving it con-trol over the House of Councillors as well as the House of Representatives. The former, the upper house of parliament, may reject a bill sent to it from the lower house, so long as it is not the budget, a treaty, or designation of a prime minister. To overturn such a rejection, the lower house requires a two-thirds majority. This makes the House of Councillors a potent force in the system.

LDP DOMINANCE AND IMPLICATIONS FOR DEMOCRACY

At an occasion in Tokyo, I was asked by the well-known businessman and academic Glen Fukushima why the Japanese electorate keeps the LDP in office despite its poor performance and widespread dissatisfaction with it.[5] Even though the premise of the question was later negated by the elections in August 2009, he put his finger on a strange paradox. We need to explore why it is so strange. In terms of normative democratic theory, if elections are rigged, or serious opposition parties are banned or restricted, then a key precondition for democracy is denied. But in Japan this is not the case. If a party in power loses an election, and then cannot reestablish its major-ity with the help of other parties, then it will lose office. This happened to the LDP in July–August 1973, though the eight-party coalition government that replaced it soon lost its cohesion. It is, therefore, perfectly arguable that (apart from the 1993 elections) the LDP was elected to power in election after election because the electorate freely exercised its right of preferring the LDP to other parties, and that this is consistent with democracy. It is also arguable that long-term dominance of a single party eases policy planning, since a compliant electorate will not demand short-term favors before each election.

Nevertheless, concerns persist about a democratic deficit resulting from single-party dominance. A party long used to power may become complacent, arrogant, and corrupt, regarding electors as those who do its bidding rather than those who hold it to account. Changes of party in power may sharpen performance and stimulate policy rethinking. Competition with uncertain outcome is analogous to free competition in business, whereas competition with certain outcome is more like monopoly or oligopoly in business.

Moreover, since the early 1990s Taiwan and South Korea, among others, have developed democratic systems in which governments actually change (though not necessarily at every general election). It is, therefore, difficult to argue that something in the common culture of East Asia inhibits government replacement. In this sense, up to 2009, Japan had become an outlier in the region.

EXPLAINING SINGLE-PARTY DOMINANCE IN JAPAN, 1950S–1990S

No single factor is sufficient to explain the dominance of a single party over Japanese politics for such an extraordinarily long period. Some factors are more important than others, some more important at one time than at another. We enumerate these below.

1. Policy Success

We may suppose that a party will continue to be elected by a grateful electorate if its policies prove successful over the long term. This assumes that the electorate recognizes "success" and "failure," and the electorate may be divided here. But a government that ensures high levels of stability, security, prosperity, and fairness is likely to be more popular than a government presiding over low levels of these conditions. So steady economic growth under a particular government should enable it to create prosperity, produce a surplus for investment in social services (promoting fairness) and in the armed services (promoting security), and buy off potentially troublesome elements (promoting stability).

But the trouble with this argument is that economic growth, especially if it is rapid, may cause disruptive social change, involving massive transfer of people from rural environments with strong social supports, to relatively anarchic and atomized urban environments. Despite material increases in living standards, this may be outweighed by social and psychological disruption. Durkheim's classic study of suicide showed that suicide rates actually increased in times of rising prosperity.[6] In Japanese electoral

Table 5.1   LDP Vote Percentages, Lower House General Elections, 1958–1972

1958	1960	1963	1967	1969	1972
57.8	57.6	54.7	48.8	47.6	46.8

Source: *Asahi Nenkan*, various dates.

Table 5.2 LDP Vote Percentages, Lower House General Elections, 1976–1990

1976	1979	1980	1983	1986	1990
41.8[7]	44.6	47.9	45.8	49.4	46.1

Source: Asahi Nenkan, various years.

Table 5.3 LDP Vote Percentages, Lower House General Elections, 1993–2005

1993	1996	2000	2003	2005	2009
36.6[8]	SM 38.6[9]	SM 41.0	SM 37.5	SM 47.8[10]	
	PR 32.8	PR 28.3	PR 35.0	PR 38.2	

Key: SM = single-member districts; PR = proportional representation blocs (the electoral system changed in 1994).

Source: *Asahi Nenkan*, various years.

results between 1958 and 1972, it was found that when growth rates were averaging 10 percent per annum, the LDP polled a slowly decreasing percentage of the vote at each general election over the period, especially in the big cities.

In elections, however, during the 1970s, which saw much lower rates of economic growth, LDP vote percentages stabilized, and even increased slightly, though in the 1980s, when rapid economic growth resumed, these rates were not adversely affected.

When we examine the figures for the economically stagnant and politically unstable decade of the 1990s and the first half of the 2000s, we find a more confused picture, reflecting the complex politics of that period, which included the emergence of new parties and a new electoral system. An inverse correlation between economic growth and LDP popularity applied in the transformational situations of the 1960s, but is harder to establish for later periods.

2. Electoral Systems

We now examine the role of the two successive electoral systems for the House of Representatives as a possible partial explanation for the long-term dominance of a single party in Japanese politics. We need to simplify complex phenomena, but may confidently point to some salient effects.

All lower house general elections between 1947[11] and 1993 were conducted under a system originating in the 1920s, whereby each elector wielded a single nontransferable vote, but each district elected multiple members (in most cases, three, four, or five). This may be termed "single nontransferable vote in multimember districts" (SNTV in MMDs). In other words, the elector's vote was cast just as in elections to the British House of Commons, but electoral districts were similar to those in elections to the Irish Dail.

There was no mandatory provision (or independent review) in the pre-1994 lower house electoral system for the redrawing of electoral boundaries to reflect population movements over time. There were ad hoc adjustments to mitigate (though never to eliminate) discrepancies in the value of a single vote in different parts of the country that took place in the 1960s, 1970s, and 1980s. At certain times, the discrepancy in the value of a vote between the most underrepresented and the most overrepresented district was almost 400 percent,[12] and for much of the time it was around 300 percent. Moreover, this malapportionment, or what the present writer has called the "negative gerrymander," was neither random nor insignificant in terms of its effects on party electoral performance. Broadly speaking, rural areas were more conservative than urban (especially big city) areas, and the LDP more firmly entrenched in the countryside than in the cities. Had malapportionment not existed at the lower house general election of 1976, 1979, and 1983 (possibly also that of 1990), the LDP might well have fallen short of a seat majority.

Multimember districts also created important effects. Let us imagine a five-member district in which one party can count on 20 percent of the vote, being about the number of its core supporters. Acting rationally, that party would run a single candidate. Two candidates would split the vote and both might fail to be elected. This is known as *tomodaore* (falling down together). But for the candidate elected, it would be against his or her interests to have a second candidate contest the district in subsequent elections. Rather than seeking to expand local support for the party, the incumbent would seek to keep party support stable, so as to retain his or her seat indefinitely, avoiding competition from other potential candidates *for the same party*. This was broadly the situation for the JSP (until the 1990s the largest opposition party), which could rely on unions for a predictable, but limited, degree of support. Paradoxically, SNTV in MMDs, while keeping the JSP (and other smaller parties) in existence at a certain level tended to stifle their further electoral development.

In the contrasting case of the LDP, it might expect to win 55 percent of the vote in a given five-member district. Here, the party would need to consider carefully how many candidates to run. If it ran two, it would probably fail to maximize its potential, and if it ran four, it would risk fragmenting its vote and losing two of them, but with three, it would stand a good chance of having all three elected. That was the party perspective, but individual candidates often saw things differently. Crucially, all three candidates would see each other as rivals just as much as they regarded as rivals candidates from other parties. This led to a style of LDP campaigning based on candidates' personal support machines (*koenkai*), and the candidates typically belonged to intraparty factions (*habatsu*) at the national party level. *Koenkai* and *habatsu* are often decried, in Japan and abroad, as obstacles to truly democratic politics, but organized rivalry between competing LDP candidates in their electoral districts boosted the total number of votes cast for the totality of LDP candidates in many districts. So for this reason as well, the system worked in the LDP's favor. It is hardly coincidental that the process of changing the electoral system was initiated, not by an LDP government, but by the Hosokawa coalition government in 1993–1994.[13] The system also promoted personality voting, where the person of the candidate was seen as more important than the character and policies of the party.

As we have seen, the lower house electoral system was abolished in 1994, and was replaced by a quite different system based on a combination of single-member districts and regional blocs electing members by proportional representation.[14] The first election held under the new system was in October 1996. The new system was a compromise between the aims of creating genuine competition on an equal footing between a very small number of large parties (in principle only two), and of protecting the interests of smaller parties. Over the 13 years from 1996 to 2009 in which it has been tested, the former aim has been achieved more convincingly than the second.

One purpose of changing the system was to make lower house elections more party- and policy-centered, with less emphasis than before on the person of the candidate and (possibly corrupt) personal linkages between the candidate and local district voters. In practice, however, things did not work out entirely like that. Most LDP (and some other party) candidates continued to cultivate *koenkai* in their now single-member districts. Personal connections and the expectation of voters that their member of parliament would bring concrete benefit for the district did not disappear with the change of system, and this benefited the LDP so long as it remained in power and could deliver on electoral promises by virtue of controlling government resources. On the other hand, the fact that many LDP parliamentarians now occupied seats safe from competition by rival LDP candidates meant that the earlier kind of competitive stimulus had disappeared.[15] LDP candidates were now relying to a large extent on the superior resources of funding and of visibility that they, as representatives of the long-time ruling party, were able to command. But with the rise of the DPJ, originally founded in 1996, rebranded in 1998 and in 2003 with the addition of the small Liberal Party, they were facing serious competition.

3. Opposition Failure

By definition, if one party was dominant and central to nearly all governments since the 1950s, then parties opposed to it constituted a long-term

Table 5.4 JSP Vote Percentages, Lower House General Elections, 1958–1972

1958	1960	1963	1967	1969	1972
32.9	27.6	29.0	27.9	21.4	21.9

Source: Asahi Nenkan, various years.

opposition. The phenomenon of permanent opposition requires explanation just as much as does single-party dominance.

The key question here is: "why did the JSP (now SDP) ultimately fail?" In 1963 Ishida Hirohide, a progressive conservative who had been minister of labour in an earlier LDP government, published an article in which he predicted that demographic and educational trends would result in the LDP losing its parliamentary majority by 1970.[16] Table 5.1 shows us that the LDP vote had been declining throughout the 1960s.[17] But whereas the JSP had been the only significant opposition party in the 1958 elections, it had lost much support to smaller parties by 1970 (see Table 5.4).

The 1960s were crucial in determining the fate of Japan's opposition parties. During that decade, the JSP failed to maintain the momentum it had built up in the turbulent 1950s, and even regressed in terms of its support. Perhaps the most obvious explanation would be that the 1960s were the decade of the "economic miracle." For the first time in history, large numbers of Japanese were experiencing prosperity, though they had to work hard for it. The political effects, however, were not so simple as this might imply. A more convincing explanation of JSP failures was that that party did not sufficiently adapt to new social and economic conditions, allowing new and revived political parties to emerge that were better adapted to the needs of people disorientated by ultrarapid changes in their circumstances. But none of these parties could grow strong enough to replace the JSP, which emerged into the 1970s debilitated, but still much the largest party outside the LDP.

The first new party to emerge was the Democratic Socialist Party (DSP), which split from the JSP in 1959–1960 protesting at the latter's hard-line leftist positions in the context of revising the Japan-U.S. Security Treaty. The DSP support base was concentrated in private sector unions, especially in the car industry. By removing centrist and right of center elements from the JSP, the latter found it difficult to adapt to an increasingly prosperous society.

Another party that came to prominence in the 1960s and 1970s was the Komeito (sometimes called "Clean Government Party" [CGP]), an offshoot of the Soka Gakkai, the most successful of the postwar "new religions." The Komeito was launched in 1964 and secured the election of all its 25 candidates in the lower house general elections of 1967. In its early years this party, like its parent religion, appealed typically to undereducated workers in small firms, and to lower class middle-aged housewives.[18] The Komeito marshalled a formidable electoral machine, exercised tight discipline over its supporters, and in most elections from the late 1960s to the early 1990s, it won around

50 seats.[19] It was thus rather more successful than the DSP, but unable to break through the glass ceiling it had reached in its early elections.

The third party to challenge JSP dominance of the opposition in the 1960s was the Japan Communist Party (JCP). This was not a new party, having been founded illegally in 1922, and legally from 1945. In the war recovery period of the late 1940s it had some successes, but lost most of its support on turning to direct action from 1950, on Moscow's orders. In the 1960s, however, it broke with Moscow and then with Beijing, and set up "clinics" all over the country to help ordinary people with their tax returns and similar matters. It reaped a sufficient electoral harvest that some in the LDP came to regard it as a greater political threat than the Socialists, so that a disinformation campaign was launched against it, to some effect.[20]

Thus the emergence of new and revived parties, in part caused by the ineffectiveness and inward-looking character of the JSP, further weakened the JSP without enabling any party to emerge that could replace it as principal opposition party. Various attempts were made to effect electoral cooperation between the various parties of opposition, but with modest results.[21] In the 1980s, however, some things began to change. In 1986 the JSP wrote a new policy platform, eliminating much previous Marxist doctrine. from it. Later in the same year, the party appointed as its chair Doi Takako, the first woman to head a political party since parties were formed. With the LDP experiencing policy difficulties and mired in corruption scandals, she mounted an effective campaign against the ruling party. Her recruitment of women to fight elections (the "Madonna Boom") further enhanced her popularity. In the House of Councillors elections of July 1989 the JSP far surpassed its normal voting levels, and since then the LDP never recovered its independent upper house majority. This became the key factor in the later formation of LDP-dominated coalition governments, since the upper house could otherwise exercise a power of veto.

The year 1989 was, however, a high point for the JSP from which it later declined in influence. This is treated later in the chapter.

4. The Governmental Machine

Another way of explaining single-party dominance in Japan is the effectiveness of the LDP organizational machine. The LDP should be seen as part of a much broader structure of interests, including the central government ministries, local administrations, and many private sector interest groups. The central government/party structure exercised a magnetic attraction for those seeking government assistance or subsidy. LDP politicians often told electors that a vote for a party other than their own was a wasted vote, since only the LDP had the contacts and clout to deliver benefits. The message was plausible, and no doubt attracted many votes.

This in turn meant that over the decades, formerly hostile and critical interest groups, especially in the labor movement, turned toward those in power, and to some extent even became incorporated into the structure itself. This discouraged opposition, since other parties could not deliver benefits

unless they formed coalitions with the LDP. Rather than setting out to criticize government policy and to develop carefully thoughtout alternatives,
non-LDP parties had two available strategies: either they could oppose in an
ideological, but hardly practical, fashion, seek to attract protest votes from
alienated sections of society; or they could attempt accommodation with the
ruling structure itself, and hope for benefits and concessions to their particular clientèles in response. In practice, the choices were not quite so clearcut.

5. LDP Organizational Superiority

Even though it makes some sense to regard the LDP up to the 1990s as
simply the political arm of a sophisticated governmental machine, the organizational structure of the party itself also has a bearing on the longevity of
its rule. First of all, the LDP was adept at organizing its electoral campaigns
effectively, maximizing its vote potential in terms of seats. We have seen that
under the former lower house electoral system, LDP candidates competed
with each other in the same districts. With no vote transferability, candidates
were on their own. The party though did not just stand aside and allow
an intraparty free-for-all in every district. Rather, it policed endorsements
to make sure the party elected the maximum number of candidates. This
required careful calculation, with two things chiefly in mind. The first was
to ensure that the right number of LDP candidates (no more and no less)
stood for election in each district. The second was to avoid a situation in
which one candidate was too popular, thus depriving others of votes and
diminishing the optimum potential of the party vote. Obviously, each candidate also should be able to attract sufficient support.[22]

Thus LDP electoral organization rested on two principles: free-market
competition between candidates on the one hand; and careful regulation of
the number and type of candidates allowed in the field, on the other. This
strategy was highly successful, as seen in the proportions of "live votes" and
"dead votes." A live vote is the vote for a candidate who is elected and a dead
vote the vote for a defeated candidate. The LDP regularly recorded about
80 percent of live votes to 20 percent of dead votes. No other party came
close to this, except on occasion the Komeito, which, however, only ever put
forward one candidate in a given district and only chose winnable districts
for its candidates.

The consequences of this way of organizing elections had an important
impact on the party's character. LDP candidates, as we have seen, normally
ran their own *koenkai*. Since it was far easier to "inherit" a *koenkai* than to
start one from scratch, a high proportion of LDP parliamentarians were the
sons, sons-in-law, nephews,[23] and so on of previous members for the same
district.[24] Hence the phenomenon of the "family seat," widely criticized but
accounting for some 35–40 percent of seats held by the LDP, and a smaller
but significant proportion of seats held by other parties.

A further aspect of LDP organizational structure (albeit informal) was fac-
tionalism at the central level. LDP members naturally gravitated to factions

in Tokyo, for access to funds, promotion support, bargaining leverage, and perhaps also for a sense of small-group solidarity. The impact of factions on how the party ran its affairs at central level was profound, in at least three senses. First, the choice of party president (who normally became prime minister) depended on an electoral contest in which the main players were the factions. Continuous rivalry between the factions for the top position meant that those who had "climbed to the top of the slippery pole" would soon find themselves sliding down.[25] Whereas in the United Kingdom between 1945 and 2010 (Attlee to Cameron) there have been 13 prime ministers, Japan over the same period (Higashikuni to Kan) has enjoyed the services of 33. Another factor adversely affecting the room for manoeuvre of a prime minister was the power of LDP committees to amend or veto prime ministerial initiatives.

Second, prime ministers had to take factional interests and claims into account in constructing their cabinets, making careful calculations about which factions most needed to be rewarded. Each faction would bargain hard with the prime minister, indicating forcefully its own list of preferred posts. It followed that the pressures on a prime minister to reshuffle his cabinet at frequent intervals, to satisfy factional demands, were immense. Cabinet ministers (and holders of party offices) were thus chosen less for their ability than in order to satisfy factional demands in a constant game of musical chairs. Not surprisingly, power gravitated toward unelected bureaucrats and away from their supposed political masters (there were some exceptions to this in the case of those appointed to head key ministries).

Third, by the 1980s, the LDP had evolved a method of promotion to ministerial office among its members based principally on seniority, calculated by the number of times a parliamentarian had been elected. In many cases, the member would be allowed just one cabinet position during his career, and only with high flyers might cabinet office become a habit. This system bore a curious resemblance to promotion practice in government ministries and large bureaucratized private companies.[26]

6. American Influence

It may also be the case that American influence facilitated single-party dominance of Japanese politics and government. There are two particular aspects and one much more general aspect of this idea.

The early years of the LDP faced conservative politicians with the daunting task of creating organizational structures capable of bringing and keeping together the disparate political elements that had sought refuge against what they saw as the Socialist threat in 1955 in the structure of a single newly constructed political party. It was no mean feat to build a new umbrella structure under which politicians from the center to the far right would find their place. The early years of the LDP were affected by frequent episodes of dissent, and the threatened defection of at least one complete faction.[27] It is now common knowledge that the U.S. authorities made financial contributions to help keep the party together at this period.

The second aspect appeared in the early 1990s, with the collapse of the USSR and the ending of the Cold War (at least so far as Europe was concerned).[28] It is hardly coincidental that left of center forces in the politics of Japan (especially the JSP) found themselves entering into government a few short years after the Berlin Wall was breached. This elicited no serious official U.S. reaction, but if the same thing had happened 10 or 20 years earlier it is hard to imagine the Americans would have been so relaxed about it.

Third, and more general, throughout the period of LDP dominance, the United States has been Japan's principal security ally and most important trading partner. The United States has been by far the most important influence on the Japanese political classes, especially those within government. This influence has served to consolidate in power those who have been the strongest proponents of Japan's alliance with the United States, and disadvantage those, particularly on the left, who have tended to criticize it or have been further removed from it.

7. Culture

Political scientists are often reluctant to tackle questions placed under the rubric of "culture," no doubt because such questions, and possible answers to them, are difficult to quantify, and contemporary political science has fallen under the influence of the hard quantitative sciences, notably economics. However this may be, it would be unfortunate to neglect the cultural aspect and we make no apology for raising it here. Cultural factors, however, can never form a total explanation for political phenomena, and cultures change over time, at different rates and in different directions.

The idea that cultural factors may have helped create a Japanese political system dominated by a single political party may seem far-fetched, but it is plausible if we understand by "culture" the concatenation of ideas relating especially to human interaction embedded in the minds of the society at large, and more particularly, in the minds of members of the political classes. If we take it in this sense, at least one aspect of culture that seems relevant to the problem of single-party dominance is the tendency in Japan to attribute to those exercising power the right to exercise power, and the duty (or need) of those not exercising power to defer to those who do. We need to tread delicately here, because such phenomena might be explained on the basis of more concrete and mundane criteria. Even so, a common sense of deference to authority may well have made it easier in Japan than elsewhere for a single party to hang onto power for a very long time. On the other hand, Japan has gone through periods of popular upheaval, which cautions us against taking such an argument too far.

POLITICAL TRANSITIONS, 1990S–2009

The 1990s may be seen as a period of transition between the norms of the old system and the painful, step-by-step transition to a new kind of system, which has still to be fully established. The following is a brief description of the main developments since 1993.

On August 9, 1993, the LDP fell from power as the result of its defeat in the lower house general elections held in July. This was entirely because the party had split, with two new parties, the Japan Renewal Party (JRP) and the New Party Harbinger (NPH), formed out of it and in opposition to it.[29] The number of seats won in the July elections by the three parties together was almost exactly the same as the previous LDP seat total, so it is difficult to argue that the LDP had fallen simply because the electorate had turned against it. Nevertheless, the defeat led to the formation of a new coalition government excluding the LDP (and the JCP), consisting of eight parties (including a small group based in the upper house), which set out an ambitious reform agenda. Its key achievement was the radical reform of the lower house electoral system described above. The government came to an abrupt end in April 1994, when the prime minister, Hosokawa Morihiro, resigned, citing an obscure corruption scandal. The coalition staggered on for another two months under Hata Tsutomu of the NRP, but the coalition's prime strategist, Ozawa Ichiro, then attempted to form a new party excluding the Socialists, who were the largest party in the coalition. He later came to regard this as his greatest mistake.[30] The Socialists reacted by promptly sealing a faustian pact with the Devil, in which they, together with the tiny NPH, would join forces with the LDP (their old enemies) in a new coalition government under a Socialist prime minister, Murayama Tomiichi. This extraordinary government took office at the end of June 1994 and lasted until January 1996, when the post of prime minister reverted to the LDP.

In December 1994 Ozawa finally put together a new party, combining most of the former parties of the Hosokawa and Hata coalitions, but excluding the JSP and the NPH, which were now in government with the LDP. The new party—in English New Frontier Party (NFP) but in Japanese *Shinshinto* (literally New Progress Party)—had some early successes and for a while attracted a trickle of defectors from the LDP and elsewhere. But three years later, in December 1997, it was disbanded, leading to another shake-up of the political parties. One of the principal reasons for its demise was its incorporation of the *Komeito*, which nevertheless maintained much of its own organization intact while operating within the new party. The strains so created proved too great for the NFP, it lost momentum, and then flew apart.

Being together with the LDP in a coalition government proved to be the kiss of death for the JSP (Social Democratic Party [SDP] from 1996). In September 1996 it split into two, with the left wing once again led by Ms Doi Takako, but was reduced in the October 1996 lower house elections to a handful of seats, a position from which it would never recover.[31] The right of center factions, however, merged with a number of different groups to form a new party, the Democratic Party (of Japan) (DPJ). the DPJ was rebranded in 1998, absorbing elements that had belonged to the NFP, and was again rebranded in 2003, when it absorbed the Liberal Party (LP), a small party founded by Ozawa from his close supporters after the demise of the NFP. The LP had entered a coalition government with the LDP in January 1999, but Ozawa, disappointed with the exiguous policy results, pulled his party out of the coalition in April 2000. About half of the LP members stayed in the coalition with the LDP and founded a new party that they called the Conservative Party (CP). It performed poorly in the next general elections and was later absorbed into the LDP. A much longer lasting coalition arrangement involved the Komeito—newly constituted after the collapse of the NFP—entering into a coalition government with the LDP in October 1999. For a decade, adherence of the Komeito served to protect the LDP from parliamentary defeat.

Finally, the JCP, like the Socialists, though they did surprisingly well in the confused 1996 elections, experienced over time a serious decline in support.[32]

Confusion and instability in the party political system persisted for most of the 1990s, overlapping with the period of economic stagnation that has come to be called the "lost decade." But by the outset of the new millennium, a reasonable degree of stability had been restored. The LDP, up to and including the 2003 lower house elections, maintained a bare majority of seats, but remained dependent for top-up votes on the Komeito as its coalition partner. The DPJ, though it changed its top leadership rather frequently, continued to make encouraging electoral progress from election to election. In the lower house elections of November 2003 it won 177 seats as against the LDP total of 237, a better score than any opposition party had ever achieved since the late 1950s. But the 2005 elections saw a serious reverse in DPJ fortunes. The maverick but enterprising prime minister from April 2001 to September 2006, Koizumi Junchiro, was defeated in the House of Councillors in August 2005 over his bill to privatize postal services, an issue that he had made into a personal crusade. He promptly dissolved the lower house and announced new elections for the baleful date of September 11. He then proceeded to expel rebel members from his party and choose alternative candidates (known as "Koizumi's children" or "the assassins") to stand against them in their electoral districts. This strategy reaped a bountiful harvest for his own party that earlier he had pledged to destroy (bukkowasu). The LDP seat total rose from 237 at the elections two years earlier to 296 in 2005, and that of the DPJ was reduced from 177 to 113.

Despite this impressive victory, Koizumi relinquished the post of prime minister one year later, in September 2006, and was succeeded in quick succession by Abe Shinzo (September 2006–September 2007), Fukuda Yasuo (September 2007–September 2008), and Aso Taro (September 2008–September 2009). None of these leaders was able to achieve the momentum or popularity of Koizumi, and in July 2007 the DPJ won a major victory in elections for the House of Councillors. This led to a situation in which the upper house had a whip hand over the lower house, and many bills sent from the latter to the former were vetoed. The situation resulted in legislative paralysis and parliament came to be referred to as "twisted" (*nejire kokkai*).

It was, therefore, hardly surprising that the DPJ should have won the lower house elections on August 30, 2009, though the scale of victory was unexpected.

EXPLAINING SINGLE-PARTY DOMINANCE, 1990S–2009

Many leading observers during the political turbulence of the 1990s were arguing that the political system was undergoing a process of fundamental change.[33] Instead, it was possible to argue at the end of the 1990s that the essentials of the party system had returned to the status quo ante. The LDP was back in a more or less dominant position, most of the new parties of the 1990s had disappeared, with the single significant exception of the DPJ, which, however, had inherited a good part of the former Japan Socialist Party. The Komeito had been reconstituted after being semisubmerged within the NFP, the Communists still existed as a small independent force, and the wheel had come back full circle.

Certain things, however, had changed.

1. Electoral System Change

The new lower house electoral system had significantly altered the parameters of campaigning, and by extension, the character of parties at various levels. Instead of multimember districts, 300 seats were on the British model, with a further 180 contested under proportional representation. This was an entirely new system of election. In single-member districts only the candidate who came first was elected. This was natural from a British perspective, but for Japanese electoral candidates it shocked their normal assumptions. To a certain extent, the 180 seats determined by proportional representation were used as a way of "resurrecting" candidates who failed in the single-member seats, since candidates could stand in both kinds of district simultaneously. But of course, resurrection was possible only to a much more limited extent than in the old system.

An important purpose of the change of system was to shift the focus of elections from the local candidate as a conduit for benefits for the local area, to the local candidate as representative of a national party with a coherent policy platform, upon which the voter was invited to pronounce. Naturally, it took some considerable time and the experience of several elections before long-entrenched habits of electioneering began to change in the directions originally envisaged. But campaign "manifestoes," pioneered by the DPJ in the new millennium, soon became general, as did the use of candidate websites, which needed to be kept up to date and focused attention on policy issues. One thing that the 2005 and 2009 elections both demonstrated was that voters generally, but especially in urban areas, responded well to policy appeals that promised change in long-established practices.

2. Koizumi

The period in office of Koizumi as prime minister between April 2001 and September 2006[34] was a crucial one of change. It is not our intention here to evaluate his policies or discuss what he did in office. In any case, he was given a useful opening since the government bureaucracy had been restructured and the powers of prime minister strengthened a few months before he came to office. The atmosphere of policy innovation experienced between 2001 and 2006 induced a greater concern with policy among both candidates and the electorate that had been seen hitherto.

OPPOSITION CONSOLIDATION

During the first decade of the twenty-first century a much higher proportion of opposition lower house members belonged to the DPJ than had belonged to the JSP in the earlier periods. In the 2005 elections, 113 DPJ candidates were elected, but only 22 from other opposition parties (9 Communists, 7 Social Democrats, and 4 from the People's New Party). In the 2003 elections, the figures were 177 for the DPJ and 21 for other opposition parties. By contrast, in the 1976 elections, no fewer than 120 members from 5 "minor" parties were elected,[35] as against 123 for the JSP. The DPJ was thus much more obviously the leading party of opposition, and projected itself as a party having a real chance of forming a government on its own, or in dominant position.[36]

THE HATOYAMA GOVERNMENT AND THE CHALLENGES OF POLITICAL REFORM

When a new government was formed on September 16, 2009, it seemed that something momentous had occurred, or in more flowery language, that we were witnessing a new dawn in the land of the rising sun. Subsequent developments suggest that this judgement was premature. Indeed, in some ways the performance of the new government appears reminiscent of that of many past LDP governments, and as we have seen, its approval ratings fell from the 70 percent range at the outset to the 20 percent range half a year later. Two leading members of the government, Ozawa, the party strategist,[37] and Hatoyama, the prime minister, found their financial dealings under investigation. Hatoyama resigned in June 2010 over his failure to resolve the Futenma Marine base relocation issue, and was replaced as prime minister by Kan Naoto. The DPJ did badly in the House of Councillors elections in July, creating another "twisted Diet" in which the government would have difficulty getting its legislation through the upper house. Ozawa unsuccessfully challenged Kan for the party leadership in September, but relations between Kan, Ozawa, and their respective followers remained tense.

The issue of moving the Futenma U.S. Marine base away from the densely populated area of Ginowan City on Okinawa island, which so exercised the government and lost it so much support, was in fact a consequence of its attempt to strike out in new policy directions. By questioning the need for Japan to follow unquestioningly American military policy in the western Pacific, and reorienting Japanese foreign policy more toward Asia, the Hatoyama government found itself in a difficult relationship with the Obama administration in Washington. On the face of it, the Futenma base relocation presents problems that are secondary to broader strategic issues. But the fact that the Japanese government was attempting to renegotiate an agreement entered into with the Clinton administration in 1996 caused severe difficulties with American officialdom (especially military). Moreover, no viable alternative has yet been found to relocation near Nago City in the northern part of the island, despite fierce local opposition and the government's best efforts.

The Hatoyama government was reformist in other ways as well, and the effects of this were important. Determined to shift the focus of power from unelected bureaucrats to elected politicians, it was working toward a different relationship between the two than that which prevailed under successive LDP governments. It was also attempting to cut back on the kind of wasteful public expenditure that gave Japan the title of "Construction State." One of its first initiatives was to freeze dam construction pending thorough cost-benefit scrutiny of the many existing projects. The Hatoyama and later Kan governments have also approached the question of increasing social inequalities with a raft of new policies designed to help deprived sections of the society, in social welfare, health, and education. This is an uphill struggle, because of the lack of available funds given the size of the national debt. Nevertheless, it is important not to underestimate the ambition of its approach.

If DPJ-based governments have faced severe difficulties, the LDP is not in a good condition either. As happened briefly in 1993–1994, the LDP, deprived of the oxygen of power, is demoralized and has already suffered defections. At the time of the August 2009 elections a new party named *Minna no to* (literally, "Everybody's Party," but officially designated in English: "Your Party"), founded by Watanabe Yoshimi, son of a former LDP faction leader, contested the elections and won five seats. Other minor parties have appeared. For the good health of Japanese democracy, a viable government party and a viable opposition party are crucial, yet on neither side of politics do the principal parties appear to be enjoying the best of health.

CONCLUSION

This chapter has sought to explain the extraordinary persistence of single-party dominance in Japan over more than half a century, with one brief hiatus in the 1990s. It has also touched on the seminal elections of August 2009 that brought single-party dominance to an end (though it could recur in the future).

No one element stands out as a uniquely persuasive explanatory factor. But policy success (and failure), various aspects of the former electoral system (and its radical reform), opposition party failure up to the 1990s (and the recasting of the opposition from the 1990s), the magnetic pull of the governmental machine (and its decline from the 1990s, as well as recasting by Koizumi), superior organizing abilities on the part of the LDP (and their decline since 2006), American involvement and backing for the regime in Tokyo (and fluctuations in American interest and pressure after the Cold War ended), and finally a cultural preference for deference to the strong, rather than determined opposition (and then cultural evolution in favor of more free-wheeling political contestation)—all these things together add up to a kind of explanation. But the salient factor is complexity.

Some general elections have the effect of changing a political system. This may be said of the British elections held on May 6, 2010, which ended 65 years of alternating government by two major competing parties, and resulted in a coalition arrangement between the Conservatives and the Liberal Democrats. What happened in Japan in August 2009 was different, but in both cases major change occurred, providing an opportunity for systemic reform. It is too soon to pronounce on the performance of the new British coalition government, but the change in Japan shows just how difficult it is to reform a deeply entrenched political system, even after opposition parties win a decisive victory at the polls. More months and years are needed before we can say clearly whether or not they have succeeded.

NOTES

1. The results of the general elections held in September 2005 were almost exactly reversed. the The LDP score of 296 seats in 2005 was reduced to 119, whereas the DPJ 2005 score of 113 seats rocketed forward to 308. The other parties of the coalition government formed in September 2009 were the Social Democratic Party (SDP), with seven7 lower house seats, and the People's New Party (PNP) with three seats.
2. Revelations in 2007 about millions of inaccurate, misattributed, and lost pension files caused deep disillusionment with the capacity of government to fulfill its responsibilities.
3. Public opinion poll reported in the *Asahi Shimbun* (henceforth *Asahi*), May 17, 2010.
4. See T. J. Pempel, ed., *Uncommon Democracies: The One-Party Dominant Regimes* (Ithac, and London: Cornell University Press, 1990). By 2009 Japan had outstripped Sweden and Italy, two comparators for Japan in the book, in the longevity of its single-party dominance.
5. A "book break" at the Foreign Correspondents Club of Japan, March 30, 2009.
6. Emile Durkheim, *Suicide* (Original French edition, 1897; in English: Simon and Schuster, Free Press, 1997).
7. LDP performance in this election was adversely affected by the defection of several of its parliamentarians to form the New Liberal Club, most of whom rejoined the LDP in 1986.
8. The 1993 elections were contested soon after the formation of two new parties by groups of LDP defectors, thus robbing the LDP of its seat majority, and creating the short-lived Hosokawa coalition government, from which the LDP was excluded.

9. The 1996 elections were the first to be fought under the new electoral system, in which there were both single-member seats and seats elected by proportional representation from 11 regional blocs. The LDP performed less well in the latter largely because party was emphasised rather than a particular candidate, whereas personality voting had been an important element in LDP successes in the past.

10. This was the "postal privatization election", in which the prime minister, Koizumi Junichiro, greatly increased his popularity by boldly challenging the postal privatization rebels within his own party.

11. The 1946 general election was conducted under a different system.

12. At the time of the 1979 lower house general elections, the rural fifth district of Hyogo prefecture had 3.87 times fewer electors on the electoral roll per seat than did the urban fourth district of Chiba prefecture. For more details, see J. A. A. Stockwin, *Governing Japan: Divided Politics in a Resurgent Economy*, 4th ed. (Oxford and Malden, MA: Blackwell, 2008), pp. 177–178.

13. It was, however, finalized in 1994 by a coalition government including the LDP and JSP, under a Socialist prime minister.

14. Initially, there were 500 seats, of which 300 were elected in single-member districts and 200 elected in 11 regional PR blocs. Later, the 200 PR seats were reduced to 180.

15. It is true that in certain circumstances, a candidate defeated in a single-member district could be "resurrected" in a PR district. See Stockwin, *Governing Japan*, p. 174.

16. Ishida Hirohide, "Hoshu seito no bijiyon" (Vision of the Conservative Party), *Chuo Koron* (January 1963): 83–97.

17. In every election, however, the LDP seat total was boosted by the adherence of a small number of unaffiliated (*mushozoku*) candidates, who accepted the LDP whip when the elections were over.

18. In later years it appealed to a more sophisticated and middle-class electorate.

19. 1969: 57; 1972: 29; 1976: 55; 1979: 57; 1980: 33; 1986: 56; 1990: 45; 1993: 51.

20. JCP seats totals in lower house general elections over this period were 1969: 14; 1972: 38; 1976: 17; 1979: 39; 1980: 29; 1983: 26; 1990: 16; 1993: 15.

21. See Stephen Johnson, *Opposition Politics in Japan: Strategies under a One-Party Dominant Regime* (London and New York: Routledge, 2000).

22. At each election some candidates refused that LDP endorsement would nevertheless contest the district, and of these a few would be elected. Most were then accepted into the LDP after the elections.

23. Less commonly widows, daughters, daughters-in-law, or nieces.

24. Substantial numbers had also been the secretaries of former members, which in a sense is an aspect of this same practice, whereby someone close to the member "inherits" his seat.

25. To Benjamin Disraeli, when he first became British prime minister in 1868, is attributed the comment: "I have climbed to the top of the slippery pole."

26. Sato Seizaburo and Matsuzaki Tetsuhisa, *Jiminto seiken* (LDP Rule), 7th ed. (Tokyo: Chuo Koronsha, 1992[1986]), pp. 216–229. J. A. A. Stockwin, "Parties, Politicians and the Political System," in J.A.A. Stockwin, Alan Rix, Aurelia George, James Horne, Daiichi Ito, and Martin Colllick, *Dynamic and Immobilist Politics in Japan* (Basingstoke: Macmillan, 1988), Table 2.1 on p. 41.

27. Kono Ichiro, a top LDP leader, threatened defection in 1960 over revision of the Japan-U.S. Security Treaty. This project collapsed after two weeks.
28. Whether the Cold War really ended in the 1990s in Asia is more disputable.
29. In addition, a new party originating outside the LDP had been formed in 1992 by Hosokawa Morihiro, who was to become prime minister in the new administration. It was titled Japan New Party (JNP).
30. Oka Takashi, private conversation.
31. SDP lower house seat totals from the 1996 elections were 1996: 15; 2000: 19; 2003: 6; 2005: 7; 2010: 7.
32. The JCP lower house seat total in successive elections 1996 was 1996: 26; 2000: 20; 2003: 9; 2005: 9; 2010: 9.
33. For instance, T. J. Pempel, *Regime Shift: Comparative Dynamics of the Japanese Political Economy.* (Ithaca and London: Cornell University Press, 1998).
34. Koizumi enjoyed the third longest tenure of any postwar prime minister, following Sato Eisaku (1964–1972) and Yoshida Shigeru (1946–1947 and 1948–1952).
35. Komeito: 55; DSP: 29; New Liberal Club: 17; JCP: 17; Social Democratic League: 2.
36. On the transition from the Socialists to the Democrats, and the development of the DPJ as a viable contender for government office, see Sarah Hyde, *The Transformation of the Japanese Left: From Old Socialists to New Democrats* (Abingdon and New York: Routledge, 2009).
37. Early in 2009 Ozawa had stepped down as DPJ leader because of questions about his financial affairs, and was replaced by Hatoyama.

6

THE FARM LOBBY

Aurelia George Mulgan

Japan's farming sector is one of the most supported and protected in the world. This is in no small part due to a powerful farm lobby. Farmers have traditionally formed a well-organized voting bloc with privileged access to policymakers in both the Ministry of Agriculture, Forestry, and Fisheries (MAFF) and the ruling Liberal Democratic Party (LDP) party, which held power almost continuously from 1955 until 2009. Because the LDP was heavily reliant on votes from the agricultural sector, farmers played a major role in Japan's domestic political process.

However, this role is not fixed and unchanging. A number of developments has served gradually to weaken the political influence of farmers. Electoral reform implemented in 1994 reduced electoral malapportionment, which favored rural areas. The size of the national agricultural electorate gradually diminished as the sons and daughters of farm households migrated to the cities and an increasingly aged farm population abandoned agriculture. The political and economic standing of the leading farmers' group—the agricultural cooperative organization known as Japan Agriculture (JA or JA Group), previously as Nokyo, also declined as numbers of farmer-members and local cooperatives continued to drop. Similarly, levels of agricultural representation in the Diet fell as LDP politicians linked to farming areas decreased in number. Known variously as "farm politicians" (*noson giin*), "agriculture and forestry Diet members" (*norin giin*), "agricultural cooperative Diet members" (*Nokyo giin*),[1] and "agricultural and forestry tribe members" (*norin zoku*), their political prominence steadily contracted over the years.

Finally, in a major setback for conservative political forces, the LDP's predominance in power came to an end in August 2009. The resounding victory of the opposition Democratic Party of Japan (DPJ) in the lower house election was a significant step toward the establishment of a two-party system. In the new political environment, the farm lobby faces increasing pressure to assume a less partisan position. The DPJ also seeks proactively to undermine the political and economic power of the JA organization because of its historically close links to the LDP. Hence, the evolving political climate is unlikely to sustain the enduring ties between the farmers and the LDP that characterized the more than five decades of almost uninterrupted LDP rule.

In this chapter I analyze the relationship between the farm lobby and the government immediately before and during this period of political transition. My focus is on JA and its links to the LDP and the MAFF, which together formed an "agricultural policy triangle." I discuss how the ties that bind the parties to the triangle have been weakened or broken. The setback that the farm lobby is suffering as a result of the break-up of this triangle by no means indicates that it will lose all its political influence, or that it will not continue to push farmers' interests in national politics. Nonetheless, some important changes are occurring, which are not necessarily favorable for agricultural interests. Moreover, consolidation of a two-party system and a further reduction in bureaucratic power, to which the DPJ is committed, will make it even more difficult for the "agricultural policy triangle" to survive in its customary form.

JA's DOMINANCE OF THE FARM LOBBY

Several key characteristics define the farm lobby in Japan. First, it is highly unified and organized within a single dominant grouping—JA or Nokyo—that consists of a three-tiered organization of national, prefectural, and local-level agricultural cooperative groups, although a number of smaller agricultural organizations exists.[2] Whereas some of these share JA's status as a statutory organization, none has JA's clout, or its economic or political weight.

Second, JA's membership, which covers the vast majority of farmers, is strongly cemented by its all-encompassing economic, social, and community roles in farming areas. These organizational features have allowed JA to claim a legitimate representative function on behalf of farming interests. Just under 5 million regular farming members (4.83 million) and 4.67 million associate members (nonfarming rural residents)[3] belonging to just over 700 local, general-purpose coops throughout Japan form JA's membership base.[4] The main businesses of JA are banking, insurance, agricultural wholesaling and retailing, and supply of farming materials. Gross profits from these businesses amount to around ¥2 trillion per year, with more than one-half of all agricultural products marketed through the cooperatives (for a total value of ¥4.3 trillion in 2007) and more than one-third of all farm inputs handled by the coops.[5] In 2010 JA deposits were just under ¥86 trillion, second only to one of Japan's megabanks, Bank of Tokyo-Mitsubishi UFJ.[6]

Third, the farm lobby is not simply a "lobby" in the usual sense of "a group of persons engaged in trying to influence legislators or other public officials in favour of a specific cause." JA does not necessarily fit neatly into the standard definition of an interest or pressure group, defined as "an association of individuals that seeks to influence the policy process, without direct election to political office, through lobbying."[7] These definitions presuppose that the government and farm lobby are two separate institutions. In Japan, considerable overlap has characterized relations between the two. Although JA presses politicians and bureaucrats to make policy favorable to its interests and to those of the farmers, in some respects, JA has functioned as part of the government's administrative and policymaking apparatus. For this reason, the term "farm lobby" does not fully capture the unique features of the representation of agricultural interests in Japan.

Corporatization: JA's Semiadministrative Role

First, there is strong state involvement in agriculture. The MAFF intervenes in the agricultural sector with the assistance of JA, which was originally legislated into existence in 1947. In this respect JA should be considered an adjunct of the state to which semiadministrative functions are delegated.

In the political science literature, the term "corporatism" is used to describe this kind of relationship between interest groups and government.[8] JA is "corporatized" into government, which has been a significant source of its power. JA benefited in many ways from its proximity to government, enjoying many officially sanctioned monopolies and concessions. Administratively allocated tasks directly supported its huge organization, almost as an auxiliary agricultural bureaucracy, as well as providing a powerful organizational rationale.

JA's corporatization was most visible in relation to various aspects of MAFF intervention in the rice market. From 1947, when the Food Control (FC) system—which strictly regulated the distribution and pricing of rice, wheat, and barley—was established until 1994 when it was abolished, JA occupied a privileged position in the rice market as the government's chief rice collection agent. It capitalized on the FC system to expand its businesses and influence.[9] Rice and other grains made up a large portion of JA's marketing business. Even after the FC system was dismantled, JA's preeminence as the principal marketing agent for rice remained. JA was also granted monopolies in the supply of fertilizer and agricultural machinery to farmers.[10] In addition, the government heavily regulated and protected JA's banking and insurance businesses.[11] Led by its peak financial institution, the Norinchukin Bank, JA's privileged position in banking and insurance bestowed many advantages in competition with private sector financial institutions.

Because JA assisted the government in administering the farm sector and its compliance was often needed to implement government measures, it was automatically consulted by policymakers in the process of formulating agricultural policy. In short, it was corporatized into both agricultural policymaking and implementation processes.[12] It occupied a legitimate place in the policy deliberations of government, even though it simultaneously conducted pressure group-type lobbying activities.

At the same time, the benefits of corporatization came at some organizational cost: loss of organizational autonomy and almost obligatory compliance with government measures. JA was constrained to follow the MAFF's policy guidelines and hence its options in confronting government were limited when it opposed policy changes.

Politicization: JA's Electoral Activities

Second, although officially politically neutral, JA effectively functioned as the largest electoral support organization for the LDP. JA benefited from this relationship because of LDP dependence on the farm vote and JA's powers as a vote-gathering organization. The LDP's electoral debt to farmers and JA was one of the principal reasons why the government continued to support farmers.

While the agricultural cooperatives were prevented by law from engaging in electoral activities, JA created its own national political organizations for this purpose. The National League of Farmers' Agricultural Policy Campaign Organizations or National Farmers' League (*Zenkoku Nogyosha Nosei Undo Soshiki Renmei* or *Zenkoku Noseiren*) established farmers' political leagues (*nomin seiji renmei* or *noseiren*) in every prefecture.

Through these political groups, JA delivered bloc votes to candidates because of its high levels of organizational mobilization and its extremely high membership rate in farm coop members were virtually synonymous with farm household voters. JA, *Zenkoku Noseiren,* and the *noseiren* enlisted coop executives, staff members, and farmers in various kinds of electoral activities (*senkyo undo*), including recommending (*suisen*) candidates; dispatching JA executives, staff, and farming members to politicians' personal support groups (*koenkai*) to provide backup to candidates' campaigns; and supplying political funding through donations and the purchase of tickets to politicians' fundraising parties (*hagemasukai*).

Organizational backup was strongest in cases where JA leaders were themselves standing for national election. In this case, the entire JA organization, including *Zenkoku Noseiren,* went into action. In the 2007 upper house election, Yamada Toshio, a former executive of JA's peak body, the National Central Union of Agricultural Cooperatives, or JA *Zenchu,* stood for the LDP in the proportional representation (PR) constituency of the upper house. He won the second highest vote tally among LDP candidates in the PR constituency, with just under 450,000 votes (about 2.5 percent of the total LDP vote in the PR constituency). In fact, Yamada obtained the highest number of votes in 20 prefectures and the second highest number in 10 prefectures. These results clearly demonstrated JA's organizational power in elections.

The chairman of *Zenkoku Noseiren* attributed Yamada's victory to "the unified campaign of the executive and staff members of JA and related groups, with each organization's voluntary and influential sphere of activities mobilized."[13] Yamada's income and expenditure report for 2007 revealed that he ranked fifth among all Diet members in the amount of political funds received. He explained that this was wholly due to the 2007 upper house election, and that as a candidate in the national PR constituency, the money was for political activities, and so he needed a large quantity of funds for the election campaign.[14]

Yamada's election was significant because he was clearly identified as a "candidate from within the organization" (*soshikinai kohosha*). Once elected, he became a direct organizational representative of JA in the Diet, acting as a conduit for the opinions and wishes of the JA organization. As the chairman of *Zenkoku Noseiren* commented, "Over and above sending Mr Yamada into national politics, the organizations [who backed him] wanted to get the ideas of JA and the farmers reflected in policy so that they could be tightly grasped. With the focus on Yamada, who is an agricultural policy veteran, we expect to enliven the JA Group's movement even more."[15]

In January 2008, *Zenkoku Noseiren* received a special commendation from former prime minister and LDP president Fukuda Yasuo as an affiliated group (*yuko dantai*) at the LDP's convention, in recognition of the cooperation and support of *Zenkoku Noseiren* in elections and other activities. Of the 170 LDP "friendship groups," *Zenkoku Noseikyo* was chosen for the special commendation. Prime Minister Taro Aso also made a special effort to visit JA *Zenchu* prior to the August 2009 lower house election. In his speech to 200 JA executives he said, "The role of the JA Group is important, and we fully appreciate and trust it. We would like to ask for your support for the LDP in this general election also."[16]

JA's LOBBYING ACTIVITIES

As a farm interest group, JA also conducts farm policy representation, known as agricultural policy activities (*nosei katsudo*). These are led by JA *Zenchu*, which sees its primary objective as "representing the interests of Japanese farmers and their agricultural co-operative organization (JA Group)."[17] JA *Zenchu* formulates agricultural policy demands and publicizes them in multiple public fora. It organizes assemblies (*shukai*) and conventions (*taikai*) attended by staff from JA and *Zenkoku Noseiren* as well as from their lower level organizations, and by JA's farming members.

In addition to providing leadership for JA's policy-related activities, JA *Zenchu* uses its executives as professional lobbyists, making direct representations to the prime minister, the MAFF minister and deputy ministers, individual politicians, and MAFF officials. Under the LDP's long-term rule, it made specific policy requests to the combined council of LDP politicians linked to agriculture and forestry (Jiminto *norin kankei no godo kaigi*), and to meetings of various agricultural committees of the LDP's Policy Affairs Research Council (PARC). For each major agricultural policy issue requiring a government decision, there was a designated LDP policy committee to deal with it. JA *Zenchu* executives attended meetings of these committees as representatives of the JA Group, alongside, on some occasions, representatives from other groups related to the agriculture, forestry, and food industries.

Pressure from the farm lobby focussed primarily on policies affecting farm incomes, particularly agricultural support and stabilization prices[18] and other kinds of agricultural subsidies including those for the provision of farm infrastructure. On budget-related matters, JA's policy objective was to maximize funding from the central government's budget for agriculture. A meeting of the board of directors of JA *Zenchu* decided its requested budgetary appropriations (*gaisan yokyu*) for the annual agricultural, forestry, and fisheries budget and supplementary budgets.

One of the most sensitive policy-related issues for JA has been agricultural trade liberalization and associated market access negotiations at the WTO and in bilateral and regional Free Trade Agreements (FTAs). JA's consistent policy position has been to resist any further lowering of import tariffs on agricultural products because of the threat it posed to domestic agricultural prices. Outside Japan, JA *Zenchu* has concentrated its efforts on forming alliances with overseas farmers' groups that also favor the protection of domestic agricultural producers. JA *Zenchu* has built cooperative relations with agricultural groups in the Group of 10 (G10) of net food-importing countries, mainly developed countries, such as Norway and Switzerland. More recently, it has developed closer ties to farmers' groups in food-importing countries in Asia, such as India, forming an alliance called the Asian Farmers' Group for Cooperation (AFGC). JA *Zenchu* makes much of Japan's similiarity to other Asian countries with small-scale family farms, which are also seeking to raise their food self-sufficiency and are resisting pressure at the WTO to lower import barriers for "sensitive items" (*juyo hinmoku*) and "special items" (*tokubetsu hinmoku*).

THE AGRICULTURAL POLICY TRIANGLE AT WORK

The original iron triangle of Japanese politics comprised the bureaucracy, big business, and the LDP. However, a version has always existed in the farm sector. Agriculture is an area of policymaking where ties among key LDP politicians, interest groups, and the relevant ministry were considered to be the closest and strongest.[19] Indeed, relations among the three groups were described as collusion,[20] or as comprising a "collusive triangle of Japan's agricultural cooperatives, Diet members defending agricultural interests, and MAFF."[21]

In elections, the triangle manifested as former MAFF officials standing in elections for the LDP with JA's backing. For many decades, many former MAFF bureaucrats won upper house national constituency (now PR) seats as well as lower house seats for the LDP by drawing on the voting power of agriculture and related interests, including JA and *Zenkoku Noseiren*.[22]

In policymaking, the triangle took the form of an institutionalized policy community or subgovernment.[23] It involved a three-way policy negotiation and consultation process among MAFF bureaucrats, JA, and *norin zoku* who were executives of LDP agricultural policy committees. As a policy community, it was typically characterized by a comparatively limited membership, a strong focus on economic interests, a stable pattern of interaction, shared values, and "a relative balance of power amongst members and exchange of resources."[24] JA furnished voting support for the LDP and organizational support for the MAFF in exchange for policy benefits that supported its own and farmers' interests. All three worked together to deliver support and protection to farmers.

As agricultural committee executives, the *norin zoku* met in the *Norin Kanbukai* (the Agricultural and Forestry Executive Committee), which had the final say on the party's policy position on agriculture. The MAFF bureaucrats played the primary role as policy coordinators within the agricultural policy triangle, whereas the final decisions on policy were taken in deliberations between the MAFF, including the minister, and executives of the LDP agricultural policy committees, representing the government and the party (*seifu-Jiminto*) respectively.

It was not usual for large numbers of LDP agricultural politicians, including the *norin zoku*, former MAFF ministers and deputy ministers, chairmen, ex-chairmen and members of the PARC and parliamentary agricultural committees, and even other ministers, to attend policy conventions and national assemblies organized by JA *Zenchu* and the *Zenkoku Noseiren*. The role of the LDP *norin giin* was to take the proposals of these conventions and assemblies back into deliberations of their committees. LDP farm politicians also gathered together in Diet members' leagues to press the government on particular policy issues, such as the Rice Paddy Agriculture Promotion Diet Members' League (*Suiden Nogyo Shinko Giin Renmei*) that pushed for extra subsidies for rice farmers.

THE VESTED INTERESTS OF THE AGRICULTURAL POLICY TRIANGLE

JA is one of the chief obstacles to reform of the agricultural sector and has consistently used its political and economic power to block reform. In particular, it opposes structural reform to create large-scale farms and encourage corporate-style farms operated on a business basis.[25]

JA has developed a vested interest in small-scale, part-time farming because this type of farming remains the principal source of its economic, political, and organizational power. Structural reform would inevitably reduce JA's membership size, farmers' patronage of its services, and profits from its marketing and purchasing businesses. Small-scale, part-time farmers who gain most of their income off the land find JA's services very convenient and are not as interested in reducing production costs and JA's marketing commissions as full-time professional farmers who depend on agriculture for their livelihood. They comprise the majority of JA's membership and are privileged organizationally within JA by the one-member-one-vote system. Hence, their views are more strongly reflected in JA's business priorities and policy interests.

In maintaining a vested interest in the continuation of small-scale farming, JA shared a common policy standpoint with the MAFF and LDP. The MAFF consistently sought to maximize government intervention in the agricultural sector in terms of its own regulatory and budgetary powers, and small-scale farming was most dependent on government intervention.[26] For the LDP, the goal was to maximize the size of the farm vote and the numbers of rural dwellers. LDP politicians were always excessively concerned with the farm vote, particularly the votes of small-scale farmers, because they formed a significant part of the country's agricultural and rural vote.

THE AGRICULTURAL POLICY TRIANGLE IN DECLINE

Several trends have eroded the foundations of the agricultural policy triangle. Small-scale part-time rice farmers, who have formed the core of JA membership, declined in number from 1.98 million households in 1990 to just 1.21 million in 2005.[27] Moreover, among rice farmers who have strongly supported JA's political and economic interests because of its role in the FC system, the aging of the farm population is particularly dramatic. More than 70 percent of farmers who grow rice for all or most of their income are 65 years or over.[28] At the same time, JA is becoming less representative of the farming community because large-scale, more efficient full-time farmers, or those who gain the bulk of their income from farming, and who are not dependent on its less competitive business services, are growing in number. Given that JA's ability to speak for all farmers has been one of the foundations of its political influence, these developments do not augur well for JA's medium- to long-term future. On top of this, JA members are losing their organizational solidarity. Those attending JA-sponsored public gatherings and conventions, especially farmers, are falling in number. JA is a large bureaucracy of several hundred thousand, and it is on these white-collar workers that JA is increasingly dependent for political and policy mobilization purposes.

Second, the outlook for a number of JA's businesses is negative in terms of profits, market share, and volume of business. JA's share of rice sales (the most important agricultural commodity it trades) has fallen to 50–60 percent.[29] Some of its previously protected businesses are now more exposed to market forces such as savings and loans. The operations of many local coops have become unprofitable because they are dependent on the patronage of small-scale, part-time farmers owning tiny plots, whose input demands and output sales are very small. Coop business operations are inefficient in relation to such farmers.[30] The local JA that run up deficits in their marketing and purchasing operations have traditionally relied on profitable credit and insurance businesses to make up the shortfall. However, even JA's financial businesses are in difficulties. *Norinchukin*'s investments were hard-hit by the global financial crisis in 2008–2009, with well over ¥1 trillion in unrealized losses. The question JA now faces is whether its financial businesses are in a position any longer to cover losses in its agricultural businesses.[31]

Third, JA is vulnerable if it loses not only economic but also political power, with the agricultural policy triangle resting solidly on the JA's organizational base as the chief intermediary organization for both farmers and the state. Despite Yamada's outstanding success as an "organizational representative candidate" (*soshiki daihyo koho*) in the 2007 upper house election, JA's individual farmer members now constitute less than 5 percent of the national voting electorate.[32] Most notable in recent years have been the electoral losses sustained by groups of farm politicians in the 2004 and 2007 upper house elections, and in the 2009 lower house election. Six *norin zoku* and *norin giin* respectively lost their prefectural or proportional representation seats in 2004 and 10 lost their seats in 2007 (including five who had held the position of MAFF deputy minister or parliamentary secretary), with several others supported by *Zenkoku Noseiren* also unsuccessful. Overall, only one-half of the *Zenkoku Noseiren*'s recommended candidates won seats in the 2007 election.[33] *Zenkoku Noseiren* itself acknowledged a fear that the voting base of the LDP's *norin giin* was sinking.[34]

Even Yamada's election could be seen as an organizational victory rather than as a demonstration of farmers' voting power, in other words, the product of farm lobbyists' votes rather than farm lobby votes. Although JA officials and their families voted for Yamada, many farmers voted for DPJ candidates, attracted by the promise of direct income support, thereby explaining the LDP losses in rural prefectural constituencies.[35]

Furthermore, one strong aspect of agricultural representation in the Diet and the agricultural policy triangle—the election of former MAFF officials to the Diet as LDP candidates with the backing of JA and other groups from the agricultural and food industries has almost completely been erased. In the 2007 election, former MAFF officials who were elected stood for the DPJ.

The 2009 election was yet another debacle with key *norin zoku* losing their seats and only 100 of the 281, or 36 percent of candidates recommended by *Zenkoku Noseiren*, victorious.[36] Furthermore, JA's political unity weakened, with differences emerging in the electoral recommendations of national and prefectural groups. *Zenkoku Noseiren* recommended LDP candidates in almost all electorates,[37] and was critical of the rise in cases of support going to the DPJ within the JA organization, including among both its staff and membership. In only 33 out of 47 prefectures did the *noseiren* decide to offer support for the LDP across all electoral districts. In 11 prefectures, the local offices said that they adopted different strategies depending on the situation in each electoral district. In one prefecture there was no decision, and in two prefectures (Mie and Aomori) the decision was for a free vote. The LDP "kingdom" of Aomori delivered a particularly strong shock to JA *Zenchu*'s management.[38] The secretary-general of the Aomori *noseiren* said: "A free vote is not equivalent to not supporting the LDP, but we're also thinking that there may be a change of government . . . If this choice is a trigger for a change of government, I want it to be a wake-up call for the LDP. We also have expectations of the DPJ."[39] The LDP's top-down strategy of shoring up organizational support focused on approaching the headquarters of groups such as JA *Zenchu* in Tokyo proved, in practice, to be no guarantee of follow-through support from the regional and local branches of these groups.[40]

Finally, in the LDP administrations of 2007–2009, signs of disagreement on key agricultural policy reforms began to appear between the MAFF, on the one hand, and JA and the *norin zoku*, on the other. The tensions in the agricultural policy triangle were due to the MAFF's seeking key agricultural policy reforms, while JA, representing the interests of small-scale farmers who were resistant to any reforms, and their backers amongst the *norin zoku*, opposed these reforms.[41]

THE DPJ AT WORK: BREAKING UP THE AGRICULTURAL POLICY TRIANGLE

The DPJ adopted a deliberate policy of undermining the key institutions in the LDP-MAFF-JA agricultural policy triangle.[42] As the biggest supporter of the LDP, the farm lobby was squarely in the DPJ's sights.

As an initial strategy, the DPJ took proactive steps to break the political and economic power of JA. First, in late 2008, the DPJ opposed *Norinchukin*'s eligibility to receive funds in the government's bailout program in response to the financial crisis. The Law on Special Measures for Strengthening Financial Functions (*Kinyu Kino Kyokaho*) was designed to allow the government to inject more public funds into troubled financial institutions. The DPJ pushed for *Norinchukin*'s exclusion, citing its relatively low level of financing for small- and medium-scale firms, but it was obvious that the DPJ was really trying to destroy JA.[43]

Second, in April 2009, the DPJ submitted a bill to the upper house to revise the JA Law (*Nogyo Kyodo Kumiaiho*) to prohibit the "political utilization of associations of farmers and fisheries—that are under administrative control of the MAFF—for a particular political party(ies)."[44] The DPJ's bill took direct aim at the role of JA groups as vote-collection organizations for LDP candidates in elections. It was a legislative attempt to make JA's involvement in such activities illegal, and to try and enforce its political neutrality, a move directly opposed by the JA Group and *Zenkoku Noseiren*.

Third, the DPJ's agricultural policies targeted a change in the conventional subsidy framework for farmers from an indirect one, where farmers were subsidized through higher support prices, from which both farmers and JA benefited, to a system focusing directly on the farmers themselves. In other words, the DPJ's scheme was offering direct support, whereas traditional LDP agricultural policy was based on an indirect system.[45] The DPJ's new direct payment system for individual farm households, which proved so successful as a vote-winner in the 2007 upper house election and which was retained for the 2009 campaign, proposed to compensate farmers directly for the gap between production costs and the sales price of their products. Although price supports and direct payments were not so different for farmers—who just wanted their income guaranteed—JA really needed the price-support system to be retained, because under the existing rice distribution system, JA made more profit from a higher rice price.[46] By switching to a direct payment system, JA would be bypassed, thus weakening JA's influence on agricultural policy and on rural votes, and further undermining its economic and political power in the countryside.[47] The DPJ's agricultural policy package thus aimed to initiate the collapse of JA.

In contrast, the agricultural subsidies in the LDP's stimulus policy package in early 2009 used an indirect system of financial assistance to farmers. One of the biggest selling points of the stimulus package, which appropriated over ¥1 trillion for agriculture, forestry, and fisheries, were subsidies for converting production to nonrice crops such as wheat and soybeans. This aimed to compete with the DPJ's manifesto for a direct payment system. However, many of these subsidy programs were implemented through associations such as JA. An executive of the local JA office in Kawauchi's district explained: "Agricultural policy needs to look at 'communities.' This is why we need organizations such as JA."[48] An LDP executive added: "'individual blessings' are not supported and appreciated by farmers."[49] In utilizing this approach, the LDP's clear objective was to reinforce loyalties among its groups of organized supporters, and in particular, to regain the support of agricultural and rural voters, who had moved in such numbers to the DPJ in the 2007 elections.

The DPJ's farm income policy, with its proposal to offer direct income compensation all commercial farm households, deliberately tried to separate the LDP from its farm voter base. The party was not interested in enticing JA away from the LDP in order to use it as a vote-collection machine itself. As a general strategy, it refrained from approaching industries and groups linked to the LDP. The Council for the Revival of Food and Agriculture, which the DPJ established in June 2009 with about 80 former JA local heads and independent farmers, limited its activities to increasing the understanding of the system of direct income compensation to farm households, which was the party's key policy.[50] A DPJ executive said: "Even if we fawn on industries whose organizational power is weakening, it won't turn into votes and it would only limit our policy options."[51] On the contrary, "we are approached by some groups, who might be trying to take action before it is too late to ride a winning horse."[52] For example, in Yamagata prefecture, some local JA executives said that they did not support the LDP, disclosing that "their aim was to ensure a link with the DPJ, which was riding the winning horse."[53]

In the 2010 upper house election, *Zenkoku Noseiren* went as far as refusing to endorse an LDP candidate in the proportional representation segment of the election who was a former leader of JA's youth organization (*Zenseikyo*) and who garnered only 80,000 votes, well down on Yamada's performance in 2007 and only 10,000 more than *Zenseikyo*'s membership of 70,000. *Zenkoku Noseiren* announced that it would allow its members to vote according to their own preferences. Its prefectural branches could also decide freely whether they would support specific candidates in their own districts. The 2010 election was further marked by the retirements of six more *norin giin* and *norin zoku*, all but one belonging to the LDP.

Fourth, once in power, the DPJ targeted JA for reform, making it a topic for examination by a Government Revitalization Unit working group with a view to requiring tighter inspection of JA's financial businesses and reviewing its antitrust exemption. Moreover, one of the DPJ administration's key policy initiatives in 2010 was to promote FTAs, including the possibility of joining the Trans-Pacific Partnership (TPP), which would require all participants, including Japan, to reduce import tariffs to 0 over 10 years. This prospect galvanized JA into a campaign for the "survival" of Japanese agriculture, but it was clear that politically, JA had become more isolated and less influential. The DPJ had designated it a "hostile" organization, and consequently restricted its access to cabinet ministers and the party leadership. Having lost the ear of government and effectively abandoned by the ruling party, it was clear that JA had forfeited its privileged position in the policy community. Furthermore, because a trade agreement such as the TPP would drive down domestic agricultural prices, it would cut into JA's marketing profits (taken as a percentage commission on the sale price of agricultural goods) as well as pose a direct threat to JA's business services to small-scale, part-time producers, who would be the primary targets of restructuring in the agricultural sector. By covering all farmers with an income safety net, the DPJ could continue to separate farmers' economic interests from those of the agricultural cooperatives.

CONCLUSION

Party competition between the LDP and DPJ on farm policy is an entirely new phenomenon in Japanese agricultural politics. Prior to the 2009 election, it was pilloried in the Japanese media as "a battle of the pork barrels," but it had much wider significance for the future of the farm lobby and how it has traditionally conducted itself. Interest groups with almost fixed and durable alignments with the LDP, such as JA, have been forced to rethink their customary political strategies in an effort to reposition themselves in the new political landscape. The 2009 election was unsettling for JA and the farmers not only because of the increasing competition between the LDP and the DPJ for the votes of farmers but also because of the DPJ victory, which put JA on the wrong side of politics. In the wake of the election, JA and its political arm, *Zenkoku Noseiren*, adjusted their political strategies to the emerging two-party system. To be permanently aligned with one side of politics risked political exclusion on a regular basis. Moreover, the DPJ's successes in rural and semirural districts in the 2007 and 2009 elections revealed major defections to the DPJ among farm voters. Even the LDP's improved performance in rural single-member constituencies in the 2010 election did not necessarily herald a reversion to the fixed voting patterns of the past, rather a greater volatility in the agricultural electorate, with farmers prepared to switch their votes between both major parties depending on circumstances. Moreover, with JA's influence on the farmers diminishing and with no political force to replace it, the farm lobby is a fading presence in national politics.

Japan's DPJ government aimed to formulate an agricultural policy that was free of the vested interests that marked the old, established agricultural policy triangle. For the farm lobby, this inevitably meant loss of its intimate ties with government as well as its automatic policy access and influence. Indeed, the DPJ initially targeted the JA with proposals, including legislation, to reduce its political and economic dominance in the farm sector, and to enforce its political neutrality. The DPJ's antipathy toward JA was based on the agricultural cooperatives' previously unchanging links with the LDP. In wanting to break JA's power, the DPJ was aiming both to destroy the agricultural cooperatives as an electoral support base for the LDP and to remove a potential obstacle to agricultural policy change. If successful, this strategy might pave the way for both the structural reform of agriculture and agricultural trade liberalization.

NOTES

1. *Nokyo giin* are Diet politicians who are former or current JA executives. By 2009 (prior to the lower house election), their numbers had decreased to an all-time low, with five in each house of the Diet, for a total of 10. This compares with a peak of 51 in 1971. After the 2009 election, there were only three *Nokyo giin* left in the lower house, for a Diet total of eight. After the 2010 Upper House election, this had shrunk to seven. Sourced from the author's personal database on farm and JA politicians.
2. They include the organizations of land improvement associations (which focus on acquiring budgets for agricultural and rural public works) and the agricultural committee system (which assists the government in agricultural land administration), as well as commodity associations and rice-roots farmers' groups (the farmers' unions). Each represents a more specialized agricultural interest (for details, see George Mulgan, *The Politics of Agriculture in Japan*). However, because of the dominance of JA in routine agricultural policymaking affecting government benefits to farmers, in this chapter I focus almost exclusively on JA and its political offshoots.
3. Regular farmer-members of the agricultural co-ops fell from 5.77 million in 1975 to 4.83 million in 2008. JA *Zenchu*, "JA Gurupu to wa" (About the JA Group); Norinsuisansho. "Norinsuisan Kihon Detashu".
4. Local co-ops amalgamated to achieve greater organizational efficiencies. The merger process dramatically reduced their numbers from 3,574 in 1990 to 716 in 2011. See Ministry of Internal Affairs and Communications, "Agriculture, Forestry and Fisheries", in *Japan Statistical Yearbook 2009*; JA *Zenchu*, "JA Gurupu to wa" (About the JA Group);
5. Central Union of Agricultural Cooperatives (JA *Zenchu*), *The Present Situation of Japanese Agriculture and JA Group: Case of Agricultural Cooperatives of Japan*.
6. Norinsuisansho. "Norinsuisan Kihon Detashu"; "'Nokyo' Losing Say in Agripolicy," *The Nikkei Weekly*.
7. Warhurst, "Interest Groups and Political Lobbying," p. 327.

8. Panitch defines corporatism as a political structure that "integrates organized socioeconomic producer groups through a system of representation and cooperative mutual interaction at the leadership level and mobilization and social control at the mass level" (Panitch, "Recent Theorisations of Corporatism," p. 173).

9. Yamashita, "The Agricultural Cooperatives and Farming Reform in Japan (1)."

10. Godo, "The Changing Economic Performance and Political Significance of Japan's Agricultural Cooperatives," p. 6.

11. Ibid., pp. 6, 9.

12. See George Mulgan, *The Politics of Agriculture*, pp. 137-158.

13. "Zenkoku Noseiren: Heisei 19-Nendo Rinji Sokai o Kaisai" (The National Farmers' League Holds a 2007-Year Extraordinary General Meeting), *Nosei Undo Jyaanaru*, p. 2.

14. "Yamada Toshio Giin Kokkai Nikki, Heisei 19-Nendo Seiji Shikin Shushi Hokoku" (Toshio Yamada's Diary from the Diet, The 2007 Political Funds Report), *Nosei Undo Jyaanaru*, p. 12.

15. "Zenkoku Noseiren," p. 2.

16. "Aso Shusho: Kikikan Arawa Keidanren, Zenchu o Homon" (Prime Minister Aso Visits the Japan Business Federation and the National Central Union of Agricultural Cooperatives, Revealing a Sense of Crisis), p. 5.

17. JA *Zenchu*, Central Union of Agricultural Co-operatives, "Objectives and Activities of JA-Zenchu."

18. Under the FC system, which governed rice distribution and pricing until its abolition in 1994, JA led an annual producer rice price (*seisansha beika*) campaign to push the government into raising the price at which it bought rice from the farmers (the Food Agency of the MAFF was a state trader). The rice price campaign (*beika undo*) was the major agricultural policy campaign of JA each year. JA's own fortunes were also very much tied up with rice farming, because higher prices of rice boosted the amount of rice passing through JA's hands as chief rice collector, and higher profits from marketing commissions. In addition, the government paid the farmers for their rice through farmers' savings accounts held with JA, which channelled large quantities of funds through JA's financial organizations. Higher rice prices also boosted sales of farm inputs purchased from the cooperatives, which could raise prices accordingly. Even after the FC system was abolished, the trading arm of JA (JA *Zenno*) was found to have manipulated rice prices in the public bidding system. It successfully lobbied the MAFF to prohibit the trading in rice futures, which would have made it harder for JA to keep rice prices high by manipulating the spot trading market. Yamashita, "The Agricultural Cooperatives."

19. George Mulgan, "'Japan Inc' in the Agricultural Sector: Reform or Regression," *Pacific Economic Papers*, No. 314, April 2001, pp. 1–2.

20. Godo, "The Changing Economic Performance," p. 5.

21. Yamashita, "The Agricultural Cooperatives and Farming Reform in Japan (2)."

22. Another important organization in this context was the National Federation of Land Improvement Groups, together with its prefectural and local land improvement industry groups.

23. George Mulgan, "'Japan Inc' in the Agricultural Sector," pp. 1-9; George Mulgan, "Where Tradition Meets Change: Japan's Agricultural Politics in Transition," p. 263; George Mulgan, "Japan's FTA Politics and the Problem of Agricultural Trade Liberalisation," pp. 172–176.

24. Hill, *The Public Policy Process*, p. 69.
25. Yamashita, "The Agricultural Cooperatives and Farming Reform in Japan (1)."
26. See George Mulgan, *Japan's Agricultural Policy Regime*; George Mulgan, *Japan's Interventionist State: The Role of the MAFF*.
27. Yamashita, "The Agricultural Cooperatives and Farming Reform in Japan (2)."
28. Ibid.
29. Yamashita, "'Nokyo' to 'Gentan' ni 'No' to Ieru Seiji ga Ima Koso Hitsuyo" (It's Necessary to Demand Politics that Says "No" to "JA" and the "Rice Acreage Reduction Program").
30. Yamashita, "The Agricultural Cooperatives and Farming Reform in Japan (2)."
31. Ibid.
32. Total regular farm membership of JA in 2007 was 4.89 million, whereas the total number of eligible voters nationwide in 2007 was 103.7 million, giving a percentage of 4.7. JA *Zenchu*, "JA Gurupu to wa" (About the JA Group); Somusho, "Senkyo" ("Elections").
33. Yamashita, "The Agricultural Cooperatives and Farming Reform in Japan (2)."
34. "Hinmoku odan, kobetsu shotoku hosho, WTO nado Yamada shi no sonzai-kan ni mo chumoku" (Paying Attention to Non-Product-Specific Management Stabilization Countermeasures, Farm Household Income Compensation, WTO etc. and also the Powerful Presence of Mr Yamada), *Nosei Undo Jyaanaru*, p. 23.
35. Yamashita, "The Agricultural Cooperatives and Farming Reform in Japan (2)."
36. "Zenkoku Noseiren Suisen Koho ga Kettei" (National Farmers' League Decides Its Recommended Candidates), pp. 2-13; "'09 Shuinsen, Kaihyo Kekka to Tosensha Ichiran" (The '09 Lower House Election, Vote Counting Results and Table of Elected Members), pp. 8-13.
37. Of the 281 candidates recommended by *Zenkoku Noseiren*, all were from the LDP (96 percent), apart from one from the DPJ, six from the Komeito, two Independents, and a candidate from the Kokumin Shinto (People's New Party). "Zenkoku Noseiren Suisen Koho ga Kettei," pp. 2-13.
38. "Jimin Shiji Dantai ni Nejire, Chiho Shibu wa Jishu Tohyo mo" (Rebellion within LDP Support Groups, Regional Branches Resolving on a "Free Vote").
39. "Senkyo: Shuinsen, Ken Noseiren ga Jishu Tohyo, Jimin Koho Suisen Sezu" (Election: House of Representatives Election, Prefectural Farmers' Political League Grants a Free Vote, We Won't Recommend LDP Candidates).
40. "Jimin Shiji Dantai ni Nejire, Chiho Shibu wa Jishu Tohyo mo" (Rebellion within LDP Support Groups, Regional Branches Resolving on a "Free Vote").
41. Yamashita, *Nokyo no Daizai (Serious Crimes of the Agricultural Cooperatives)*, p. 128.
42. Iinuma, "What Are Its Goals? DPJ in Power," *The Oriental Economist*, p. 8.
43. Yamashita, "Minshuto no Seiken Dasshugo ni Otozureru 'Nogyo Kaikoku' no Rasuto Chansu" (The Last Chance for "Agricultural Opening" Coming with the DPJ Administration).
44. "Kawaida san, Minshuto to Taiwa Shimasu ka: FTA Teiketsu wa Danko Soshi" (Head of Agricultural Cooperatives' Political Arm Calls for Firm Resistance to FTA with US), *Asahi Shimbun*, p. 7.
45. "Nogyo Seisaku: Minshu 11-Nendo Kara Kobetsu Hosho, Jimin Suiden Furu Katsuyo de Shunyuzo e" (Agricultural Policy: DPJ to Start Income Subsidies for Farming Households From FY11, LDP to Increase Income by Full Utilization of Paddy Fields), *Tokyo Shimbun*, p. 7.

46. Yamashita, "Minshuto no Seiken Dasshugo ni Otozureru 'Nogyo Kaikoku' no Rasuto Chansu" (The Last Chance for "Agricultural Opening" Coming with the DPJ Administration).

47. Iinuma,"What Are Its Goals?" p. 9.

48. "09 Seiken Sentaku Manifesuto, Sosenkyo, Doko Mite Erabu (Jo): Kuni no Okane no Tsukaikata" (The Manifesto Choice 2009, The General Election, What We are Looking At [Part I]: How the Government Spends Our Tax), p. 3.

49. Ibid., p. 3.

50. "Jimin Shiji Dantai ni Nejire, Chiho Shibu wa Jishu Tohyo mo" (Rebellion within LDP Support Groups, Regional Branches Resolving on a "Free Vote")".

51. Ibid.

52. Ibid.

53. "Noseiren, Jishu Tohyo 8 Senkyoku ni Baizo Tohoku" (Agricultural Policy Leagues, a Rise in the Free Vote to 8 Electoral Districts in Tohoku).

BIBLIOGRAPHY

Asahi Shimbun, "Kawaida san, Minshuto to Taiwa Shimasu ka: FTA Teiketsu wa Danko Soshi" (Head of Agricultural Cooperatives' Political Arm Calls for Firm Resistance to FTA with US), August 14, 2009.

——, "09 Seiken Sentaku Manifesuto, Sosenkyo, Doko Mite Erabu (Jo): Kuni no Okane no Tsukaikata" (The Manifesto Choice 2009, The General Election, What We are Looking At [Part I]: How the Government Spends Our Tax), June 29, 2009.

Central Union of Agricultural Cooperatives (JA *Zenchu*), *The Present Situation of Japanese Agriculture,* available online at www.agricoop.org/resources/resources _UpFile/IDACA_Nakashimal.pdf (accessed June 16, 2009).

George Mulgan, Aurelia, *The Politics of Agriculture in Japan* (London and New York, Routledge, 2000).

——, "'Japan Inc' in the Agricultural Sector: Reform or Regression," *Pacific Economic Papers,* No. 314, April 2001.

——, "Where Tradition Meets Change: Japan's Agricultural Politics in Transition," *Journal of Japanese Studies* 31, no. 2 (2005).

——, *Japan's Interventionist State: The Role of the MAFF* (London and New York: RoutledgeCurzon, 2005).

——, *Japan's Agricultural Policy Regime* (London and New York: Routledge, 2006).

——, "Japan's FTA Politics and the Problem of Agricultural Trade Liberalisation," *Australian Journal of International Affairs* 62, no. 2 (June 2008).

Godo, Yoshihisa, "The Changing Economic Performance and Political Significance of Japan's Agricultural Cooperatives," *Pacific Economic Papers,* No. 318, August 2001.

Hill, Michael, *The Public Policy Process,* 4th ed. (Edinburgh Gate: Pearson Education, 2005).

"Hinmoku Odan, Kobetsu Shotoku Hosho, WTO nado Yamada shi no Sonzaikan ni mo Chumoku" (Paying Attention to Non-Product-Specific Management Stabilization Countermeasures, Farm Household Income Compensation, WTO etc. and also the Powerful Presence of Mr Yamada), *Nosei Undo Jyaanaru*, No. 75, October 2007.

Iinuma, Yoshisuke, "What Are Its Goals? DPJ in Power," *The Oriental Economist*, August 2009.

JA *Zenchu*, Central Union of Agricultural Co-operatives, "Objectives and Activities of JA *Zenchu*," www.zenchu-ja.or.jp/eng/objectives/index.html (accessed September 1, 2009).

——, "JA Guruupu to wa" (About the JA Group), http://www.zenchu-ja.or.jp /profile/b.html (accessed December 11, 2010).

"Jimin Shiji Dantai ni Nejire, Chiho Shibu wa Jishu Tohyo mo" (Rebellion within LDP Support Groups, Regional Branches Resolving on a "Free Vote"), www. yomiuri.co.jp/election/shugiin2009/news1/20090802-OYT1T00024.htm (accessed August 10, 2009).

Mainichi Shimbun, "Aso Shusho: Kikikan Arawa Keidanren, Zenchu o Homon" (Prime Minister Aso Visits the Japan Business Federation and the National Central Union of Agricultural Cooperatives, Revealing a Sense of Crisis), July 23, 2009.

——, "'09 Shuinsen, Kaihyo Kekka to Tosensha Ichiran" (The '09 Lower House Election, Vote Counting Results and Table of Elected Members), August 31, 2009.

Ministry of Internal Affairs and Communications, "Agriculture, Forestry and Fisheries," in *Japan Statistical Yearbook 2009*, www.stat.go.jp/english/data /nenkan/1431-07.htm (accessed September 10, 2009).

The Nikkei Weekly, "'Nokyo' Losing Say in Agripolicy," May 24, 2010, http://e. nikkei.com/e/ac/20100524/TNW/Nni20100524FTOFARM1.htm (accessed September 30, 2010).

Norinsuisansho. "Norinsuisan Kihon Detashu" (Agriculture, Forestry and Fisheries Basic Data Collection), http://www.maff.go.jp/j/tokei/sihyo/index.html (accessed January 11, 2011).

"Noseiren, Jishu Tohyo 8 Senkyoku ni Baizo Tohoku" (Agricultural Policy Leagues, a Rise in the Free Vote to 8 Electoral Districts in Tohoku), GOO News, http: //news,goo.ne.jp/article/kahoku/region/20090810t71033.html?fr=rk (accessed August 12, 2009).

Panitch, Leo. "Recent Theorisations of Corporatism: Reflections on a Growth Industry," *British Journal of Sociology* 31, no. 2 (1980).

The Present Situation of Japanese Agriculture and JA Group: Case of Agricultural Cooperatives of Japan, Institute for the Development of Agricultural Cooperation in Asia (IDACA) for JA *Zenchu*, 2007, www.agricoop.org/resources/resources _UpFile/IDACA_Nakashimal.pdf (accessed June 27, 2009).

"Senkyo: Shuinsen, Ken Noseiren ga Jishu Tohyo, Jimin Koho Suisen Sezu'" (Election: House of Representatives Election, Prefectural Farmers' Political League Grants a Free Vote, We Won't Recommend LDP Candidates), http://mainichi.jp/area /aomori/news/20090711ddlk02010121000c.html (accessed July 13, 2009).

Somusho, "Senkyo" (Elections), http://www.soumu.go.jp/senkyo/senkyo_s/data /sangiin21/index.html (accessed December 11, 2010).

Tokyo Shimbun, "Nogyo Seisaku: Minshu 11-Nendo Kara Kobetsu Hosho, Jimin Suiden Furu Katsuyo de Shunyuzo e" (Agricultural Policy: DPJ to Start Income Subsidies for Farming Households from FY11, LDP to Increase Income by Full Utilization of Paddy Fields), August 14, 2009.

Warhurst, John, "Interest Groups and Political Lobbying," in Andrew Parkin, John Summers, and Dennis Woodward, eds., *Government, Politics, Power and Policy in Australia* (Frenchs Forest: Pearson Education Australia, 2006).

Yamashita, Kazuhito, "'Nokyo' to 'Gentan' ni 'No' to Ieru Seiji ga Ima Koso Hitsuyo" (It's Necessary to Demand Politics that Says "No" to "JA" and the "Rice Acreage Reduction Program"), *Diamond Online*, September 5, 2008, http://diamond.jp/series/agric/10005/.

———, "The Agricultural Cooperatives and Farming Reform in Japan (2)," The Tokyo Foundation, February 25, 2009, www.tokyofoundation.org/en/articles/the-agricultural-cooperatives-and-farming-reform-in-Japan-2 (accessed February 8, 2009).

———, "Minshuto no Seiken Dasshugo ni Otozureru 'Nogyo Kaikoku' no Rasuto Chansu" (The Last Chance for "Agricultural Opening" Coming with the DPJ Administration), *Diamond Online*, July 1, 2009, http://member.diamond.jp/series/agric/10015/.

———, *Nokyo no Daizai* (*Serious Crimes of the Agricultural Cooperatives*) (Tokyo: Takarajimasha, 2009).

"Yamada Toshio Giin Kokkai Nikki, Heisei 19-Nendo Seiji Shikin Shushi Hokoku" (Toshio Yamada's Diary from the Diet, The 2007 Political Funds Report), *Nosei Undo Jyaanaru*, No. 76, December 2008.

"Zenkoku Noseiren: Heisei 19-Nendo Rinji Sokai o Kaisai" (The National Farmers' League Holds a 2007-Year Extraordinary General Meeting), *Nosei Undo Jyaanaru*, No. 75, October 2007.

"Zenkoku Noseiren Suisen Koho ga Kettei" (National Farmers' League Decides Its Recommended Candidates), *Nosei Undo Jyaanaru*, No. 86, August 2009.

7

CIVIL SOCIETY AND
GLOBAL CITIZENSHIP IN JAPAN

Jennifer Chan

INTRODUCTION

During those years of militarism and war, the Japanese were said to be imbued
with the notion that Japan was the land of the gods, inhabited by a people
uniquely superior in the world, who lived together, the whole nation as a single family, under the benevolent guidance of a divine emperor. This picture
of a society mobilized by its *mythology in service to the national cause* was the
backdrop against which the subject of *tennosei ideorogii*, the ideology of the
emperor system, was articulated in the early postwar period.

        —Carol Gluck (1985, p. 4, emphasis mine)

And yet, amid the profusion of neologisms that sought to stabilize the cate-
gorical flux of Meiji society, *"citizen" does not stand out*. It may be only a slight
exaggeration to say that *"citizen" was at best the conceptual and moral stepchild
of Japan's modernization*. Instead, the official bearer of the tasks of development, and in this sense of making history, was the imperial subject, *shinmin*,
clad in a neotraditionalist mantle of loyalty, filial piety, and self-sarifice on
behalf of the national community . . . Vis-à-vis that of "subject," other collective identities were to be negotiated from positions of unequal strength,
their descriptors reflective of greater or lesser consciousness of difference from
official subjecthood, with difference extending by degrees toward more radical estrangements.

        —Andrew Barshay (2004, p. 64, emphasis mine)

If modern Japan is about a process of ideology making as Carol Gluck suggests, the comment by Andrew Barshay perhaps best sums up the struggle of
civil society in Japan, to strive from state-subject to state-citizen relations. If
a *tennosei ideorogii*, disseminated by an elaborate, but loose network of ideologues and institutions, represented both "internal psychological constric-
tion and external political submissiveness,"[1] the role of Japanese civil society,
I argue, lies precisely in undoing that ideology by constructing new values as
well as institutions for the expressions of citizenship.

In this chapter I take the observations of Gluck and Barshay on the modern Japanese state as a departure point for an analysis of the critical role of civil society in Japan. To borrow from a powerful image of Masao Maruyama, to counteract a Meiji ideology that had "succeeded in spreading a many-layered, though invisible, net over the Japanese people,"[2] the function of civil society consists of poking holes in the mythical net of the modern Japanese state. Using a postmodern theoretical stance that emphasizes heterogeneity, locality, and dissension from metanarratives,[3] I make a threefold argument concerning the *what, where, and how* of civil society in Japan. First, concerning the role, I contend that, while the intellectual and political project of Japanese civil society entail the construction of counterhegemonic narratives against modern Japanese state ideology, civil society needs to be considered in its own right, independent of the state. Second, concerning the site, I argue for a multilevel analysis of Japanese civil society, that is, one embedded in global civil society, Asian regionalism, and Japanese democratic institutional development. Third, concerning the mechanism, I posit the centrality of education in creating and negotiating a new set of norms and institutions.

Drawing on my observations from fieldwork and over 150 interviews with a diverse spectrum of civil society actors in Japan over the past decade, the remainder of this chapter is structured in five parts. In the second part I delineate a postmodern approach to Japanese citizenship and civil society. In the third part I situate the development of Japanese civil society within a postwar global human rights multilateral system. In the fourth part I take Asia as a unit of analysis and embed Japanese civil society within the development of people-centric regionalism. In the fifth part, through the example of postwar grassroots pacifism, I examine the pedagogic role of Japanese civil society in forging alternative narratives and institutions against a predominant state ideology. I conclude the chapter by outlining some challenges faced by Japanese civil society.

POSTMODERN CONCEPTIONS OF JAPANESE CITIZENSHIP AND CIVIL SOCIETY

The postmodern condition is marked by a crisis of legitimation of grand truth claims, or metanarratives, such as theories of the nation-state.[4] Instead of accepting a certain ideology, a postmodern theoretical stance asks the critical question: Who decides the conditions of truth? Michel Foucault,[5] for example, looks at how the French state exercises power over its subjects through various techniques of power. He argues that "the state is superstructural in relation to a whole series of power networks that invest the body, sexuality, the family, kinship, knowledge, technology, and so forth . . . [Its power] is rooted in a whole series of multiple and indefinite power relations."[6] The power of the modern state lies in its efficient capacity to control the minds of the people:

A stupid despot may constrain his slaves with iron chains; but a true politician binds them even more strongly by the chain of their own ideas; it is at the stable point of reason that he secures the end of the chain; this link is all the stronger in that we do not know of what it is made and we believe it to be our own work; despair and time eat away the bonds of iron and steel, but they are powerless against the habitual union of ideas, they can only tighten it still more; and on the soft fibres of the brain is founded the unshakable base of the soundest of empires.[7]

Hence, the postmodern project entails deconstructing the legitimacy claims of the state by emphasizing heterogeneity, locality, and dissension (see Figure 7.1).

The application of a postmodern approach to the study of Japanese citizenship requires the simultaneous task of deconstructing the claims of the modern Japanese state and reconstructing multiple, local narratives of citizenships. By using a postmodern approach to understand Japanese civil society, we are compelled to go beyond the traditional focus on voluntary associations to emphasize diverse expressions of activism at the local, regional, and global levels. The women's movement in Japan provides a good example. The movement has fought against a state definition of women's role in the making of modern Japan.[8] In a postmodern stance, gender relations are understood as a regime of power, but only in relation to other formations of power such as class, race, and disability. In the case of Japan, minority women—particularly, Buraku, Korean, Ainu, and Okinawan—began to question the foundationalist assumptions and claims of mainstream Japanese feminists that "women" in Japan constituted a singular category in the 1990s.[9] Perhaps the best example of omission by mainstream Japanese feminists of an intersectional approach to discrimination (tying gender to race, class, and nationality) is the "comfort women" redress issue. The mainstream Japanese women's movement has a long history of activism on issues of sexuality and sexual violence. Women's groups were instrumental in successfully pushing for the 1956 Anti-Prostitution Law and raising the issues of corporate-sponsored sex tours to Asia in the 1970s. But it was not until the late 1980s that Japanese women's groups (notably Japan Anti-Prostitution Association) worked with Korean women's groups to seek redress for roughly 200,000 women from different Asian countries who were drafted during World War II to serve as sex slaves for the Japanese army.[10] Similarly, in the areas of caste, race, and disability, different Buraku, Ainu, Okinawans, Koreans, Chinese, and foreign resident groups have formed to challenge the unitary, linear history of modern

Modernist Claims of Citizenship	Postmodernist Claims of Citizenship
State-based	Postnational, global
Unitary, linear history	Multiple, different histories
State-controlled expressions of citizenship	Local expressions
Singular identity	Multiple identities

Figure 7.1   A Postmodern Approach to Citizenship.

Japan.[11] These include the Buraku Liberation League, Citizens' Diplomatic Centre for the Rights of Indigenous Peoples, Association of Rera (an Ainu group), Association of Indigenous Peoples in the Ryukyus, Mirine (a Korean women's group), Issho Kikaku (foreign residents' group), Filipino Migrants Center Nagoya, Japan Association for Refugees, Japan National Assembly of Disabled Peoples' International, and International Movement Against All Forms of Discrimination and Racism (pan-racial group).[12] In the area of environment, a wide variety of advocacy groups that go beyond the traditional leisure and local focus (e.g., birdwatching) have also sprung up. They include the Advocacy and Monitoring Network on Sustainable Development (AM-Net in Kansai), Japan Center for a Sustainable Environment and Society, and Japan Climate Policy Center.

Scholars on Japanese citizenship point to a "citizenship gap"[13] between the predominant state ideology of a homogenous Japan and the historical making of modern Japan. But few have made an explicit link between the issue of a citizenship gap and the critical role of civil society. In this chapter, I use Muthiah Alagappa's open definition of civil society as "a space, a site, and an actor"[14] and argue that civil society has emerged to occupy a critical role in Japan since the 1980s precisely in the context of a shift away from a singular statist definition of Japanese national citizenship to multiple narratives of postmodern and postnational citizenship in Japan.

DEFINING AND LOCATING JAPANESE CIVIL SOCIETY: BEYOND A STATE-CENTRIC APPROACH

The rise of new social forces did not necessarily occur in opposition to the state. By 1900, civil society and the state were considerably more intertwined than they had been during the first three decades of the Meiji period. In retrospect, the civil society of those earlier decades strikes us as anomalous in its autonomy and its often spirited resistance to the government. Thereafter, most societal groups preferred to work with the state to realize their objectives, while state officials increasingly sought to mobilize society for the purposes of governance.

—Sheldon Garon (2004, p. 48)

It is crucial to view civil society as an arena of governance in its own right, not just an adjunct or means to influence the state, political society, or the market. The notion of civil society as an end in itself is relevant not only to totalitarian and authoritarian states but also to liberal-democratic states.

—Muthiah Alagappa (2004, p. 32)

There are probably as many conceptions of civil society as there are kinds of civil society actors. I use two contrasting approaches by Sheldon Garon and Alagappa as a basis for discussion. Garon, in looking at Japanese state-social group relations since the Meiji era, argues that, historically, societal groups preferred to work with the state.[15] This state-centric approach that tends to gauge civil society in relation to the state dominates the existing literature on Japanese civil society. In particular, the bulk of studies focus on the relationship between voluntary associations (including neighborhood, welfare, and business groups) and the state. Robert Pekkanen posits that nonprofit organizations (NPOs) are "members without advocates."[16] Mary Haddad discusses volunteering in Japan but restricts her analysis to participation patterns.[17] Akihiro Ogawa examines how the Japanese state institutionalizes a volunteer subjectivity through the regulation of NPOs.[18] Apichai Shipper makes a nuanced argument on the relationship between associative activism and democratic governance by distinguishing the type of associations.[19] Even though ethnic associations weaken national identity through the promotion of their members' attachment to the homeland and hence foster psychological and political detachment from Japanese society, immigrant rights groups have "forced government officials to reflect on Japan's national identity and to negotiate a new social contract with citizens on agreed rules, procedures, and responsibilities for all those who reside on their islands."[20]

Although it is important to focus on associations in Japan for both historical and political reasons, a "myopically domestic" and "myopically state-centric" paradigm[21] confines our understanding of Japanese civil society. Often in explicit or implicit comparison with its Western counterparts, Japanese civil society has been characterized as small, underdeveloped, fragmented, and ineffectual in bringing about political change. If we conceptualize civil society to exist in its own right, as Alagappa suggests, it would allow for a more complex and dynamic understanding of a heterogeneous sector, populated by more than voluntary associations and able to change in tandem with global, regional, and local factors.[22] Despite the call for a transnational approach to study Japanese civil society,[23] few empirical studies have taken up that challenge. In this chapter, I propose to broaden our analysis of Japanese civil society to include a multilevel and multisite analysis.

As a student of Japanese civil society in the past decade, I have found the international human rights system to be an indispensable unit of analysis for Japanese civil society. The intensification of institutionalization of a global human rights system since the 1970s—complete with conventions, optional protocols, declarations, world conferences, special rappporteurs, complaint procedures, and country reports—has encouraged the development of a global civil society as a new space, site, and actor. Although often politically invisible and marginalized, a wide spectrum of nongovernmental organizations (NGOs) and coalitions on issues—ranging from gender to children, environment, caste, racism, indigenous peoples' rights, disability, disarmament, trade, migration, trafficking, access to essential medicines, and food sovereignty—has emerged in Japan to take advantage of the new opportunity presented by structures offered by an international human rights system, on the one hand, and a global civil society, on the other. I have detailed elsewhere the development over the past three decades of these Japanese networks grouped under three broad categories of alterglobalization, antiwar, and antidiscrimination.[24] My contention is that one cannot understand contemporary Japanese civil society without looking at the new spaces, sites, and actors outside the Japanese state. In many areas such as torture, women's rights, children's rights, disability, environment, and indigenous peoples' rights, civil society actors pushed for new human rights norms. Japanese advocacy networks have been an integral part of such a global justice movement, variously called by scholars "globalization from below"[25] and "grassroots globalism."[26] The extent of conceptual and organizational linkages between Japanese nongovernmental networks and its regional and international counterparts vary, but they all draw on similar mobilization frames by utilizing diverse human rights discourses. Blocked by domestic political institutions, Japanese NGOs have been practicing "boomerang" politics[27] by bypassing the Japanese state to lobby international organizations to exert pressure on Japan from above.

JAPANESE CIVIL SOCIETY AS AN ASIAN PROJECT

> Notwithstanding the differences in orientation, considerations relating to civil society have become a significant factor in the calculations of the Asian political elite. Except in a case like North Korea, political leaders can no longer hold on to state power or govern on the assumptions that society does not matter or that they know best what is good for society. For their part, leaders and members of nonstate organizations and participants in mass movements regard themselves and their organizations as belonging to civil society. They seek to create public spaces and organizations free of state control.
>
> —Muthiah Alagappa (2004, p. 3)

Increasingly, scholars have also begun to address national civil societies in a regional context. As Alagappa argues, civil society has entered Asian political discourse. A twelve-country study, for example, concludes that "there is no necessary connection between civil society and democratic change."[28] Although we gain great insights from this nascent, regional, Asian civil society literature, it is still structured in a national framework, that is, civil society is analyzed as country case studies before they are put in a comparative context. Few studies have paid attention to the emergence of intraregional NGO networks in a wide variety of areas that range from women's human rights to environment and HIV/AIDS. Many reasons support the importance of Asia as a unit of analysis in the study of Japanese civil society. Here I conjecture three of those reasons: specificity in Japanese history in Asia; people-centric, regional institution building; and the emergence of mass movements in the context of rapid political change.

One of the persistent problems in Japanese foreign relations within Asia is the issue of historical responsibility. A major omission in existing Japanese civil society research is the intimate link between historical memory and civil society. Civil society literature, dominated by comparativist political scientists, focuses primarily on domestic political institutions (relationships with the state, legal and regulatory framework, etc.); historical memory literature, dominated by historians, rarely mentions the role of civil society. In the gap between these two streams of literature is the role of emergent, regional, rights-based networks that address a range of issues concerning Japan's military past from the emperor system to Yasukuni Shrine, "comfort women," forced labor redress, and pension denial for Korean and Taiwanese soldiers. One example of such a Japan-focused, Asian, regional human rights movement is the Violence Against Women in War (VAWW)-Net Japan. VAWW-Net Japan emerged in the 1990s as a coalition of women's groups in Japan, South Korea, and the Philippines who are seeking redress for the military sex slaves drafted during World War II. The "comfort women" issue has forced the women's movement in Japan to reexamine its own racial omission (the majority of the 200,000 women were non-Japanese).[29] Although the network did not succeed in receiving an official apology and compensation from the Japanese government, it has managed to raise public consciousness of the issue through the UN human rights system and a popular tribunal. The 1996 report by the UN Special Rapporteur on Violence against Women as well as the 1998 report by the UN Special Rapporteur on Contemporary Forms of Slavery, for example, both define the Japanese "comfort system" as sexual slavery.

Japan's specific historical role in the Asian region calls for an active civil society and a segment of Japanese civil society has begun to respond. Here I do not mean that nongovernmental advocacy networks working in the areas of military sexual slavery, forced labor, and the Yasukuni Shrine are similar in terms of memberships, claims, or strategies. Indeed, often these are fairly different and work apart from each other. However, one can conceptualize a field of inquiry within Japanese civil society by focusing on historical memory. For example, public concern about the Japanese constitutional revision movement is substantial in both Japan and in the region. As long as Japan's past is not properly addressed or redressed, it remains, in the words of Eric Santner, "indefinitely postponed."[30] "Narrative fetishism," that is, "the construction and deployment of a narrative consciously designed to expunge the traces of the trauma or loss that called that narrative into being in the first place . . . typically by situating the site and origin of loss elsewhere," would only serve to accentuate the "battle of discourse and memory."[31] It is in this specific Asian geopolitical context that Japanese civil society inherits a considerable burden against state narrative fetishism. International and regional advocacy networks such as Article 9 Association have taken themselves to task in terms of peace education, in constantly forging a counterhegemonic narrative against the *tennosei ideorogii.*

Another compelling reason for considering Asia as a unit of analysis for the study of Japanese civil society is the process of regional institutionalism in the past few decades. Scholars of Asian regionalism contrast the development of people-centric regionalism versus state-centric regionalism, or normative versus functional regionalism.[32] Unlike the European project where institution building has spread to social, cultural, and human rights areas, the process of regionalism within Asia has thus far focused mainly on economic cooperation. Tanaka Akihiko, for example, has consistently argued for people-centric regionalism that focuses on capacity building for new norms and values. Such a process includes but goes beyond market- and state-centric institution building such as the Association of Southeast Asian Nations (ASEAN). Scholars such as Gilbert Rozman have gone so far as to ask the critical question: to what extent is the region ready to deal with diversity and social justice?[33] Various kinds of networks—economic, inter-governmental, and scientific—already exist. Positing Asian regionalism as a unit of analysis for Japanese civil society entails asking new questions: What constitutes an Asian community? What is the role of leadership? What kinds of values and institutions need to be created for civil society to act, not as troublemakers, but as a legitimate actor in its own right with its own gover-nance structure and mechanisms?

Beyond Japan's historical responsibility and regional institutionalism, a third conjunctural factor that favors a regional understanding of Japanese civil society is the process of democratic transition and the blossoming of civil society activities in the region. For a majority of countries in Asia, including South Korea, Taiwan, the Philippines, and Indonesia, civil soci-ety consists of mass movements that seek political change. Their history, organizational makeup, and mobilization strategies differ significantly from that of Japanese civil society. As shown in the areas of labor movements, food sovereignty, and the environment, a diverse array of Asian nongov-ernmental networks of civil society actors, ranging from community-based organizations to nonprofit groups, mass movements, and advocacy coali-tions, have emerged. For example, Labor Net, an informal gathering of labor union activists in Japan, was formed in 1998 after a few Japanese union activists attended the International Labor Media program in Seoul. Labor Net goes beyond the traditional company-based and industry-based unions under the national umbrella union structure known as Rengo.[34] Regional labor coalitions have also emerged to lobby for the inclusion of basic workers' rights in free trade agreements. For example, in November 2004, a coalition of 54 Japanese NGOs and labor unions, together with 52 South Korean counterparts, protested in front of the Japanese Ministry of Foreign Affairs in their campaign against the Japanese-Korean Free Trade Agreement. In the area of agriculture, many regional linkages have also been formed in civil society activities, such as in fair trade, resistance against genetically modified food, and monitoring the impact of cheap food imports from Asian countries to Japan under free trade agreements.[35] Another active area of regional NGO networking is the environment. For example, in 2001, a Kansai-based group, AM-Net, formed a Ramin (tropical hardwood tree) research group after inviting a member of an Indonesian NGO, Telapak Indonesia, which focuses on the illegal logging and trade of Ramin. The research group found that more than one-half of 500 Japanese companies imported rare species of Ramin, registered with the Appendix II of the Convention on International Trade in Endangered Species of Wild Flora and Fauna. AM-Net mounted a successful campaign that stopped many Japanese companies from continuing the practice.[36]

INSTITUTIONAL DEVELOPMENT OF
CIVIL SOCIETY WITHIN JAPAN

> Notwithstanding its compelling prehistory, the moment for the articulation of citizenship as a positive ideal did not come until 1945, and it would take still longer for it to assume the status of an "objective" category for social analysis. From either point of view, the history of civil society in Japan—that is, a "self-conscious" or "self-aware" history—belongs to the postwar era.—Andrew Barshay (2004, p. 65)

The expansion of Japanese civil society activities since the 1980s in parallel with the development of an international human rights system and Asian regionalism, as I argue above, draws on antecedents of vibrant social movements in postwar Japan. As Barshay pinpoints, modern Japanese civil society developed only after 1945. The postwar constitution lays down the foundations of a democratic society. The Japanese antisecurity treaty protests and antinuclear movements following World War II gave birth to the ideological and organizational forms that dominated other national social movements until the 1980s. The 1960 ANPO (Treaty of Mutual Cooperation and Security between the United States and Japan) protests, in particular, were a turning point in Japanese protest historiography: "The galvanized and convergent energies of a range of quite disparate social groups, the huge scale and variety of protests, the sense that individual commitment and engagement need not come at the price of ideological subordination to any party—all of this was new. This was civil society."[37]

The intellectual and political project of postwar Japanese civil society entails the construction of counterhegemonic narratives against diverse modern myths of Japan: the family state (*kazoku kokka*), enterprise state (*kigyo kokka*), social harmony (*wa*), and monoethnic nation (*tanitsu minzoku*). In the name of the emperor, under the ideology of a family state, modern Japan was built through conquest and colonization. Grassroots pacifism provides one of the best angles to look at the role of civil society development in postwar Japan in countering the dominant state.

Pacifism (*heiwa shugi*) in Japan is a postwar consciousness based on the direct experience of war-weariness and repudiation of wartime ideology.[38] This consciousness is anchored in the 1947 Japanese constitution. Article 9 states that "the Japanese people forever renounce war as a sovereign right of the nation and the threat or use of force as a mean of settling international disputes."[39] For a long time, antinuclear and antisecurity treaty protests dominated grassroots pacifism in Japan. The leadership often came from organized labor, strong student movement, close links to left-wing political parties, and women's participation groups. Strong state repression, ideological differences, and violence among New Left sects led to a rapid decline of the once vibrant movement. Many peace activists consider the postwar movement to be at an impasse since the 1980s.[40]

It was not until the 1990s that the mainstream peace movement began to address its own gender and racial biases. On the one hand, women's groups in Japan, South Korea, and other Asian countries came together to use a variety of international human rights instruments to seek redress for the "comfort women." On the other, the rape incident on September 4, 1995, when three U.S. servicemen kidnapped and raped a 12-year-old sixth-grade Japanese girl brought the issue of violence against women to the mainstream public and galvanized the mainstream Okinawan peace movement that had traditionally focused on antimilitary base activism. Further, U.S. plans to move the Futenma Marine Corps Air Station to a sea-based facility off the east coast of the main island of Okinawa, near the village of Henoko, in December 1999 spurred the creation of peace coalitions within Japan, and spurred connections with international NGOs such as Greenpeace.

From a civil society perspective, what we observe in the development of civil society activism in the area of peace is the emergence of multiple over-lapping discourses, including gender, race, colonialism, and ecology, away from the traditional socialist orientation and organizational tactics of labor unions.[41] Besides gender-based violence, increasing recognition also exists for the connection between race, colonization, and military occupation.[42] Many Okinawans believe that Emperor Hirohito sacrificed them in 1945 in the Battle of Okinawa in order to delay surrender, and that Tokyo sacrificed them again in 1952, that is, Japan could regain its independence from the Allied Occupation Force and felt comfortable with the Japan-U.S. Security Treaty as long as most bases are located in Okinawa.[43] For many Okinawans, the island's tourism and cultural boom since the 1990s only serve to hide the ignorance and unconscious role of continuous colonization of Okinawa by mainland Japanese.[44] Like the feminists who began regional and global net-working after the Beijing Conference in 1995, some young Okinawans have formed networks, such as the Indigenous Peoples' Rights Network Japan, to mobilize at the UN level from the perspective of indigenous peoples' rights. Okinawan peace activists have also begun to use an environmental framework for their cause. They lobby for the removal of military bases on ecological grounds.

Since the early 2000s, grassroots mobilization against the war in Iraq and constitutional revision has led to the formation of new networks such as World Peace Now. What is common across this diverse spectrum of civil society actors, including youth groups, women's movements, labor unions, ecologists, and indigenous and minority rights activists, is the constant con-struction of alternative narratives on Japanese citizenship beyond the pre-dominant state ideology.

Central in this process of debunking the myths of "family," "homoge-neous nation," "enterprise state," "sense of love and respect for the country," and "becoming a 'normal' country" is elaborate educational efforts. If mod-ern Japanese state ideology was built over a century, it requires conscious, concerted effort on the part of civil society to deconstruct the normalized values and institutions that had spread a nebulous net over Japanese society.

The role of Japanese civil society is less to create another metanarrative about Japanese state-citizen relations, but more to forge new norms and institutions through the daily practices of citizenship. As Chandra Mohanty stresses,

> Resistance lies in self-conscious engagement with dominant, normative discourses and representations and in the active creation of oppositional analytic and cultural spaces. Resistance that is random and isolated is clearly not as effective as that which is mobilized through systemic politicized practices of teaching and learning. Uncovering and reclaiming subjugated knowledge is one way to lay claim to alternative histories.[45]

Instead of judging Japanese civil society in relation to the state, a pedagogic conception of it focuses on its role in knowledge production through participation. Civil society actors negotiate between global human rights frames and local cultural narratives to translate global governance issues into accessible terms and to introduce an international human rights language to the Japanese public. Against state metanarratives on efficiency and harmony, NGO networks construct alternative sets of knowledge by drawing on and mixing international human rights standards with local subjugated histories (of women, labor, children, minorities, foreigners, indigenous populations, disabled peoples, etc.)

CONCLUSION: JAPANESE CIVIL SOCIETY AND COUNTERHEGEMONIC NARRATIVES FOR GLOBAL CITIZENSHIP

> The paramount concern of civil society leaders has been to bring about change in the state and its politics; lesser attention has been devoted to the institutionalization of civil society of the development of governance that is independent of the state.
>
> —Muthiah Alagappa (2004, p. 455)

In this chapter, I have tried to argue for a different conceptualization of Japanese civil society based on three tenets. First, concerning the unit of analysis, a complete, dynamic understanding of Japanese civil society must take global, regional, and local developments into consideration. Second, the intellectual and political project of Japanese civil society is to construct counterhegemonic narratives against the predominant modern state ideology. Civil society needs to be considered in its own right, independent of the Japanese state. Finally, I go beyond a political efficacy approach to focus on the civic and educational functions of civil society. Building Japanese civil society is more than just a legal and political process. It is an important pedagogical process centered on participation and knowledge production.

Leading Japanese intellectuals such as Uchida Yoshihiko (1913–1989) have commented that "Japan capitalism has developed thanks to the weakness of civil society."[46] If the citizen was at best the conceptual and moral stepchild of Japan's modernization, as Barshay suggests, the struggle of post-war Japanese civil society has been to create new norms and institutions for the practices of citizenship beyond the confines of the Japanese state.[47] Like their counterparts elsewhere in Asia, civil society actors in Japan suffer from an "institutionalization lag."[48] Most NGOs in Japan are small and face considerable practical constraints, from resource mobilization to governance issues, and political and cultural marginalization. Cross-issue networking, at the local, regional, and global levels, is filled with tensions in terms of gender, class, ability, ideological as well as tactical dynamics. Despite persistent calls for a legally protected space for autonomous organization, the Japanese government fails to recognize NGOs beyond a service delivery or public welfare model. In the backdrop of continuing political and economic crises, civil society in Japan faces both opportunities and challenges in becoming a legitimate actor in the changing landscape of Japanese, Asian, and world politics. The recognition and development of Japanese civil society, in my opinion, becomes a litmus test for the new Yukio Hatoyama administration. Nongovernmental networks within and beyond Japan are watching closely as to whether and how new political leadership will translate into a supportive environment for civil society actors to assume their much belated role locally, nationally, regionally, and globally.

NOTES

I would like to acknowledge the support of the Center for Japanese Studies at the University of British Columbia for the conference travel that led to this publication.

1. Gluck, *Japan's Modern Myths*, p. 5.
2. Maruyama 1963, quoted in Gluck, *Japan's Modern Myths*, p. 4.
3. Lyotard, *The Postmodern Condition*.
4. Ibid.
5. Foucault, *Power/Knowledge: Selected Interviews and Other Writings: 1972–1977*.
6. Foucault, *Power/Knowledge: Selected Interviews and Other Writings: 1972–1977*, p. 122.
7. Foucault, *Discipline and Punish: The Birth of the Prison*, pp. 102–103.
8. Chan, *Gender and Human Rights Politics in Japan*.
9. Chan, "Gender as Intersectionality."
10. Groups involved include VAWW-Net Japan. For a detailed analysis, see Chan-Tiberghien, *Gender and Human Rights Politics in Japan*.
11. Chan, *Gender and Human Rights Politics in Japan* and *Another Japan Is Possible*.
12. For interviews with these groups, see Chan, *Another Japan Is Possible*.
13. Murphy-Shigematsu, *Multicultural Encounters*; Douglass and Roberts, *Japan and Global Migration*; Ryang, *Koreans in Japan*; Lie, *Multiethnic Japan*; Morris-Suzuki, *Re-Inventing Japan*; Weiner, *Japan's Minorities*; Siddle, *Race, Resistance, and the Ainu of Japan*; Denoon, McCormack, Hudson, and Morris-Suzuki, *Multicultural Japan*; Miyazaki, *Kokusaika jidai no jinken to dowa mondai* (Human Rights in an Era of Internationalization; Tomonaga, "Buraku

mondai" (Buraku Issue); Neary *Political Protest and Social Control in Pre-war Japan*; and Neary, "Burakumin in Contemporary Japan."

14. Alagappa, "Civil Society and Political Change," p. 32.
15. Garon, *From Meiji to Hesei: The State and Civil Society in Japan.*
16. Pekkanen, *Japan's Dual Civil Society.*
17. Haddad, *Politics and Volunteering in Japan.*
18. Ogawa, *Failure of Civil Society?*
19. Shipper *Fighting for Foreigners*
20. Ibid., p. 200.
21. Khagram, Riker, and Sikkink, *Restructuring World Politics*, p. 6.
22. Alagappa, "Civil Society and Political Change."
23. Schwartz, "What Is Civil Society?"
24. Chan, *Another Japan Is Possible.*
25. Brecher, Costello, and Smith, *Globalization from Below*; Falk, *Predatory Globalization: A Critique.*
26. Ezzat, "Beyond Methodological Modernism," p. 40.
27. Keck and Sikkink, *Activists Beyond Borders.*
28. Alagappa, "Civil Society and Political Change," p. 10.
29. Chan, *Gender and Human Rights Politics in Japan* and Dudden, "We Came to Tell the Truth' Reflections on the Tokyo Women's Tribunal."
30. Santner, "History Beyond the Pleasure Principle," p. 144, quoted in Breen, *Yasukuni, the War Dead, and the Struggle for Japan's Past,* p. 160.
31. Ueno, *Nashonarizumu to Jendaa* (Nationalism and Gender).
32. Tanaka, "Dynamism and Uncertainty in Asia."
33. Rozman, presentation at the Conference on Sustainability, "Global Governance Reforms, Social Movements in Asia and Education for Sustainability." Science Council of Japan, Kyoto, Japan. September 9–10, 2005.
34. For an interview with Labor Net, see Chan, *Another Japan Is Possible.*
35. Chan, *Another Japan Is Possible.*
36. Ibid.
37. Barshay, *Capitalism and Civil Society in Postwar Japan*, p. 71.
38. Yamamoto, *Grassroots Pacifism in Post-war Japan.*
39. Japanese Constitution, http://www.solon.org/Constitutions/Japan/English/english-Constitution.html (accessed March 9, 2010).
40. Takada, *Goken wa kaiken ni katsu* (Constitutional Protection will Win over Constitutional Revision).
41. For a detailed account, see Chan, "Le Mouvement Pacifiste Japonais Depuis les Années 1990."
42. Nomura, *Muishiki no shokuminchi: Nihonjin no beigun kichi to Okinawajin* (Unconscious Colonialism: Japanese' U.S. Military Bases and the Okinawans).
43. Johnson, *Okinawa.*
44. Medoruma, *Okinawa "sengo" zero nen* (Okinawa "Postwar" Year Zero); Nomura, *Muishiki no shokuminchi: Nihonjin no beigun kichi to Okinawajin* (Unconscious Colonialism: Japanese' U.S. Military Bases and the Okinawans).
45. Mohanty, quoted in Hooks, *Teaching to Transgress*, p. 32.
46. Summarized by Yama 1967, quoted in Barshay, "Capitalism and Civil Society in Postwar Japan."
47. Barshay, "Capitalism and Civil Society in Postwar Japan."
48. Alagappa, ""Civil Society and Political Change" and "The Non-state Public Sphere in Asia," p. 470.

BIBLIOGRAPHY

Alagappa, Muthiah, "'Civil Society and Political Change' and 'The Non-state Public Sphere in Asia: Dynamic Growth, Institutionalization Lag,'" in Muthiah Alagappa, ed., *Civil Society and Political Change in Asia: Expanding and Contracting Democratic Space* (Palo Alto: Stanford University Press, 2004).

Aldrich, Daniel, *Site Fights: Divisive facilities and Civil Society in Japan and the West* (Ithaca: Cornell University Press, 2008).

Barshay, Andrew, "Capitalism and Civil Society in Postwar Japan: Perspectives from Intellectual History," in Frank Schwartz and Susan Pharr, eds., *The State of Civil Society in Japan* (New York: Cambridge University Press, 2004).

———, *The Social Sciences in Modern Japan: The Marxian and Modernist Traditions* (Berkeley: University of California Press, 2004).

Brecher, Jeremy, Tim Costello, and Brendan Smith, *Globalization from Below: The Power of Solidarity* (Boston, MA: South End Press, 2000).

Breen, John, ed., *Yasukuni, the War Dead, and the Struggle for Japan's Past* (New York: Columbia University Press, 2003).

Chan, Jennifer, "Le Mouvement Pacifiste Japonais Depuis les Années 1990," *Critique Internationale* 36 (2007): 51–69.

———, *Another Japan Is Possible: New Social Movements and Global Citizenship Education* (Palo Alto, CA: Stanford University Press, 2008).

Chan-Tiberghien, Jennifer, *Gender and Human Rights Politics in Japan: Global Norms and Domestic Networks* (Palo Alto, CA: Stanford University Press, 2004).

———, "Gender as Intersectionality: Multiple Discrimination against Minority Women in Japan," in M. Nakamura and P. Potter, eds., *Comparative International Studies of Social Cohesion and Globalization in Asia: Japan* (New York: Palgrave Macmillan, 2004), pp. 158–181.

Denoon, Donald, Gaven McCormack, Mark Hudson, and Tessa Morris-Suzuki, eds., *Multicultural Japan: Paleolithic to Postmodern* (Melbourne: Cambridge University Press, 1996).

Douglass, Mike and Glenda Susan Roberts, eds., *Japan and Global Migration: Foreign Workers and the Advent of a Multicultural Society* (Honolulu: University of Hawaii Press, 2002).

Dudden, Alexis, "'We Came to Tell the Truth' Reflections on the Tokyo Women's Tribunal," *Critical Asian Studies, 33*, no. 4 (2001): 591–602.

Ezzat, Heba Raoul, "Beyond Methodological Modernism: Towards a Multicultural Paradigm Shift in the Social Sciences," in Helmut Anheier, Marlies Glasius, and Mary Kaldor, eds., *Global Civil Society 2004/5* (London: Sage, 2005).

Falk, Richard. *Predatory Globalization: A Critique* (Malden: Polity Press, 1999).

Foucault, Michel, *Discipline and Punish: The Birth of the Prison* (New York: Vintage Books, 1979).

———, *Power/Knowledge: Selected Interviews and Other Writings: 1972–1977* (New York: Vintage Books, 1980).

Garon, Sheldon, "From Meiji to Heisi: The State and Civil Society in Japan," in Frank Schwartz and Susan Pharr, eds., *The State of Civil Society in Japan* (New York: Cambridge University Press, 2004).

Gluck, Carol, *Japan's Modern Myths: Ideology in the Late Meiji Period* (Princeton: Princeton University Press, 1985).

Haddad, Mary Alice, *Politics and Volunteering in Japan: A Global Perspective* (Cambridge: Cambridge University Press, 2007).

Hooks, Bell, *Teaching to Transgress* (New York: Routledge, 2004).

Japanese Constitution, http://www.solon.org/Constitutions/Japan/English/english-Constitution.html (accessed March 9, 2010).

Johnson, Chalmers, ed., *Okinawa: Cold War Island* (Tokyo: Japan Policy Research Institute, 1999).

Keck, Margaret, and Katherine Sikkink, *Activists Beyond Borders* (Ithaca and London: Cornell University Press, 1998).

Khagram, Sanjeev, James Riker, and Kathryn Sikkink, *Restructuring World Politics: Transnational Social Movements, Networks, and Norms* (Minneapolis: University of Minnesota, 2002).

Lie, John, *Multiethnic Japan* (Cambridge, MA: Harvard University Press, 2001).

Lyotard, Jean Francois, *The Postmodern Condition: A Report on Knowledge* (Minneapolis: University of Minnesota Press 1984).

Medoruma, Syun, *Okinawa "sengo" zero nen* (Okinawa "Postwar" Year Zero) (Tokyo: NHK Shuppan, 2005).

Miyazaki, Shigeki, ed., *Kokusaika jidai no jinken to dowa mondai* (Human Rights in an Era of Internationalization) (Tokyo: Akashi Shoten, 1999).

Morris-Suzuki, Tessa, *Re-Inventing Japan: Time, Space, Nation* (London: ME Sharpe, 1998).

Murphy-Shigematsu, Stephen, *Multicultural Encounters: Case Narratives* (New York: Teachers College Press, 2002).

Neary, Ian, *Political Protest and Social Control in Pre-war Japan: The Origins of Buraku Liberation* (Manchester, UK: Manchester University Press, 1989).

———, "Burakumin in Contemporary Japan," in Michel Weiner, ed., *Japan's Minorities: The Illusion of Homogeneity* (London: Routledge, 1997).

Nomura, Koya, *Muishiki no shokuminchi: Nihonjin no beigun kichi to Okinawajin* (Unconscious Colonialism: Japanese' U.S. Military Bases and the Okinawans) (Tokyo: Ochanomizu Shobo, 2005).

Ogawa, Akihiro, *Failure of Civil Society? The Third Sector and the State in Contemporary Japan* (New York: SUNY Press, 2008).

Pekkanen, Robert, *Japan's Dual Civil Society: Members without Advocates* (Palo Alto, CA: Stanford University Press, 2006).

Rabinow, Paul, *The Foucault Reader* (New York: Pantheon Books, 1984).

Rozman, Gilbert. Presentation at the Conference on Sustainability, "Global Governance Reforms, Social Movements in Asia and Education for Sustainability." Science Council of Japan. Kyoto, Japan. September 9–10, 2005.

Ryang, Sonia, ed., *Koreans in Japan: Critical Voices from the Margin* (London: Routledge, 2001).

Santner, Eric, "History Beyond the Pleasure Principle: Thoughts on the Representation of Trauma," in Saul Friedländer, ed., *Probing the Limits of Representation: Nazism and the Final Solution* (Cambridge, MA: Harvard University Press, 1992), pp. 143–154.

Schwartz, Frank, "What Is Civil Society?" in Frank Schwartz and Susan Pharr, eds., *The State of Civil Society in Japan* (New York: Cambridge University Press, 2004).

Shipper, Apichai W., *Fighting for Foreigners: Immigration and its Impact on Japanese Democracy* (Ithaca: Cornell University Press, 2008).

Siddle, Richard, *Race, Resistance, and the Ainu of Japan* (London: Routledge, 1996).

Takada, Ken. *Goken wa kaiken ni katsu* (Constitutional Protection will Win over Constitutional Revision) (Tokyo: Gijutsu to ningen, 2004).

Tanaka, Akihiro,Presentation at the Science Council of Japan Conference on Sustainability, "Dynamism and Uncertainty in Asia," Kyoto, Japan, 2005.

Tomonaga, Kenzo, "Buraku mondai" (Buraku Issue), in *Wocchi! Kiyaku jinken iinkai: Doko ga zureteru? Jinken no kokusai kijun to nihon no genjo* (Watch! Human Rights Committee: Where Is the Gap? International Human Rights Standards and the Situation in Japan), edited by International Human Rights NGO Network (Tokyo: Nihon Hyoronsha, 1999).

Ueno, Chizuko, *Nashonarizumu to Jendaa* (Nationalism and Gender) (Tokyo: Seitousha, 1998).

Weiner, Michel, ed., *Japan's Minorities: The Illusion of Homogeneity* (London: Routledge, 1997).

Yamamoto, Mari, *Grassroots Pacifism in Post-war Japan: The Rebirth of a Nation* (London, UK, and New York, NY: Routledge/Curzon, 2004).

8

WELFARE POLICY

Gregory J. Kasza and Takashi Horie

Welfare policies are the first preoccupation of the Japanese people in opinion surveys and the biggest challenge confronting the Japanese government today. At a glance, it may seem hard to understand why. The Japanese have one of the lowest infant mortality rates and the longest life expectancy of any people in the world. There is universal public health insurance at modest cost, and since 1960 the economy has sustained comparatively low levels of unemployment. However, the financial and demographic underpinnings of Japan's welfare system are degenerating.

Current welfare benefits were fixed during a prolonged period of rapid economic growth that began in the early 1950s. Bountiful government revenues financed continuous improvements in health care and old-age pensions, and the state supported employment in the less dynamic sectors of the economy. However, when the price of oil skyrocketed in the 1970s, economic growth slowed, and in 1990 a financial crisis caused by speculation in stocks and real estate halted expansion. Since then, the government has struggled to sustain its welfare commitments.

Demographic change poses another threat to Japan's welfare state. The elderly receive most welfare benefits, and the percentage of elderly in Japan's population has grown. Working people pay insurance premiums to finance the welfare system, but their percentage of the population is falling. A decline in the fertility rate has accompanied these changes, which are also occurring in other industrialized countries. It requires 2.07 children per woman to sustain the size of a population, but Japan's fertility rate has not reached that level since 1973. The fertility rate fell to 1.57 children per woman in 1989 and to an all-time low of 1.26 in 2005. These figures not only reflect a slowed economy but also changes in the family structure and gender relations. If the government cannot reverse these trends, Japan's welfare programs will soon become unaffordable, and hence the public's apprehension about welfare policy.

This chapter describes the evolution of Japan's welfare state and recounts the characteristics of Japan's welfare programs. It then analyzes Japan's current welfare difficulties, most especially the low fertility rate and rising social inequality, and the obstacles to overcoming them.

WHAT IS WELFARE POLICY?

Welfare policies protect people from the effects of injury, sickness, old age, unemployment, and poverty, and alleviate the costs of raising a family. Although relief for the poor has existed throughout history, only modern states have provided wide-ranging welfare services to the majority of people. Most public welfare measures are expensive and administratively complex, so that the requisite resources are available mainly in industrialized societies. Although people rely on private sources of welfare as well, states are the primary providers of welfare in most developed countries.

The costliest welfare programs are those that furnish income to the elderly. About one-half of Japan's welfare expenditures serve this purpose. The government requires people to contribute to a social insurance fund during their working lives, and they then receive a monthly payment or pension to support their livelihoods between retirement and death. Most of Japan's welfare programs rely on social insurance funds of this type. The amount of a person's pension varies with the amount of his or her contributions, although in Japan noncontributors, such as the disabled, the poor, and the nonworking wives of salaried employees, also receive pensions from the government.

Japanese must also contribute to a social insurance fund for public health care. This is Japan's second most expensive welfare program. Recently the government has introduced a new social insurance program for long-term care of the elderly, which finances nursing homes and home-help services. Yet another social insurance fund provides temporary benefits to the unemployed. The government also uses other means to bolster employment, including job training programs, subsidies to private employers, and support for inefficient economic sectors.

Two Japanese welfare policies that do not rely on social insurance are public assistance for the poor and child allowances for families. Support for the poor comes from the government's general tax revenues, whereas child allowances are financed jointly by the government and employers.

A BRIEF HISTORY OF JAPAN'S WELFARE STATE

Japan's first law to compensate victims of industrial accidents was passed in 1911, its first major health insurance law in 1922, its first large-scale pension program in 1941, its first unemployment insurance law in 1947, and its first child allowance program in 1971.[1] There are several noteworthy features of Japan's welfare history. First, although different forms of government have adopted welfare measures for various purposes, there has been much continuity in policy. Many traits of Japan's welfare policies today originated before 1945. Second, conservative policy sponsors and conservative social values have often generated Japan's welfare programs. Although conservatives and liberals launched the welfare state in the West as well, Socialist and Christian Democratic political parties expanded public welfare in many nations after World War II. In Japan, parties of labor and the left have never established prolonged rule over the government, and thus conservative policymakers have guided welfare policy. Finally, at every stage foreign models have swayed welfare policymaking. All of Japan's welfare programs are based partly on foreign models.

Japan began to experiment with modern welfare policies in the late nineteenth century, providing welfare services mainly for government officials and the workers in some state-owned enterprises, but its first major policy was the Factory Law of 1911. This bill required that employers pay for workers' medical treatment due to injury or sickness on the job. It applied to all firms of 15 or more employees, although opposition from business owners delayed its enforcement until 1916. Bureaucrats initiated Japan's early welfare policies. A burst of industrialization in the early twentieth century had alerted them to the poor working conditions in Japanese factories, and they wished to avoid the radical labor politics they observed in Europe. German ordinances, which also aimed at enticing workers away from socialism, inspired Japan's earliest welfare policies, much as they inspired emulation elsewhere in Europe.

Japan's Health Insurance Law of 1922 (implemented from 1926) is reputed to be the first social insurance program adopted outside the West.[2] It, too, sought to undermine the attractions of socialism and anarchism among workers. The health law was adopted against the background of the Rice Riots of 1918 and Russia's Bolshevik Revolution. Political parties controlled the government in the 1920s, and the Kenseikai (Constitutional) Party promoted the Health Insurance Law. The law applied to workers in the same firms covered by the earlier Factory Law, and coverage later expanded until by 1934 it included all regular workers in firms of five or more employees. Workers were covered for sickness and injuries whether sustained on the job or not, and they also received benefits for childbirth and death. The larger companies participated in the law's implementation, and they continue to do so today.

Japan's welfare state expanded greatly under military rule during the war years of 1937 to 1945.[3] The armed forces promoted welfare policy to strengthen Japan's "human resources" for total war. Wartime policymaking also reflected a strong sense of egalitarianism, since everyone contributed to the war effort. At the army's urging, the government created the Ministry of Health and Welfare (MHW) in 1938, and it remains the chief agency responsible for welfare policy today. Its first task was to promote a new health insurance law to cover people excluded from the 1922 legislation, and by 1944 two-thirds of the population had public health insurance. The government also introduced in 1941 pension insurance for workers. Although insurance premiums were used to help finance the war, enrollees totaled 8.44 million people by the end of 1944.[4] Officials also increased public assistance for the poor to support soldiers' families and to improve the physical well-being of a population at war. These policies had long-term consequences. For instance, Japan's public health insurance system is still characterized by the jurisdiction of the renamed Ministry of Health, Labor, and Welfare (MHLW), compulsory participation by physicians, fixed prices for medical treatments and drugs, and copayments for service by patients.

The U.S. Occupation of Japan over 1945–1952 saw few policy innovations in welfare, since Japan's welfare system was already more advanced than that of the United States. However, the Occupation forces did advance a Livelihood Assistance Law to aid the poor in 1946 and Japan's first unemployment insurance law in 1947. The U.S. authorities forbade the Japanese government to enact special measures to help war veterans. The only way to assist them was to pass laws that applied to everyone, and that is what the government did. The Livelihood Assistance Law was the weightiest welfare policy adopted during the Occupation. In 1950, over 2 million people received benefits.[5] The Americans also inserted welfare provisions in Japan's postwar constitution, which granted people "the right to maintain the minimum standards of wholesome and cultured living" and enjoined the government to promote "social welfare" and "public health."[6]

Japan's welfare programs recovered fully from defeat only in the mid-1950s, and thereafter new policies bolstered the dominance of the Liberal Democratic Party (LDP). Though the LDP is known for championing economic growth, it was equally zealous in promoting public welfare. Universal public health insurance and pensions were prominent in the LDP's early electoral platforms. Prime Minister Nobusuke Kishi declared a national pension to be the party's first goal in the electoral campaign of 1958, and in 1960 Prime Minister Hayato Ikeda proposed expanding social security as part of his famous income-doubling plan.[7] Over 1958–1961, Japan reportedly became the fourth country in the world to implement universal public health insurance, and the twelfth to make old-age pensions universal.[8] At that time, Japan's gross domestic product per capita was sixteenth among the industrialized countries.

Why did the conservative, pro-business LDP support public welfare? In the late 1950s, the party was battling the Japan Socialist Party for political supremacy, and welfare policy attracted mass support. The LDP's governments realized that just as rapid growth enriched workers in heavy industry, it disadvantaged those in sectors such as small business and agriculture. To generate mass appeal, the party expanded welfare coverage to the economically disadvantaged under the politically neutral rubric of "structural adjustment."[9] During the mid-1960s, the LDP improved the terms of its health or pension policies almost every year, and over 1960–1975 the government's real social expenditures grew at an annual rate of 12.8 percent while the real GDP grew at 8.6 percent.[10] Japan's Socialists did not challenge the LDP's leadership in welfare policy until the late 1960s, when opposition-led local governments instituted some popular welfare innovations. But the LDP quickly made those policies its own and responded by introducing child allowances and raising other welfare benefits in the early 1970s. Thus the LDP strengthened its political dominance by exploiting an issue that in many countries has favored the leftist parties.

Initially, rapid economic growth provided the revenues that financed the welfare state. When growth slowed during the international oil crises of 1973 and 1979, the industrialized countries strove to cut welfare expenditures. In the 1980s, the Japanese government lengthened the period of work required to qualify for a full pension, reintroduced modest copayments for medical treatment for the elderly, and shifted funds from the prosperous health insurance pools managed by large enterprises into those managed by local governments, which enrolled more old people.

The main lesson learned in the 1980s was the resilience of the more costly welfare programs. The government protected the welfare budget from cutbacks during the recession of 1974–1975, and spending on public welfare over 1975–1984 increased at the same rate that it had during the previous 10 years. In the 1980s, Japan's welfare benefits rose faster than those of all but three other industrialized countries.[11] What accounts for the durability of welfare policy in the face of economic slowdown? The welfare state had strong cross-class support. People who contributed to social insurance funds during their working lives viewed welfare benefits as "entitlements" they had earned, not as arbitrary gifts from the state. Moreover, the aging of the population made the same pension and health policies more expensive over time. Japan's economic boom in the mid-late 1980s eased the strain of rising welfare costs somewhat, but the government had to use deficit spending to sustain its commitments.

The real challenge to the welfare system came in 1990, when financial and demographic crises rocked Japan. Stock and real estate prices plummeted and the fertility rate fell to its lowest postwar level. The MHW marked 1990 as the year when the focus of policy shifted to the problems of sustaining public welfare in an aging society.

THE TERMS OF JAPAN'S CORE WELFARE POLICIES
Public Health Care

Health insurance is arguably Japan's most effective welfare program. Citizens have universal coverage for an unlimited duration of treatment, including general care, hospitalization, surgery, medicine, and dentistry. Health expenditures per person are the nineteenth highest among the wealthy Organization for Economic Co-operation and Development (OECD) countries, and less than one-half of the expenditures per person in the United States.[12] Athough waiting periods for treatment vary between health care providers, the insured may choose their place of treatment. Many doctors are in private practice and health care providers receive payment from the government according to the actual services they perform. The system thus retains some benefits of a competitive market.

The financing of Japan's health care system is complex but effective. A government commission fixes the costs of all medical services. Overall the government pays about 35 percent of total health costs from general tax revenues (this percentage is rising), the insured and employers cover about 50 percent with insurance premiums, and the insured cover the remaining 15 percent in the form of copayments when they receive treatment.[13] Public health insurance includes separate programs for government employees, the employees of large firms, the employees of small firms, the self-employed and nonemployed, the elderly in different age categories, and several smaller groups.[14] Despite this complexity, financing is fairly egalitarian. The insurance premiums of the employees of both large and small firms cost about 8 percent of income, and copayments are set at the same rate for most people. Individuals' monthly health expenditures are capped at a low level; the elderly and people of low income pay lower fees; the impoverished pay nothing. Government surveys reveal that income levels have no effect on citizens' utilization of public health care in Japan.[15] A flaw in the system has been the shortage of health care providers in some sparsely populated areas.

In most respects, Japan's public health insurance is comparable to that of Western European countries. Common features include reliance on social insurance and general tax revenues, near universal coverage for citizens, free treatment for the poor, the patient's choice of health care provider, official price regulation, the unlimited duration of coverage, and the range of services.

Old-Age Pensions

The average elderly household in Japan relies on public pensions for over two-thirds of its income.[16] All Japanese must participate in a "basic" pension plan that pays a flat-rate benefit. In addition, salaried employees whose income exceeds a minimal level must participate in an earnings-related pension plan, whose benefits vary with contributions. There were 69 million people enrolled in the earnings-related pension program in 2005. A full earnings-related pension is based on a work life of 40 years, and the most recent rules provide people with full basic and earnings-related pensions at age 65. Separate public pension plans cover government officials, private school teachers, seamen, and workers in agriculture and fisheries.

The funding of pension programs depends mainly on social insurance. Contributions to the earnings-related pension are scheduled to reach 18.3 percent of income within the next 10 years.[17] Employer and employee each pay one-half of the insurance premium. As in most industrialized countries, the system operates on the "pay-as-you-go" principle, meaning that the government uses the pension premiums of today's working population to pay pension benefits to those already retired. In addition, general government revenues cover 20 percent of the cost of the earnings-related pension and 50 percent of the basic pension. In 2009, the government estimates that earnings-related pensions will equal 62 percent of the average after-tax wage in the economy, which is a comparatively high replacement rate. However, the government is committed to sustaining the pension at only 50 percent of the average wage, and the MHLW has questioned whether even that will be possible in the future.[18] The state pays a noncontributory pension to the poor and a noncontributory basic pension to the spouses of salaried employees.

Most traits of Japan's pension system are shared by other industrialized democracies, including the use of social insurance, near universal coverage for the working population, noncontributory pensions for the poor, pay-as-you-go budgeting, the joint payment of insurance premiums by employers and employees, and a standard retirement age of 65.

In recent years, the administration of Japan's pensions has been disastrous. In mid-2007 it was revealed that the Social Insurance Agency had mishandled the contribution records of 50 million people, who then had to reconstruct their pension records with the help of former employers. It is impossible to recover accurate data for many individuals, and consequently many retirees have not been receiving the correct benefits. Given the heavy reliance on public pensions for retirement income and the fact that benefits vary with contributions, the public is outraged.

Another scandal concerns the delinquency of many contributors to the basic pension plan. The social insurance premiums of salaried employees are automatically deducted from paychecks, but the self-employed and their spouses, students over 20, and other nonsalaried individuals must also contribute to the basic pension. In fiscal 2002, some 40 percent of the 18 million people in the latter groups neglected to pay premiums.[19] Moreover, politicians are categorized as "self-employed" in the pension system, and it came to light in 2004 that seven cabinet members and two opposition party leaders had also failed to pay premiums. These are problems of execution rather than program design, but they have damaged the program's reputation.

Employment and Poverty

Employment policy and public assistance for the poor serve complementary goals. While unemployment insurance assists people who are temporarily out of work, public assistance aids those suffering long-term poverty.

The terms of assistance to the unemployed and the poor in Japan are comparatively harsh. Employers and workers contribute 1.05 and 0.70 percent of the worker's salary, respectively, into a social insurance fund supporting the unemployed. This policy does not cover the self-employed, most part-time and seasonal workers, or some who labor in agriculture or fisheries. To become eligible for benefits, one must have worked for six months during the previous year, and the maximum time one can receive benefits is 150 days, a shorter period than that covered by most Western states. In one study of 10 industrialized countries, Japan was ninth in the percentage of salary replaced by unemployment benefits in the first month of unemployment.[20] The formal terms of public assistance for the poor resemble such programs elsewhere, but in practice Japanese officials use their discretion to discourage applicants. According to scholarly estimates, the proportion of people living below the official poverty line who actually collect public assistance falls below 50 percent.[21]

Although the government's aid to the destitute has been meager, its active measures to promote employment have been effective. The Japanese state has subsidized jobs in lavish fashion, especially for farmers, construction workers, and the self-employed. After World War II, the government continued a wartime policy to purchase the entire rice crop, paying farmers up to eight times the world market price for their product. In the 1970s, this "food control" budget amounted to as much as 15 percent of total government expenditures. In addition, Japanese farmers pay almost no income tax. In 1980 Japan's agricultural subsidies were 1.75 times higher than a weighted average of those in six European countries.[22]

Construction is Japan's biggest industry, employing 10 percent of the workforce. As of the late 1990s, the government's spending per capita on construction was double the average in Western Europe and the United States, and the main reason is that public works supplied about 40 percent of the construction business. Like agriculture, construction is not a competitive industry in Japan. Builders do not compete on the world market, and a system of bid-rigging limits their competition for government contracts. Yet the government continues to support needless construction projects because it views construction as an "employment absorbing sector."[23]

Until recently, a Large Retail Store Law protected the self-employed by making it difficult to build new supermarkets and department stores. Consequently, small shopkeepers probably account for a larger share of the workforce than in any other industrialized country, with the exception of Italy. The smallest shops are even exempt from collecting the sales tax.

In sum, Japan's approach to unemployment and poverty has been to subsidize jobs in inefficient industries rather than pay allowances to the poor and unemployed. For many years, Japan's work policies were effective. Over 1960–1995, unemployment averaged 1.9 percent, compared to 5.9 percent in the prosperous countries of the OECD as a whole.[24] But Japan's proactive employment policies were expensive and thus dependent upon rapid economic growth for their funding. Since the economy began to stagnate in 1990, the government has had to emasculate these policies (see below).

Child Allowances

Nearly all other industrialized countries adopted family support programs earlier in their economic development than did Japan, which did not legislate child allowances until 1971. Local governments had been introducing child allowances, and this may have provoked the central government to adopt the policy. Another motivation was that welfare bureaucrats wanted to add the one major welfare program common to other advanced nations that Japan had yet to adopt. Whatever the cause, the government did not initially invest sufficient resources to make the policy effective.

Before 2010, families received ¥5,000 (about $50) per month for their first and second children, and ¥10,000 per month for their third child and beyond. The program excluded wealthier families, and these amounts were too small to influence anyone's decision to bear children. Moreover, until 2000, families received this allowance only during the first three years of their child's life. After 2000, the payments were extended to age six, but the state simultaneously reduced the annual tax deduction for dependent children by ¥100,000, taking away with one hand what it was granting with the other.[25] Child allowances have been Japan's least popular welfare program.

This changed after the lower house election of 2009. The victorious Democratic Party of Japan (DPJ) touted a massive boost in children's allowances as part of its campaign. It promised to increase the monthly allowance to ¥26,000 (about $260) for every child until the end of junior high school; all families would receive the allowance regardless of income. The plan was to pay half of this amount (¥13,000) in fiscal 2010 and to institute the full amount in 2011. Alas, budgetary realities intervened. The government instituted half-payments in 2010, but as of this writing, it has decided to freeze the allowance at this amount in 2011 for children over three, and to increase it to ¥20,000 only for children under that age. Fear of public opinion thwarted the DPJ's initial plan to eliminate spousal income tax deductions to finance the new program.

Thus far Japan's welfare state has served mainly the elderly. The elderly receive most pensions and require the most health care, and these programs take most of the welfare budget. Except for the state's proactive employment policies, which are disappearing due to cost, aid to the poor and the unemployed has received less emphasis, and until recently support for families raising children has been insignificant. Some Japanese argue that the government should reverse its priorities. In their view, the problem of low fertility demands greater investment in young families; changes in the employment system demand better programs for the poor and the unemployed; and the elderly should shoulder more of their own expenses. The current debate over the future of welfare policy thus raises fundamental questions regarding the Japanese system.

THE IMPENDING CRISIS I: DEMOGRAPHICS

Increasing longevity and declining fertility pose great challenges to Japan's welfare system. Japanese live longer than any other people in the world. In 2007 the average life expectancy at birth was 82.6 years, compared to 81.0 years in Sweden and France, 79.8 years in Germany, and 78.1 years in the United States. This is a tribute to Japan's welfare system and also to healthy living habits. Adult obesity, for example, is 3.4 percent in Japan, but 10.2 percent in Sweden, 10.5 percent in France, 13.6 percent in Germany, and 34.3 percent in the United States.[26] Nonetheless, due to the decline in fertility, Japan's aging society portends severe welfare problems.

In 2008 and 2009 the average number of children born to Japanese women between the ages of 15 and 49 was 1.37. Thanks to relatively benign economic conditions and a baby boomer generation entering its thirties, the rate for 2008 actually followed three years of rising fertility. Still, this rate remains far below the number of 2.07 children per woman required to sustain the population size, and it stands among the lowest fertility rates in the industrialized countries.

Due to rising longevity and declining fertility, people aged 65 years or older constituted a high 21.5 percent of the population in 2007, and this figure is projected to rise to 31.8 percent by 2030 and 40.5 percent by 2055. Although some less developed Asian societies are aging even faster, Japan's pace exceeds that of other industrialized societies, and the fertility rate is unlikely to rebound soon. The result is population decline. Officials estimate that Japan's population of 127 million today could fall to 89.9 million by 2055 unless current trends are reversed.[27]

Because the elderly receive most welfare benefits, the costs of public pensions and health care have risen inexorably. This has increased the financial burden on a shrinking working population, whose contributions to social insurance are used to pay welfare benefits to today's elderly under pay-as-you-go financing. Public welfare expenditures have been rising by about $9 billion annually, and they will account for 53 percent of the government's general account budget in 2011.[28] The government's budget deficit was almost 175 percent of GDP in 2008, when no other developed country had a deficit over 125 percent of GDP.[29] This financial burden has put welfare reform atop the list of public demands of government in opinion polls.[30] What has the government done to cope?

When rising welfare costs became an issue in the late 1970s, the ruling LDP initially responded with rhetoric about a "Japanese-style welfare society." This welfare "society" was contrasted to welfare "states" elsewhere. The LDP eulogized Japan's traditional family values as "hidden assets" that would lighten the government's welfare burden. Encouraged by the high number of elderly still residing with their children, the government appealed to housewives to provide more care for the elderly and needy family members. This rhetoric fell on deaf ears. The number of elderly living with their children has been declining by about 1 percent annually, and the welfare burden in the home is one reason for the falling birth rate, since some young women refrain from marrying to avoid it. The government soon discovered that basic welfare entitlements had strong public support.[31] The LDP protected the welfare budget during the oil crises of the mid-late 1970s, and thereafter official attention shifted from traditionalist rhetoric to action.

Starting in the 1980s, officials strove to cut welfare costs and make better use of available funds. They increased pension premiums and raised the required work years and age for receiving a full pension. They increased copayments for medical treatment and moved funds from the health insurance pools serving big businesses into the residential health insurance pools that had more elderly members. Administrative deregulation encouraged private enterprise to build more day nurseries and long-term care facilities. On a less positive note, the government reduced support for low-income fatherless families and rammed an unpopular sales tax through the Diet in 1988, raising it to 5 percent in 1997. In part, the neoliberal agenda then being pursued by the U.S. and British governments inspired these steps.

Many of these measures made sense, but the experience highlighted the difficulty of bolstering welfare finances and cutting benefits. The LDP's first declaration of intent to introduce a sales tax resulted in an electoral setback in 1979, and the public backlash against its eventual passage in 1988 was one cause of Prime Minister Noboru Takeshita's resignation. Japan's retirees do not pay income tax, but they do pay the sales tax, and they are a growing segment of the electorate. Politically the government is caught between the public's attachment to welfare and its equally fervent dislike of new taxes. Following a resounding electoral victory in 2005, the neoliberal administration of Junichiro Koizumi proposed to cut welfare spending by $10 billion over five years. But the popular enthusiasm that met this proposal was not in evidence when the government proposed a sharp increase in pension premiums by 2017.

The state has greatly improved welfare conditions for the elderly. Beginning in 1989, it adopted a series of "Gold Plans" to increase care facilities and home helpers for the aged. A program of long-term care insurance was then launched in 2000, boosting revenues while improving welfare services. Japan joined Germany as one of the few countries to adopt such a program.

New policies to boost fertility were less impressive until the DPJ launched its new child allowance policy, whose impact on the fertility rate is not yet clear. Low fertility did not capture the public's attention until 1990, thus it is a newer item on the policy agenda than the aging society. It is also a multi-faceted problem involving a syndrome of distinct but related behaviors:

- An increasing number of women do not marry. The proportion of women who never marry has risen from 1.87 percent in 1960 to 4.45 percent in 1980 and 5.82 percent in 2000.
- Women who marry do so later in life. The average age of women on their first marriage has risen from 25.1 years in 1980 to 28.6 years in 2000.
- Women who marry have fewer children. Today's fertility rate of 1.37 children per woman contrasts with a rate of 2.00 in 1960 and 1.75 in 1980.[32]

Diverse attitudes underlie these behaviors. Some women are disinclined to marry or bear children because they wish to pursue careers. Some are more concerned about making time for recreation and personal enjoyment. Some shun marriage to avoid the heavy responsibilities of being a home-maker, which may include care for elderly parents-in-law. Many do not have larger families due to the rising cost of children's education. It is difficult to weigh the relative importance of these attitudes, let alone to modify them as a matter of public policy.

The government has striven to make it easier for working women to raise families. A series of "Angel Plans" began in 1994 to increase day-care centers for children in businesses and residential areas. Public day care has also been made available for nonworking mothers. The government has encouraged fathers to become more involved in childrearing. In 1999 the MHW issued a famous poster declaring that "We don't call a man a father unless he raises his children." The government also urges men as well as women to take parental leave from work when a child is born, setting numerical targets for this purpose in 2002. (In 2007 89.7 percent of female employees took parental leave, in contrast to only 1.6 percent of male employees.)[33] Officials strengthened the Gender Equal Employment Law in 1997 by imposing concrete penalties on employers who discriminate against female employees. The government's Second Basic Plan for Gender Equality, adopted in 2005, proposes further steps to eliminate indirect discrimination by employers, and it posits the goal that women should occupy 30 percent of leadership positions in all spheres of society by 2020.

Steps to promote gender equality have received a mixed reaction from women, thus complicating the task of policymakers. For instance, in the 1980s the government increased the tax deduction for the nonworking spouses of salaried employees and provided them with noncontributory public pensions. These steps compensate women who devote themselves to child-rearing. However, women who seek equality in the labor market protest that such steps discourage women from taking regular jobs, thus reinforcing the male-breadwinner model of the family. When the government imposed fines on firms that discriminated against women workers in 1997, it removed certain clauses from the Labor Standards Law that had protected women, the rationale being that regular female employees should do the same work as men. But since Japanese men work exceedingly long hours, some feminists have criticized this measure for dissuading women from taking managerial-track jobs.

The government's efforts have alleviated the effects of demographic change somewhat but will not suffice to rescue welfare finances from the strains of expanding longevity and declining fertility. Considerable political courage and ingenuity are required to save the situation. Should the government fail, Japanese society may experience severe intergenerational conflict over welfare policy.

Currently, about 70 percent of the public welfare budget is spent on the elderly, but only 4 percent on children, an imbalance that is less pronounced in Western states such as Sweden and France.[34] Moreover, the government calculates that the amount of welfare benefits minus contributions for a Japanese born between 1974 and 1983 is about ¥65,350,000 (or $653,500 at ¥100/$1) less than that for a Japanese born before 1943.[35] This lopsided advantage of the elderly in Japan's welfare system has attracted considerable attention. Popular journals have issued special editions with titles such as "Are the Elderly Really the Weak?"[36] and "Silver Democracy Endangers Japan."[37] Some speculate that the higher voter turnout of the elderly has won them priority in social policy. In the general election of 2009, only 49 percent of people in their twenties voted, compared to 84 percent of people in their sixties.[38]

Younger Japanese realize that pay-as-you-go financing has them supporting a level of pension benefits for the elderly today that they may never be able to collect themselves in the less favorable demographic conditions of coming decades. When asked if they felt disadvantaged by the pension system, 67 percent of Japanese in their twenties agreed, but only 19 percent of those over 65.[39] The many nonsalaried youth who decline to pay pension premiums reflect these attitudes. In short, the intergenerational solidarity that was once a pillar of the welfare state is at risk. Referring to the pension systems of Japan, Italy, and Germany, Anthony Giddens comments that "Rather than creating greater social solidarity, as it is supposed to do, in this situation welfare institutions can undermine it."[40]

Scholars sometimes suggest that the forging of the welfare state after World War II was based on a metaphorical social contract between the working and managerial classes. The workers abandoned their radical designs to eliminate private property, and in exchange management accepted welfare policies that granted the average worker health care and a comfortable retirement. The welfare state's continued viability may depend on the forging of a similar social contract between the young and the old. In the meantime, however, the social contract between economic classes is itself suffering strains.

THE IMPENDING CRISIS II: THE ECONOMY

Adverse economic conditions have exacerbated the financial difficulties arising from demographic change. In the 1980s, Japan experienced an artificial economic boom owing to speculative investment in land and stocks, whose monetary value rose much faster than their real productive value. This speculative "bubble" burst in 1990, causing a sharp drop in asset prices and leaving a mountain of nonperforming loans in the banking system. This ended some 40 years of almost uninterrupted economic growth. One reason that Japan's welfare finances are in such straits today is that benefits were always predicated upon continued economic expansion.

The government was slow to react to the financial crisis. Japanese had enjoyed unparalleled confidence in their economy in the late 1980s, and bureaucrats and bankers strove to conceal the financial collapse, partly to hide their own culpability. Its implications for the welfare system first became evident in employment policy. During the recession that has followed the bursting of the bubble economy in 1990, three important changes have occurred: (1) Japan has experienced higher unemployment than it had known for several decades; (2) budget deficits have forced the government to curb the proactive work policies that formerly boosted employment in inefficient economic sectors; and (3) employers have hired fewer long-term employees, causing a sharp rise in temporary and part-time workers.

Since 1990 the Japanese have ceased to enjoy the low unemployment rates that accompanied their postwar economic boom. The unemployment rate of 2.1 percent in 1990 had risen to 4.7 percent by 2000, and since then it has ranged from 3.9 to 5.7 percent. Thus far the government has neglected to strengthen its miserly programs of unemployment insurance and poor relief to meet this challenge.

Budget deficits have compelled the government to diminish its once robust work policies. In 1997 the government's purchases of the rice crop shrank to 19 percent, diluting its support for the rural population. After electoral reform in 1994, rural dwellers lost the disproportionately high representation in the Diet that they had had previously. In 1999, under foreign pressure, Japan revoked the Large Retail Store Law that had protected small shopkeepers. Foreign business interests had complained that they could not market their products effectively through Japan's multitude of small retailers. The self-employed fell from 17.5 percent of total employment in 1997 to 13.4 percent in 2007.[41] Finally, the government has reduced public works spending under public criticism that it is wasteful.[42] Public works had kept many low-income workers employed in the construction industry, but construction workers decreased from 6.32 million in 2001 to 5.37 million in 2008.[43] However successful these work policies were in the past, the economic slowdown has forced cutbacks.

Japanese big business has been renowned for hiring long-term employees who might spend their entire working lives with the same firm. While the economy was growing rapidly, there was little risk in making long-term commitments to a core work force, but the economic crash of 1990 induced firms to lower their fixed costs by hiring fewer permanent employees. Many companies pressed long-term workers into early retirement to survive.

The government's figures on "irregular" employees, who include various temporary and part-time workers, reflect the economy's decline. Before 1990 most irregulars were housewives, young unmarried women, students, and the elderly, people who labored to supplement other income from spouses, parents, scholarships, or pensions. Their employment was more a means to participate in society than a necessity to earn a living. But irregular workers have increased from 20.2 percent of total employment in 1990 to 34.1 percent in 2008, and their number now includes many individuals who depend on their incomes to live. Irregular male workers rose from 8.8 percent to 19.2 percent of all male workers over 1990–2008, and the ratio of irregulars among 25–34-year-old male workers rose from 3.2 to 14.2 percent.[44]

Besides straining the government's unemployment and livelihood assistance programs, irregular workers hurt the welfare system in other ways. Part-timers earning below a certain amount do not contribute to the social insurance fund for old-age pensions. Thus the pension fund loses contributors and the government faces the prospect that many people will reach old age without adequate incomes. Irregular employment also exacerbates the demographic crisis, since the poor and the unemployed are less likely to raise large families. Many students who graduated during the economic downturn of the 1990s and early 2000s are caught in an endless cycle of irregular jobs. Japanese refer to them as the "lost generation."

The U.S. financial collapse of 2008 worsened Japan's employment situation and underscored the plight of irregular workers. One category of irregulars comprises "dispatch workers" (*haken rodosha*) who are hired out to companies on temporary assignment by private labor services. The impact of the U.S. financial crisis saw many of these workers dismissed, losing not only their jobs but also the dormitory housing that companies often provided. Many became homeless, taking refuge in Internet cafes or living on the streets. During New Year's week of 2009, labor and social movement activists organized a "dispatch workers' village" in Tokyo's Hibiya Park, providing over 500 dismissed dispatch workers with food, tent shelters, and legal aid. As their numbers grew, the organizers asked the MHLW to shelter them in its auditorium, which the ministry did. The dispatch workers' village became a major media event, as politicians of all parties rushed to the scene to show their sympathy.

Public concern about income inequality had actually been growing for some time. From the wartime period to the 1980s, both the government's social policies and corporate labor practices had earned Japan the reputation of a highly egalitarian society, at least outside the area of gender relations. Granted, the long-term employees of large businesses always enjoyed a higher standard of living than other workers, but the government's work policies and welfare programs narrowed the income gap between the two. In the 1980s, this commitment to social equality weakened, and after 1990 there was a decline in long-term employment at the top of the labor market and an erosion of government support for less secure workers at the bottom. Consequently, the dwindling minority of long-term employees became even more of a labor aristocracy, and the gap between this group and the growing number of irregular workers widened. Neoliberal values bred greater tolerance for income inequality through the 1990s, and this trend influenced the Koizumi government (2001–2006), which sought to deregulate labor markets and reduce official employment policies such as public works programs. Lately, however, the economic hardships of the post-bubble economy have moved public opinion away from neoliberalism and back toward egalitarian values.

In recent years, terms such as "unequal society" (*kakusa shakai*) and "poverty" (*hinkon*) have become major topics of discussion. Table 8.1 tracks the number of articles devoted to those subjects in magazines since 2000.

In 2006, Japan's public television network NHK broadcast a documentary on the "working poor," a concept unknown during the years of rapid economic growth. According to the OECD, in 2004 the percentage of people earning less than one-half of the median income was higher in Japan (14.9 percent) than in any other industrialized nation except the United States.[45] In 2008 children living in poverty became the subject of scholarly studies, special magazine editions, and television programs. A survey of 20 countries by the BBC and the *Yomiuri* newspaper found that 72 percent of Japanese considered their society unequal, the sixth highest figure in the group. The *Yomiuri* reported on September 22, 2009, that only 16 percent of Japanese still viewed Japan as an egalitarian society.

In the lower house election campaign of 2009, LDP and DPJ politicians offered competing solutions to the aging society, low fertility, unemployment, and income inequality. The DPJ won this contest with promises to boost child allowances, increase support for farmers and fatherless families,

Table 8.1 Number of Journal Articles Including the Terms "Inequality" (*kakusa*), "Poverty" (*hinkon*), or "Working Poor" (*waakingu pua*) in the Title

Year	2000	2001	2002	2003	2004	2005	2006	2007	2008
kakusa	392	384	340	387	366	537	1282	1560	1201
hinkon	170	153	148	176	177	258	370	486	654
Working Poor	0	0	0	0	1	8	51	65	96

Source: NII (National Institute of Informatics); *Ronbun Joho Navigator* (Article Information Navigator); CiNii, http://ci.nii.ac.jp/ (accessed October 2009).

and otherwise combat the trend toward unequal incomes. The new government even appointed the chief of the dispatch workers' village, Makoto Yuasa, as an advisor.

There are no simple solutions to Japan's current welfare problems. The financial straits of the pension system alone will make it impossible to sustain current entitlements and simultaneously meet new welfare challenges. If the government wishes to increase support for young families, it will have to reduce welfare commitments to the elderly. If it hopes to bolster income equality, it will have to find alternatives to the expensive employment policies of the past. If it hopes to boost fertility, it will have to find ways to further gender equality while also making it easier for families to raise children. The task of sustaining the welfare state amid today's adverse demographic and economic conditions may prove just as challenging as the creation of the welfare state was in the past century.

NOTES

1. On Japan's welfare history, see Sugaya, *Nihon Shakai Seisaku Shi Ron* (Discourse on the History of Japan's Social Policy).
2. Roemer, *Comparative National Policies on Health Care*, p. 39.
3. Kasza, *One World of Welfare: Japan in Comparative Perspective*, Chapter 2.
4. Koseisho 50-Nen Shi Henshu Iinkai, *Koseisho 50-Nen Shi: Kijutsu Hen* (A 50-year History of the Ministry of Health and Welfare: Narrative Volume), pp. 558–564.
5. Koseisho, *Kosei Hakusho: Heisei 11 Nenban* (Welfare White Paper: Heisei 11), p. 16.
6. Reischauer, *The United States and Japan*, p. 352.
7. Campbell, *How Policies Change: The Japanese Government and the Aging Society*, p. 21; Watanuki, "Is There a 'Japanese-Type Welfare Society'?" p. 261.
8. Shinkawa, *Nihongata Fukushi no Seiji-keizaigaku* (The Political Economy of Japanese-Style Welfare), p. 69.
9. Milly, *Poverty, Equality, and Growth: The Politics of Economic Need in Postwar Japan*, pp. 180–181, 200–207.
10. Organization for Economic Co-operation and Development, *Social Expenditures, 1960–1990: Problems of Growth and Control*, p. 21.
11. International Labor Office, *The Cost of Social Security: Fourteenth International Inquiry, 1987–1989: Comparative Tables*, pp. 96–98, Table 6.

12. Kosei Tokei Kyokai, *Hoken to Nenkin no Doko: Kosei no Shihyo* (Trends in Insurance and Pensions: Welfare Indicators), p. 13.
13. Ibid., p. 17.
14. Campbell and Ikegami, *The Art of Balance in Health Policy: Maintaining Japan's Low-Cost, Egalitarian System*, pp. 89–90; Kosei Tokei Kyokai, *Hoken to Nenkin no Doko: Kosei no Shihyo* (Trends in Insurance and Pensions: Welfare Indicators), pp. 17, 27.
15. Peabody et al., *Policy and Health: Implications for Development in Asia*, p. 229.
16. Kosei Tokei Kyokai, *Hoken to Nenkin no Doko: Kosei no Shihyo* (Trends in Insurance and Pensions: Welfare Indicators), p. 29.
17. Premiums are not charged against every individual's total income, but only up to a certain maximum amount of income.
18. Matsutani, "Grimmer Pension Forecast Released," *Japan Times*, April 16, 2009.
19. Yoshida, "Distrust in Pension Framework Growing," *Japan Times*, May 3, 2004.
20. Martin, *What Works among Active Labour Market Policies: Evidence from OECD Countries' Experiences*, p. 25.
21. Nakagawa, "Seikatsu Hogo no Taisho to Hinkon Mondai no Henka" (The Objects of Public Assistance and Changes in the Poverty Problem), pp. 33–38.
22. Sheingate, *The Rise of the Agricultural Welfare State: Institutions and Interest Group Power in the United States, France, and Japan*, p. 223; Calder, *Crisis and Compensation*, pp. 238–239.
23. Ministry of Land, Infrastructure, and Transport, *White Paper on Land, Infrastructure and Transport in Japan, 2001*, p. 22; Woodall, *Japan under Construction*.
24. Organization for Economic Co-operation and Development, *Historical Statistics, 1960–1995*, p. 45.
25. *Japan Times*, "Bill for Child Allowance Receives OK," May 19, 2000.
26. Organization for Economic Cooperation and Development, "OECD in Figures: 2009," *OECD Observer 2009, Supplement 1*.
27. For all figures in this paragraph, see Kaneko et al., "Population Projections for Japan: 2006–2055, Outline of Results, Methods, and Assumptions," pp. 1, 9.
28. "Editorial: Budget with Stop-Gap Funding," *Japan Times*, January 4, 2011.
29. Organization for Economic Cooperation and Development, "OECD in Figures: 2009," *OECD Observer 2009, Supplement 1*.
30. *Yoron Chosa*, November 2004, p. 87; Naikakufu, "*Kokumin Seikatsu ni Kansuru Yoron Chosa*" (Cabinet Office, Public Opinion Poll on Japanese Citizens' Lives).
31. Koseirodosho, *Koseirodo Hakusho: Heisei 20 Nenban* (Ministry of Health, Labor, and Welfare White Paper: Heisei 20), p. 5.
32. All figures from National Institute of Population and Social Security Research, *Population Statistics of Japan 2008*.
33. Koseirodosho, "*Heisei 19 Nendo Koyo Kinto Kihon Chosa*" (Ministry of Health, Labor, and Welfare, 2007 Basic Research on Equal Employment).
34. Horie, "*Shoshika Mondai-wo-meguru Aidia to Seiji*" (Ideas and Politics Concerning Low Fertility in Japan), p. 20; Naikakufu, *Shoshika-shakai Hakusho: Heisei 19 Nenban* (Cabinet Office, White Paper on the Low Fertility Society: Heisei 19), p.77.

35. Naikakufu, *Keizai Zaisei Hakusho: Heisei 17 Nenban* (Cabinet Office, White Paper on the Economy and Public Finance: Heisei 17), p. 77.
36. "Koreisha wa Honto ni Jakusha na no Ka?" (Are the Elderly Really the Weak?), *Chuo Koron*, August 2008.
37. "Nihon o Ayauku Suru Shirubaa Minshushugi" (Silver Democracy Endangers Japan), *Wedge*, August 2008.
38. Akarui Senkyo Suishin Kyokai (The Association for Promoting Fair Elections).
39. "Sasaeai Magarikado ni Futanzo Jiwari Teikokan" (Mutual Support at a Turn in the Road, Increase in Welfare Burden is Not Welcomed), *Asahi Shimbun*, June 21, 2003, p. 17.
40. Giddens, *The Third Way and Its Critics*, p. 103.
41. OECD, "OECD in Figures: 2009," *OECD Observer 2009, Supplement 1.*
42. Ministry of Land, Infrastructure, and Transport, *White Paper on Land, Infrastructure and Transport in Japan*, Chapter 3.
43. Somusho Tokeikyoku Seisakutokatsukan Tokei Kenshujo, www.stat.go.jp/.
44. Somusho Tokeikyoku Seisakutokatsukan Tokei Kenshujo (Ministry of Internal Affairs and Communications, Statistics Bureau, Director General for Policy Planning and Statistical Research and Training Institute).
45. OECD, stats.oecd.org (accessed November 2009); *Japan Times*, October 21, 2009.

BIBLIOGRAPHY

Akarui Senkyo Suishin Kyokai (The Association for Promoting Fair Elections), www.akaruisenkyo.or.jp/070various/sg_nenrei.html (accessed March 2010).
"Bill for Child Allowance Receives OK," *Japan Times*, May 19, 2000.
Calder, Kent, *Crisis and Compensation: Public Policy and Political Stability in Japan, 1949–1986* (Princeton: Princeton University Press, 1988).
Campbell, John Creighton, *How Policies Change: The Japanese Government and the Aging Society* (Princeton: Princeton University Press, 1992).
Campbell, John Creighton and Naoki Ikegami, *The Art of Balance in Health Policy: Maintaining Japan's Low-Cost, Egalitarian System* (Cambridge: Cambridge University Press, 1998).
"Editorial: Budget with Stop-Gap Funding," *Japan Times*, January 4, 2011.
Fukue, Natsuko, "First Ever Poverty Rate Released by Ministry Stands at Relatively High 15.7%," *Japan Times*, October 21, 2009.
Giddens, Anthony, *The Third Way and Its Critics* (Cambridge: Polity Press, 2000).
Horie, Takashi, "Shoshika Mondai-wo-meguru Aidia to Seiji" (Ideas and Politics Concerning Low Fertility in Japan), *Jinbungakuhou* 394 (2008).
International Labor Office, *The Cost of Social Security: Fourteenth International Inquiry, 1987–1989: Comparative Tables* (Geneva: ILO, 1996).
Kaneko, Ryuichi, Akira Ishikawa, Futoshi Ishii, Tsukasa Sasai, Miho Iwasawa, Fusami Mita, and Rie Moriizumi, "Population Projections for Japan: 2006–2055, Outline of Results, Methods, and Assumptions," *The Japanese Journal of Population* 6, no. 1 (March 2008).
Kasza, Gregory J., *One World of Welfare: Japan in Comparative Perspective* (Ithaca: Cornell University Press, 2006).
"Koreisha wa Honto ni Jakusha na no Ka?" *Chuo Koron*, August 2008.

Kosei Tokei Kyokai, *Hoken to Nenkin no Doko: Kosei no Shihyo* (Trends in Insurance and Pensions: Welfare Indicators) 55, no. 14 (special issue 2008).

Koseirodosho, *Heisei 19 Nendo Koyo Kinto Kihon Chosa* (Ministry of Health, Labor, and Welfare, Basic Research on Equal Employment, Heisei 19), 2007, www.mhlw.go.jp/houdou/2008/08/h0808-1.html (accessed April 2008).

Koseirodosho, *Koseirodo Hakusho: Heisei 20 Nenban* (Ministry of Health, Labor, and Welfare White Paper: Heisei 20) (Tokyo: Gyosei, 2008).

Koseisho, *Kosei Hakusho: Heisei 11 Nenban* (Welfare White Paper: Heisei 11) (Tokyo: Gyosei, 1999).

Koseisho 50-Nen Shi Henshu Iinkai (Editorial Board of the Fifty-Year History of the Ministry of Health and Welfare), ed., *Koseisho 50-Nen Shi: Kijutsu Hen* (A 50-year History of the Ministry of Health and Welfare: Narrative Volume) (Tokyo: Kosei Mondai Kenkyūkai, 1988).

Martin, John P., *What Works among Active Labour Market Policies: Evidence from OECD Countries' Experiences*, Labour Market and Social Policy Occasional Papers No. 35 (Paris: OECD, 1998).

Matsutani, Minoru, "Grimmer Pension Forecast Released," *Japan Times*, April 16, 2009.

Milly, Deborah J., *Poverty, Equality, and Growth: The Politics of Economic Need in Postwar Japan* (Cambridge, MA: Harvard University Asia Center, 1999).

Ministry of Land, Infrastructure, and Transport, *White Paper on Land, Infrastructure and Transport in Japan, 2001*, www.mlit.go.jp/english/index.html (accessed July 2005),

Naikakufu, *Keizai Zaisei Hakusho: Heisei 17 Nenban* (Cabinet Office, White Paper on the Economy and Public Finance: Heisei 19) (Tokyo: Kokuritsu Insatsukyoku, 2005).

———, *"Kokumin Seikatsu ni Kansuru Yoron Chosa"* (Cabinet Office, Public Opinion Poll on Japanese Citizens' Lives), www8.cao.go.jp/survey/h21/h21-life/index.html (accessed November 2008).

———, *Shoshika-shakai Hakusho: Heisei 19 Nenban* (Cabinet Office, White Paper on Low Fertility Society: Heisei 17) (Tokyo: Gyosei, 2007).

Nakagawa, Kiyoshi, "Seikatsu Hogo no Taisho to Hinkon Mondai no Henka" (The Objects of Public Assistance and Changes in the Poverty Problem), *Shakai Fukushi Kenkyu* no. 83 (January 2002).

National Institute of Population and Social Security Research, *Population Statistics of Japan 2008*, www.ipss.go.jp/index-e.html (accessed November 2009).

"Nihon o Ayauku Suru Shirubaa Minshushugi" (Silver Democracy Endangers Japan), *Wedge*, August 2008.

Organization for Economic Co-operation and Development, *Historical Statistics, 1960–1995* (Paris: OECD, 1997).

———, *Social Expenditures, 1960–1990: Problems of Growth and Control* (Paris: OECD, 1985).

———, "OECD in Figures: 2009," *OECD Observer 2009, Supplement 1* (Paris: OECD, 2009).

———, stats.oecd.org (accessed November 2009).

Peabody, John W. et al., *Policy and Health: Implications for Development in Asia* (Cambridge: Cambridge University Press, 1999).

Reischauer, Edwin O., *The United States and Japan*, 3rd ed. (New York: Viking Press, 1965).

Roemer, Milton Irwin, *Comparative National Policies on Health Care* (New York: M. Dekker, 1977).

"Sasaeai Magarikado ni Futanzo Jiwari Teikokan" (Mutual Support at a Turn in the Road, Increase in Welfare Burden is Not Welcomed), *Asahi Shimbun*, June 21, 2003, 17.

Sheingate, Adam D., *The Rise of the Agricultural Welfare State: Institutions and Interest Group Power in the United States, France, and Japan* (Princeton: Princeton University Press, 2001).

Shinkawa, Toshimitsu, *Nihongata Fukushi no Seiji-keizaigaku* (The Political Economy of Japanese-Style Welfare) (Tokyo: Sanichi Shobo, 1993).

Somusho Tokeikyoku Seisakutokatsukan Tokei Kenshujo (Ministry of Internal Affairs and Communications, Statistics Bureau, Director General for Policy Planning and Statistical Research and Training Institute), www.stat.go.jp/ (accessed March 2009).

Sugaya, Akira, *Nihon Shakai Seisaku Shi Ron* (Discourse on the History of Japan's Social Policy) (Tokyo: Nippon Hyoronsha, 1990).

Watanuki, Joji, "Is There a 'Japanese-Type Welfare Society'?" *International Sociology* 1, no. 3 (September 1986).

Woodall, Brian, *Japan under Construction: Corruption, Politics, and Public Works* (Berkeley: University of California Press, 1996).

Yoron Chosa 36, no. 11 (2004).

Yoshida, Reiji, "Distrust in Pension Framework Growing," *Japan Times*, May 3, 2004.

9

Japan's Subnational Government: Toward Greater Decentralization and Participatory Democracy

Purnendra Jain

The term "subnational government" (SNG) is less common than "local government" in the English language literature that examines *jichitai*—governments below the central government in Japan.[1] But "local government" may be mistakenly understood as small government units that function at the lowest level of government structures and perform limited local tasks, such as garbage collection, maintenance of street lights, and paving of footpaths, as many local councils do in a range of countries. In Japan, the unitary government structure is such that the responsibilities of many of the subnational units stretch beyond those ordinarily performed by local councils to include primary and secondary education, water supply, firefighting services, city planning, environmental management, and so forth. In federal systems many of these are generally the responsibilities of state governments. To avoid potential confusion, given the vast range of responsibilities, including management of huge budgets, "subnational" is more appropriate than "local" when referring to this level of government in Japan.

Although legally recognized in the postwar constitution, Japan's SNGs operate under a centralized structure that affords them little legal and financial autonomy and very little room for initiative and innovation. Japan's unitary system of government requires SNGs to comply with central laws, bureaucratic directives, and other forms of tight central control, especially financial. Yet as government units whose work touches the everyday life of local residents, they are under constant pressure from demands emanating from local communities, through organized civic groups, such as nonprofit and nongovernmental organizations (NPOs and NGOs), citizen movements, and individual citizens. Thus SNGs must effectively answer to two sets of masters in different realms: the national government working within nationally defined parameters, and citizens on the ground requiring attention to their everyday needs as local residents. Satisfying both sets of demands is usually difficult and sometimes irreconcilable from conflict of interests between local and national needs. It fuels the constant quest by SNGs to achieve a more autonomous space in which to perform tasks effectively for their constituents, with less regulation from the central government master.

In this chapter I examine the competing forces of centralization and the quest for autonomy as a continuing theme in the postwar Japanese political landscape. Although central government forces maintain a tight grip on the full government sector and are steadfastly unwilling to relinquish power to lower levels, forces from the periphery of this sector have upped the ante against the center and in the process have made some gains, even if piecemeal. The tug continues in this zero-sum game, with no sign of a satisfactory outcome. A clear consensus is unlikely to emerge until a power-sharing formula is produced in which both parties regard the outcome as a win-win situation in which national and subnational levels are at ease with each other.

The main argument advanced here is that despite a centralized government structure with relatively firm central control, Japan's SNGs have created opportunities for leadership, particularly through new policy initiatives and innovative ideas. SNGs' actions have served to foster citizen participation and bolster civic society, which both strengthen democratic processes. In the face of resistant forces seeking to preserve centralized government, SNGs have not only successfully implemented policies in the interests of local residents but on many occasions have raised the bar by setting higher policy standards locally, thus forcing the national government to revise its own laws based on local standards. Their interest in local concerns has led some SNG leaders to look even beyond the national boundary to address problems, following through on the twin slogans "think globally, act locally" and "think locally, act globally." Overall, the forces pushing for decentralization and local autonomy, and the desire to work for local interests, have made significant progress in recent years. Nevertheless, centralist cultures remain strong, especially within the bureaucracy. Although the current Naoto Kan government claims to be committed to revising the system to give greater fiscal and administrative independence to subnational governments,[2] only time will tell the fate of statements promising more power to localities made by the new DPJ national government, repeating the DPJ's claim in its election manifesto.[3]

I begin this chapter detailing the formal structure of SNGs in Japan and the types of policy innovation and groundbreaking results that SNGs have achieved. Here I consider how these have fostered grassroots democracy and encouraged citizen participation through a process that began in the 1960s and 1970s under progressive (*kakushin*) leadership. I then examine the types of policies adopted in the 1980s and 1990s by a range of reformist (*kaikakuha*) leaders, maintaining the momentum for policy innovation, the demand for autonomy, and greater civic participation.[4] Finally, I consider the legislative changes that have been introduced since the late 1990s, some of which have significantly altered the roles, functions, and even the territorial boundaries of SNGs while debate for further reforms continues under the DPJ government. National-subnational government relations and the issues of decentralization and citizen participation at grassroots level are not front-page news items in Japan and are even less so internationally. They are, nevertheless, some of the critical developments that will shape Japan's politics and society in the second decade of the twenty-first century.

THE STRUCTURE OF JAPAN'S SNG SYSTEM

Local units in Japan were given constitutional recognition for the first time under the 1947 constitution. Consisting of four articles (92–95), Chapter VIII of the constitution recognizes "the principle of local autonomy" and broadly defines the structure and functions of local public entities. It makes provision for the establishment of law for the "organization of operations of local public entities" (Article 92). It stipulates that the chief executive officers and members of local assemblies "shall be elected by direct popular vote within their several communities" (Article 93). Details of structures and financial matters were codified separately in the Local Autonomy Law and Local Finance Law.

Broadly, the SNG structure consists of two levels. One comprises the larger units: prefectures that include the Tokyo Metropolis, Osaka and Kyoto in central Japan, and Hokkaido in the north, plus 43 other units (*to, do, fu, ken*). These have existed since the Meiji period and their number has not changed even after World War II and under U.S. Occupation reform. The other level of units consists of cities, towns, and villages (*shi, cho, son*)—all of varying sizes and financial capacities. Some cities have been given special status because of their large size, such as "designated cities" (*seirei shitei toshi*) whose functions extend beyond those carried out by ordinary cities.[5] Unlike the prefectures, municipalities have undergone a number of amalgamations over the past 120 years, including the most recent between 1999 and 2006, known as the *Heisei daigappei* or the great Heisei amalgamation.[6]

Chief executive officers—prefectural governors and municipal mayors—are political heads elected for a term of four years. Each SNG has a single-chamber assembly elected directly for a term similar to that of the chief executive officer. Unlike the central-level political structure in Japan that operates under the Westminster parliamentary system, the structure at the SNG level resembles that of the presidential system where both the chief executive officers and local assembly members are elected by a direct vote.[7] This "dual representation system" has a mechanism of checks and balances in which the assembly is empowered to pass a motion of nonconfidence in the chief executive officer, and the chief executive officer has the right to dissolve the assembly.[8]

EARLY POSTWAR YEARS

With the end of the U.S. Occupation in 1952, conservative ruling parties at both central and local levels reversed the decentralization process introduced by the Occupation authorities and flagrantly recentralized to the extent that the new constitution allowed. Japan's rapid economic takeoff in early postwar served to legitimize this reversal by creating broad acceptance of a centralized state as the essential means to national economic growth.[9] In this period, both national and local politics were dominated by conservative forces with the national government providing financial support to SNGs, and in turn, commanding their political loyalty. Rapid economic growth through industrialization in the 1950s and 1960s brought with it a range of challenges, including dangerous levels of industrial pollution and severe social problems like urban housing shortage and inadequate health and family welfare. The national government, held solidly by the Liberal Democratic Party (LDP), focused on further economic growth and ignored ordinary people's suffering. Popular resistance inspired a strong, creative, and motivated grassroots movement against the center's neglect of urban living conditions, particularly industrial pollution that caused severe harm to human health.[10]

PROGRESSIVE LOCAL LEADERS

Since the conservative local leadership ignored the rising mountain of social and welfare issues faced especially by urban communities, a large number of left-leaning political chief executives were swept into office through elections. Most progressive leaders were backed by leftist parties, mainly comprising the socialists and communists that languished politically at the national level. These leftist political parties supported popular movements at the local level and demonstrated willingness to address their concerns. Leaders of such popular movements received support from leftist parties that helped them win elections in urban and metropolitan areas. Tokyo, Kyoto, Yokohama, and many other major urban centers had progressive leaders as their chief executives.

Unlike their conservative predecessors, these new leaders were not afraid to lock horns with the central government on issues vital to their local communities, with which the central government was demonstrably way out of touch or was unwilling to address their concerns. They bravely initiated innovative policies in the interests of local residents, even when that meant flying in the face of central government policies. Their strong will, forthright policy initiatives, and concern to truly serve the localities that elected them, produced de facto decentralization and a vibrant democratic process at the grassroots level.

The late 1960s to early 1980s were years of "progressive administrations" at the subnational level in Japan. A good number of studies in English appeared in this period, analyzing the policy initiatives of progressive administrations in a range of areas, including social welfare, industrial pollution management, housing, and human rights issues that also extended to the rights of foreign nationals, such as long-term Korean residents.[11] In many of these policy areas, progressive SNG units set standards higher than those of the national government, challenging and at times compelling the national government to follow the lead provided by the SNG leadership.[12] Here at last was a counterbalance to the national government. Yet no constitutional or major legislative changes were introduced to promote decentralization. In essence, SNGs pursued innovative policies within the highly centralized structure and in the face of firm central control.

Soon, however, local activism lost the wind from its sails. National economic boom and resulting widespread prosperity from the late 1970s enabled the central government to rein in the pressure for reform and, importantly, retain its tight fist on local administrations. The gains of SNGs during the 1970s were put on hold.

THE ERA OF LOCALITIES

The end of progressive administrations could not halt the momentum toward autonomy. Demand for greater power to subnational units instead evolved into a different form. After all, as representative of their localities, local-level leaders have to work in the interest of their constituents, who are generally much closer to SNG than to the central government when it comes to pressing their claims. Many of the new chief executives were elected as independents with support from a coalition of parties of different political persuasion. In some cases they were supported jointly by both conservative and progressive parties (*ainori*). Although they shunned the confrontational approach of their progressive predecessors, they continued to push new policy frontiers and press for more autonomy with the national government through negotiation. The era of localities or *chiho no jidai* emerged as a major theme throughout the 1980s.[13]

Many SNG leaders introduced new policy initiatives that furthered the cause of democracy through greater transparency of their administrations and more inclusive citizen participation within them. These leaders also took up the challenge of managing environmental issues and providing services needed for a changing society characterized by a greying population. Good governance and civic participation began to capture the imagination of many chief executives who eagerly put their innovative ideas into practice.

Greater access to government information was one particular area where SNGs began to make solid progress. Many established freedom of information ordinances, after the first in 1982 by the small SNG of Kaneyama in Yamagata prefecture. In 1994 the mayor of Niseko town, with a population of about 4,500 in Hokkaido prefecture, set a precedent by making many kinds of information publicly available, including public access to all meetings held at the level of section chiefs. SNGs nationwide dispatched teams to observe Niseko's initiatives.[14] By 2005 almost all SNGs in Japan had passed ordinances to broaden information disclosure. Similarly, SNGs have moved to recognize the importance of personal privacy and after the first personal-information protection ordinances were established in the mid-1980s, by 2006 more than 98 percent of SNGs had adopted these ordinances.[15] It is important to remember that in all of these issues, as in many since the 1970s, SNGs took the lead role. The national government then followed SNGs' initiatives.

Mechanisms encouraging political participation also began to take firm root at the SNG level. More referenda were carried out at the local level on issues such as construction of dams, airports, and nuclear power plants, putting pressure on SNGs to consider popular voice and the consequences when accepting such projects to implement on behalf of the national government.[16] On waste management, Terry MacDougall noted that "local authorities have engaged residents in thoroughgoing discussions of the siting of plants, their designs, what facilities to include, and what public amenities (from heated pools to recreation facilities for the elderly) will go along with them."[17] Other mechanisms include access to government through digital means, such as online discussion and feedback to local administrations.[18]

In more recent years, municipal charters (*jichi kihon jorei*) are becoming a norm of local governance in Japan.[19] Their purpose is to build trust between citizens and administrative bodies of SNGs and clarify the role that both sides are to play in local governance. According to a database developed by Takanobu Tsujiyama of Jichi Soken—a leading SNG research institute in Tokyo—by the end of April 2008, 126 municipal governments in Japan had established a municipal charter since 2001 when the first was established by Niseko town, which was at the forefront of freedom for information action in the early 1990s.[20] Many municipalities now use the term "citizens" (*shimin*) rather than "residents" (*jumin*). The charter of the city of Tama in Tokyo, for example, includes under the category of its "citizens" all those who live, work, study, or are engaged in business and other forms of activity within the city's municipal areas (Article 3 [2]) irrespective of their actual place of residence.[21] Through these charters, municipalities are establishing new bylaws leading to greater participation of local residents in administration and decision-making processes.

Furthermore, like most communities worldwide, globalization and the rapid movement of people across borders for business, education, migration, and through marriage have shaped local communities in Japan. The center's firm hold has ensured that only a few doors have been opened for SNGs to connect to the world beyond the national border. Nonetheless, SNGs have been amazingly active in a range of international areas, including international trade, cultural exchanges, scientific and technical collaboration, and economic cooperation, with some extending to hard-core issues of foreign policy and national security. The profile of their international involvement indicates that Japan's SNGs have forged extensive international links and connected themselves to global communities in ways that the central government, partly because of its status, is unable to do.[22] Similarly, SNGs have taken the lead role in recognizing foreigners' rights, including access to welfare and medical facilities and voting in local elections. Even so, a national law recognizing foreigners' right to vote in local elections is yet to be established. Some SNGs such as the city of Takahama and the city of Yamato through bylaws and municipal charters have already granted the right to vote to foreigners with permanent resident status, aged 18 years and above, with a continuous resident status of a certain period.[23]

REFORMS FROM ABOVE

Pressure from below for the national government to grant greater autonomy to SNGs and decentralize responsibilities for governance has produced some systemic results. Over the past decade the national government has established a number of commissions, reports have been presented, and some of the recommended changes have been implemented. A number of legislative changes have also been made and more are in the pipeline.

Japan's stagnating economy and the LDP's ouster from national government in the early 1990s injected a fresh round of momentum for decentralization from above. After almost four decades of LDP rule, the election in 1993 of the eight-party coalition, led by Morihiro Hosokawa, raised expectations of reform within the nation's political system. Non-LDP coalitions could not hold power for long, but when the LDP returned to government in 1994, it decided prudently to continue with its predecessor's decentralization process.

The first phase began in 1995 when the new Law for Promotion of Decentralization was established and a committee was formed to recommend changes. On the basis of the report issued by the Decentralization Promotion Committee and through a cabinet decision in May 1998, the government began to formulate a decentralization promotion plan. In March 1999 a bill was submitted to the national parliament and in July 1999 the Diet passed the Omnibus Decentralization Law.

One of the major achievements under the 1999 law was to give municipalities some independence in a range of functions that they previously carried out on behalf of the national government, such as city planning, school education, and social welfare policies. Abolition of agency-assigned functions (*kikan inin jimu*) in 2000 was a major landmark in Japan's SNG postwar history.[24] Under the agency-assigned function system that operated since the Meiji period, heads of local units performed functions as agents of the national government. In the postwar period this system was continued even though the principle of local autonomy was enshrined in the constitution. Some calculations suggest that between 70 and 80 percent of tasks carried out by prefectures and between 30 and 40 percent of tasks carried out by municipalities were within the agency-assigned functions category.[25]

These functions created tensions between the national government and SNGs. They truly made localities an agency of the national government, spending much of their time working on behalf of the national government and receiving instructions from Tokyo. Negotiations between the decentralization committee and national ministries made reform to abolish the agency-assigned function system possible, but according to Wataru Omori, the contribution and cooperation provided by SNGs and the six associations of the SNGs (*chiho roku dantai*) representing local chief executives and local assemblies were also crucial.[26]

SNGs still perform assigned functions, but these are now categorized into self-governing functions and statutory-entrusted functions. The major departure is that central intervention was removed, which meant, as noted by Hiroshi Ikawa, "the autonomy and independence of local governments was greatly enhanced."[27] In many fields of responsibility, central control was removed. For example, the minister of education's approval was no longer required for appointment of a superintendent of the education board; central government permission was no longer essential to issue local bonds; and instead of permission through consultation with central government, mutual agreement is now required for the creation of nonstatutory local ordinary taxes.[28]

While some achievements were made through the 1990s reform process, a final report of the Decentralization Promotion Committee, published in June 2001, pointed to a number of pending tasks. These were made part of the broader agenda of reform and restructuring taken up by Junichiro Koizumi as prime minister (2001–2006). The Koizumi administration put forward the so-called trinity reform (*sanmi ittai kaikaku*) agenda for tax reform (issues related to tax and finance are discussed below). The Shinzo Abe administration (2006–2007) continued this project, and as prime minister (2007–2008) Yasuo Fukuda endorsed his predecessors' initiatives. A new Decentralization Reform Promotion Act was legislated in 2006 and the government set up a Decentralization Reform Promotion Committee in April 2007 to consider issues related to further devolution of power and functions.

The Abe cabinet appointed the first special minister in charge of decentralization reform. This position was continued under Prime Minister Fukuda. Hiroya Masuda, minister of internal affairs, also served as minister for decentralization reform. A former governor of Iwate prefecture in northern Japan, Masuda strongly advocated decentralization while in the gubernatorial position. He announced his firm commitment to Decentralization Reform on the basis of the idea of "self-reliance and mutual cooperation." He was, of course, not the only governor favoring decentralization. Many of his contemporaries, and some before him, have raised this issue at different forums.

STRUCTURAL CHANGES

Decentralization of functions has pushed SNGs toward policies that promote increased efficiency and cost-saving. One such structural change has sought to reduce the number of SNGs through amalgamation. Amalgamation has been conducted many times before, but only at the municipal level, leaving prefectures intact since their creation in 1888.[29] This time a debate is in full swing to consider restructuring the prefectures through a regional state system or *doshusei*.[30]

Following the Omnibus Decentralization Law in 1999, a new municipal merger law was passed in 2004 that led to significant reduction in the number of municipalities. A major merger of SNGs reduced the total number from about 3,230 in the 1990s to 1771 in early 2010. The number of cities has been increased alongside substantial decreases in the number of towns and villages. Amalgamation of municipalities was part of the reform process to enhance efficiency and cut costs. Amalgamation is a difficult process; it means reducing numbers of both heads of municipalities and assembly members as well as staff across the board. Yet the financial situation nationally and at the local level presented SNGs with no choice but to swallow this bitter medicine. The full impact of recent amalgamation is difficult to assess as these are still early days, but some studies have been conducted of earlier amalgamations and their impact.[31]

As part of the devolution process, the ruling LDP, especially since the Koizumi administration, promoted the *doshusei* idea. The DPJ as main opposition party and its former leader Ichiro Ozawa also lent support. Here, Ozawa advocated a structure somewhat different from that in his renowned 1994 book *Blueprint for a New Japan: The Rethinking of a Nation*, where he considered decentralization a core issue and recommended "transfer of substantial national authority and finances to local governments." The now retired governor of Oita in southern Japan, Morihiko Hiramatsu, has authored many books on the issue, including *The Road to the United States of Japan*, where he sets out a path to decentralization through a quasi-federal model. Osaka Governor Toru Hashimoto has long pushed for the *doshusei* regional administrative system, arguing that it will lead to a streamlined bureaucracy and political system, which will use tax money more efficiently than the current prefectural system.[32] Popular governor of Miyazaki, Hideo Higashikokubaru, also advocates introducing the *doshusei*.[33] While this system is being debated, seven prefectural governors in the Kansai region that includes Osaka and Kyoto have established a regional alliance called the Kansai Regional League through which they share resources and services. This may be a beginning toward creating superstates in Japan.[34]

FINANCIAL

One of the most pressing issues surrounding national-subnational relationships is the primary lever that the national level uses to exercise power over subnational units. That lever is financial. SNGs are heavily dependent on the national government to fund the bulk of their budgets, which sets up conditions that effectively ensure SNG compliance with the center's directives. Japanese literature mostly uses the term *sanwari jichi* (30 percent autonomy), meaning that only 30 percent of SNG finances come from sources independent of the national government and for the remainder SNGs must depend on national government coffers. The national government transfers to SNGs some general-purpose grants, such as the local allocation tax, using a number of indicators, and these grants are free from political strings. But other grants and subsidies from the national government are highly political and the dependence on the national government that this produces for SNGs remains the cause of ongoing tension. For a long time SNGs have argued that the center should allow SNGs greater autonomy in both raising their own funds independent of the center and how they spend their money. Graph 9.1 and Table 9.1 below outline SNG's various sources of financing over the past 12 years.

What the above graph and table do not indicate is the mismatch between the revenue and actual expenditure of SNGs and those of the national government. SNGs collect roughly a little over 30 percent in revenue independently, but when all transfers and subsidies from the national government are added, SNGs' total revenue far exceeds that of the national government. In fiscal 2005, for example, their combined expenditure was 89.4 trillion yen, which was 1.5 times greater than that of the national government's total expenditure of 61.2 trillion yen.[35] A lot of money from the local budget is spent on nationally driven projects and functions that make SNGs follow central directives rather than acting independently.[36]

The political nature of the center's subsidies, and requirements for SNGs to match national grants with local financial sources have encouraged some SNGs recently to resist or refuse national grants. The national treasury subsidy system and obligatory share system have also come under great criticism because they make SNGs dependent on the national government, restrict SNG independence, and force SNGs to contribute local resources to projects that the national government asks them to undertake without due consideration for local requirements.

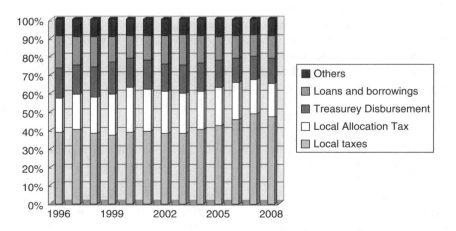

Graph 9.1   Annual Revenue of Local Governments 1996–2008

Table 9.1 Revenue Settlement (100 Million Yen)

	1996	1997	1998	1999	2000	2001	2002	2003	2004	2005	2006	2007	2008
Local taxes	350,937	361,555	359,221	350,261	355,464	355,187	333,785	326,657	335,388	348,041	365,061	402,668	395,585
%	38.8	40.2	38.4	37.2	39.0	39.3	38.4	38.5	40.6	42.6	45.8	48.9	47.1
Local Allocation Tax	168,891	171,275	180,488	208,642	217,764	203,497	195,448	180,692	170,201	169,587	159,953	152,027	154,060
	18.7	19.1	19.3	22.2	24.0	22.5	22.5	21.3	20.6	20.7	20.1	18.5	18.4
Treasury Disbursement	146,656	142,563	156,283	164,829	143,503	144,132	130,689	130,303	123,197	117,780	104,155	102,215	115,827
	16.2	15.9	16.6	17.5	15.8	16.0	15.1	15.4	14.9	14.4	13.1	12.5	13.8
Loans and borrowings	156,153	140,786	151,356	130,733	111,161	118,156	133,185	137,894	123,752	103,763	96,222	95,844	99,220
	17.3	15.7	16.2	13.8	12.2	13.1	15.3	16.3	15.1	12.7	12.1	11.6	11.8
Others	82,129	82,442	89,134	87,418	82,119	81,871	75,476	72,624	72,653	78,691	71,444	70,177	75,167
	9	9.1	9.5	9.3	9.0	9.1	8.7	8.5	8.8	9.6	8.9	8.5	8.9
Total	904,766	898,621	936,482	941,883	910,011	902,843	868,583	848,170	825,191	817,862	796,835	822,931	839,859
	100	100	100	100	100	100	100	100	100	100	100	100	100

Source: Compiled from Somusho (Ministry of Internal Affairs and Communication), *Chiho zaisei tokei nempo Heisei 20 nen-do* (Annual Statistics of Local Finance, 2008).

In recent years, some SNG leaders have resisted national government public work projects (such as road and dam construction) that are driven through
national plans but require financial contributions from SNGs. Earlier SNGs
readily embraced these pork-barrel projects. But now that localities are feel-
ing the financial squeeze they tend to set their own priorities. They do not
view such projects as being of much help to local people and prefer to spend
money on services such as welfare and education, and on areas that are close
geographically to residents' needs. For example, the popular governor of
Osaka Toru Hashimoto has openly opposed SNGs contributing to nationally driven projects that serve little purpose to local communities.[37] Osaka
residents support him, especially as the prefecture faces a more than ¥5-tril-
lion debt. Hashimoto used cost-cutting measures to trim ¥110 billion off
the 2008 fiscal budget.[38] In times of financial hardship when localities have
trouble providing essential services to their residents and are forced to slash
funding, it makes sense not to commit budgets to nonessential, nationally
driven projects.

Although the 1999 decentralization law produced some changes, especially
in the administrative area, SNGs were critical of the absence of progress on
financial reform. No headway on expanding their financial autonomy meant
SNGs would remain under central control. In response to this criticism, the
trinity reform (*sanmi ittai kaikaku*) process reviewed three financial issues as
one set: (1) national subsidies; (2) the distribution of tax resources, including
the transfer of tax resources; and (3) the local allocation tax. As Stockwin
notes, "The new idea was to give a substantial proportion of these tax revenues directly to the local authorities, thus empowering them with greater
freedom of choice about how the money should be spent."[39] Following this,
some reductions were introduced in specific grants, but reform in the financial area remains incomplete due to its highly contentious nature.[40]

SUPPORTERS AND DETRACTORS

There is now general agreement on a new structure for financing aimed at
greater autonomy for SNGs, but reform supporters are driven by different
agendas. The central government, represented through the Cabinet Advisory
Council on Economic and Fiscal Policy, supports a new structure for administrative efficiency and fiscal gains. Subnational leaders and various national-
level associations of SNGs support a new structure to gain more power and
authority over their work, although they are not clear about how the new
system may deliver the financial autonomy they seek. Japan's premier business
organizations, such as the *Nippon Keidanren* and *Keizai Doyukai*, support
decentralization, and especially the *doshusei*, purely for business advantages.

The main opposition comes from the central bureaucracy, especially from
line ministries that recognize that a new financing structure will significantly erode their hold over SNGs.[41] Even implementation of the Law for the
Promotion of Decentralization passed in 2007 faces challenges due to the
reluctance of government ministries and agencies to accept financial reform.[42]

The new structure will leave central bureaucrats with few opportunities to control localities through both their field offices and transfer of central personnel to key local administrative positions. It was not surprising that as prime minister, Koizumi broke from the past and made the Cabinet Office responsible for decentralization instead of leaving the matter in the hands of the Ministries of Finance and of Internal Affairs and Communication, the two key ministries that control SNGs. During consultation on this matter, Koizumi asked for suggestions from local organizations, such as the Six Local Bodies (*chiho roku dantai*), comprising representatives from local chief executives and local assemblies.

Implementation of financial reforms will change the current situation of "30 percent autonomy" for SNGs and the structure of the system as it now stands. Already the central government has agreed to transfer a greater portion of income tax to localities. Maintaining a sound balance of power between national and regional interests will be critical to the success of this reform. How this balance will be achieved to the satisfaction of various levels of SNGs, however, remains unclear.

IMPACTS OF REFORMS AND CHALLENGES

The reform and restructuring processes perhaps inevitably produce winners and losers among SNGs, and disparity in income and resources between SNGs is growing quickly. The larger and more resourceful SNGs are doing well through this process, whereas smaller units and those endowed with few financial resources (industries, business, etc.) are struggling financially. Inequity between SNGs leads to disparities in the provision of services to local residents.[43] Some local governments such as Yubari city in Hokkaido have been declared bankrupt because of their deteriorating financial circumstances.[44] Clearly SNGs cannot be regarded as a monolithic body. There are wide variations in the size, population, and relative wealth of their localities, in their capacities to generate finance, and in the costs and benefits that flow from recent reforms. SNGs do not speak in a uniform voice and because of the "dual representation" system, local assemblies and chief executives often have not just different but opposing political agendas and pursue similarly conflicting outcomes.[45]

HISTORICAL POLITICAL SHIFT AND SNGs

The August 2009 general elections in Japan brought a major political shift through the defeat of the long-ruling LDP and huge electoral success of the DPJ under Yukio Hatoyama. One of the five pledges the DPJ made in its election manifesto was "regional sovereignty" (*chiiki shuken*), and the first step toward that end was to increase the funds under SNGs' independent control.[46] Other steps have been listed to revitalize the regions, including a pledge to transfer to local government matters that can be handled locally, while the central government focuses on matters of national concern, such as foreign policy and security.[47] Even before the DPJ came to power, Hatoyama wrote elaborately about "Empowering Local Authorities within the Nation State" in an essay published in the September 2009 issue of *Voice* magazine titled "My Political Philosophy." In an interview at the end of 2009, Prime Minister Hatoyama even raised the possibility of amending the constitution so SNGs can be endowed with more power and autonomy, an about-turn in the current power balance between the national and local governments. He observed, "I would like to see the Constitution revised in the sense that the positions of the central government and local governments would be reversed."[48]

A series of LDP governments also signalled, from time to time, their intention to transfer power to localities and during the late 1990s and early 2000s made several legislative changes to carry out reforms. The DPJ from the very outset has made clear statements about decentralizing power. The DPJ's second prime minister, Naoto Kan, is also committed to decentralization and to handing greater administrative and financial autonomy to SNGs. He appointed Yoshihiro Katayama as international affairs minister to push through the agenda of decentralization. Katayama is a former governor of Tottori Prefecture and a great advocate of both decentralization and unlocking tied subsidies so that SNGs can spend this money at their discretion.[49] It is, therefore, likely that a redistribution of power will be implemented more systematically under the DPJ government than under the series of LDP governments that preceded it.

CONCLUSION

The preceding discussion clearly shows the initiative, innovation, and policy change carried out at the subnational level. We have also seen how SNGs have served as a fostering ground for democracy and civic participation in Japan. These are processes that SNGs began when progressive administrations had come to the fore in the 1960s and 1970s, at the height of the central government's ability to exercise control over SNGs. Today in Japan, whether progressive, independent, or conservative, popularly elected leaders at the local level see no choice but to voice the needs and demands of the citizens they serve and to work to satisfy their constituents' interests. SNGs of all political persuasions have often put the central government on notice and pressed for greater autonomy and more financial resources. Of course, SNGs are not a monolithic body; their views and ideas differ among them as do the costs and benefits flowing from reforms. And although not all SNGs have been at the forefront of innovation and reform, the trend toward greater efficiency and effectiveness through innovation is clear.

SNGs have compelled the central government to grant them more autonomy and independence in administrative and financial matters. They have persuasively argued that the "one-size-fits-all" policy of the past does not work in a rapidly changing globalized society. Some scholars have also argued strongly that the centralized system that emphasized uniformity of services and financial oversight through centralization served the nation well during a catch-up stage of development, but does not work effectively now.[50]

Although the national leadership in the past was resistant to relaxing central control, it has come to recognize that central resources are becoming scarce in a shrinking economy. Therefore, it is no longer possible for the national government to look after the varied interests of local communities. It has become imperative for the national government to relinquish its tight grip on localities and recognize that SNGs require autonomy to serve the needs of their residents. Through a number of commissions, wide-ranging discussions, and consultations, reforms have been introduced and legislative changes made in the past decade. These have led to restructuring and decentralizing some functions. Progress has been made, but debate on further restructuring and devolution of power, especially financial, continues to dominate the political landscape of contemporary Japanese politics. The DPJ government has indicated its intention to secure greater autonomy and more devolution of functions at the local level.

Any restructuring and reform comes with a price. The reforms introduced since the 1990s have produced winners and losers, as is very clearly evident in the growing financial disparities between SNGs. Further reforms and restructuring that the DPJ has signalled are likely to be introduced while Japanese society faces further challenges. These will arise from declining central revenue alongside increasing demand for services, resulting partly from an aging population. Other social challenges will be associated with education, youth and employment, and growth in the non-Japanese population. And those arising from demographic changes and social welfare concerns mean that more and more issues will require local responses. It is abundantly clear that many of these issues so far have been tackled most successfully at the subnational level, and it is likely that this response strategy will continue.

Certainly, to respond effectively to those challenges, SNGs need more financial resources, policy flexibility, and support from above and each other, rather than rigidity and central control. Community ownership and political inclusiveness are also needed. For these SNGs have an impeccable record, fostering democracy through grassroots participation. They have pushed for such empowering means of civic participation as local referenda, freedom of information, personal privacy, digitalization, and municipal charters, outlining their goals and their missions. Although the forces of centralization and decentralization will continue to pull in opposite directions, Japan is undoubtedly moving steadily in the direction of a more decentralized political system. Time will be needed for this structure to evolve into a more mature decentralized form. After all, it is by no means simple to remove the barriers that undergirded Japan's unitary system of governance and have nurtured and preserved its culture of firm centralization for over a century since the Meiji reform began in the 1880s. Today Japan faces a shrinking supply of national resources and rapid demographic shifts with concomitant demands in services. These can be addressed more efficiently and effectively by empowering the SNGs, as they have demonstrated over the past few decades. Both local and national leaders recognize this, so we may expect that the process, which started in the past 10 years or so, is set to accelerate in the second decade of the twenty-first century.

NOTES

1. Japanese SNGs include all government bodies below the national government: 47 prefectures and all other municipal bodies from large to small cities, towns, and villages.
2. "Policy speech by Prime Minister Naoto Kan," October 1, 2010, http: //www.kantei.go.jp/foreign/kan/statement/201010/01syosin_e.html (accessed December 14, 2010)
3. Minshuto, *Minshuto seiken koyaku*, p. 19
4. *Kakushin* leaders were supported by the leftist parties, whereas *kaikakuha* leaders emerged from a range of political backgrounds and were generally *ainori* (literally, sharing a ride) candidates supported by most political parties except the Japan Communist Party. See Jain, "Local Political Leadership in Japan."
5. Designated cities are Chiba, Fukuoka, Hamamatsu, Hiroshima, Kawasaki, Kita Kyushu, Kobe, Kyoto, Nagoya, Niigata, Okayama, Osaka, Saitama, Sakai, Sapporo, Sendai, Shizuoka, and Yokohama.
6. Through the first round of mergers between 1888 and 1889 during the Meiji period, the number of municipalities was reduced from 71,314 to 15,859; the Great Showa amalgamation between 1953 and 1961 reduced their numbers from 9,868 to 3,472, and, finally, the Heisei amalgamation reduced their numbers to 3,332 in 1999 and to 1,820 in 2006. See Kohara, "The Great Heisei Consolidation." In February 2010, the number was reduced to 1,771, www. soumu.go.jp/english/lab/index.html (accessed January 27, 2011).
7. Elected assembly members numbered some 85,000 at the end of December 2006. Ohsugi, "Local Assemblies in Japan," p. 19.
8. Ohsugi, "Local Assemblies in Japan," p. 22.
9. For a most comprehensive study detailing the functioning of local government until the mid-1960s, see Steiner, *Local Government in Japan*.
10. For a scholarly examination of the main issues of this period, see MacDougall, "Political Opposition and Local Government".
11. Some cities such as Kawasaki and Yokohama provided national health insurance to foreigners, including North Korean residents, directly in opposition to national government wishes. See various articles in *Toshi Mondai*, February 1996.
12. This was a particularly vibrant period as far politics and policy dynamics at the subnational level were concerned, generating a great deal of interest not just inside Japan but also beyond. The Japanese literature on subnational politics of this period is very rich, but some non-Japanese scholars also produced some very detailed studies of this period. One of the most outstanding is by Steiner et al., *Political Opposition and Local Politics in Japan*, comprising a number of essays that capture the essence of political and policy development during this period. For more specialised studies, see, for example, Reed, *Prefectures and Policymaking*; Jain, *Local Politics and Policymaking in Japan*.
13. Nagasu, *Chiho no jidai to jichitai kakushin* .
14. *Asahi Shimbun*, July 11, 1999.

15. Takao, *Reinventing Japan*, pp. 76–78.
16. Jain, "*Jumin Tohyo* and the Tokushima Anti-Dam Movement in Japan."
17. MacDougall, "Toward Political Inclusiveness," p. 33.
18. Jain, "The Catch-Up State: E-Government in Japan."
19. Tsujiyama calls it *jichitai no kenpo* (local constitution). See Tsujiyama, *Jichi kihon joreiwa naze hitsuyoka*, p. 32; Kisa and Osaka, *Watashitachi no machi no kenpo* (2003).
20. Prof Tsujiyama made a copy of the database available to this author in November 2008.
21. Ohsugi, "People and Local Government," p. 7.
22. Jain, *Japan's Subnational Governments in International Affairs*; Jain, *Nihon no jichitai gaiko*.
23. Ohsugi, "People and Local Government," p. 7.
24. For details in English on *kikan inin jimu*, see Kume, "The Agency-Delegated Function and Its Implications."
25. Ikawa, "Fifteen Years of Decentralization Reform in Japan," p. 8.
26. Omori, *Henka ni chosen suru jichitai*, p. 4.
27. Ikawa, "Fifteen Years of Decentralization Reform in Japan," p. 14.
28. Ibid., pp. 14–15.
29. Mabuchi, "Municipal Amalgamations"; Yokomichi, "The Development of Municipal Mergers in Japan."
30. Yokomichi, "Nihon ni okeru doshusei no donyu rongi."
31. Mabuchi, "Municipal Amalgamations"; Yokomichi, "The Development of Municipal Mergers in Japan."
32. Yet public opinion polls show that not many Osaka residents are as enthusiastic as Hashimoto about *doshusei*; Johnston, "A Year In."
33. Higashikokubaru, "Doshuseiwa kanchi shuken kara jichi shuken e no iko," pp. 330–333.
34. Johnston, "Is Prefectural Alliance a Step toward Superstates?"
35. Ikawa, "Fifteen Years of Decentralization Reform in Japan," p. 2.
36. For financial dependency arguments see Dewit and Ikegami, "Back on the Agenda."
37. Editorial, "Hashimoto's Revolt," asahi.com, February 11, 2009.
38. Johnston, "A Year In."
39. Stockwin, *Governing Japan*, p. 116.
40. Kanai, "The Recent Decentralization Reform in Japan," p. 72; Dewit and Ikegami, "Back on the Agenda."
41. Sasaki, "The Central Government vs Local Governments," pp. 13–14
42. Niwa, "Chiho bunken ga katsuryoku aru Nihon wo tsukuru to iu kakushin: bunkeni wa zettai hikanai," p. 328.
43. Tamura, *Jichitai kakusa ga kuni o horobosu*.
44. Omori, *Henka ni chosen suru jichitai*, p. 25.
45. The governor of Tokyo opposed the proposal to move part of the corporate tax (*hojin jigyozei*) from prosperous to less prosperous SNGs. See Omori, *Henka ni chosen suru jichitai*, p. 26.
46. In its first draft budget compiled in December 2009, the DPJ increased the grants in aid to local governments by ¥1.073 trillion to ¥16.893 trillion, search. japantimes.co.jp/cgi-bin/ed20091227a1.html (accessed December 27, 2009); *Minshuto, Minshuto seiken koyaku*, p. 12.
47. Ibid., pp. 19–20.

48. Japan Times, "DPJ Eyes Changing Constitution," http://search.japantimes.
    co.jp/cgi-bin/nn20091227a3.html (December 27, 2009).
49. Takahara, "Katayama; Empowering Local Government Is Key."
50. Ikawa, "Fifteen Years of Decentralization Reform in Japan," p. 12.

BIBLIOGRAPHY

Dewit, Andrew and Takehiko Ikegami, "Back on the Agenda: Decentralization and
    the Japanese Political Economy," *Social Science Japan Journal*, 13, no. 1 (2010):
    143–148.
Higashikokubaru, Hideo, "Doshuseiwa kanchi shuken kara jichi shuken e no iko"
    (From Centralization to Local Sovereignty through Doshusei), in Bungei Shunju,
    eds., *Nihon no ronten* (Tokyo: Bungei Shunju, 2009).
Ikawa, Hiroshi, "Fifteen Years of Decentralization Reform in Japan," *Up-to-Date
    Documents in Local Autonomy in Japan,* No. 4 (Tokyo: CLAIR/COSLOG/
    GRIPS, 2008).
Jain, Purnendra, *Local Politics and Policymaking in Japan* (Delhi: Commonwealth,
    1989).
———, "*Jumin Tohyo* and the Tokushima Anti-Dam Movement in Japan: The People
    Have Spoken," *Asian Survey,* 40, no. 4 (2000): 551–570.
———, "The Catch-Up State: E-Government in Japan," *Japanese Studies,* 22, no. 2
    (2002): 237–255.
———, "Local Political Leadership in Japan," *Policy and Society,* 23, no. 1 (2004).
———, *Japan's Subnational Governments in International Affairs* (London and
    New York: Routledge, 2005).
———, *Nihon no jichitai gaiko: Nihon gaiko to chuo chiho kankei e no impakuto*
    (Japan's Local Diplomacy and Its Impact on National-Subnational Relations)
    (Tokyo: Keibundo, 2009).
Johnston, Eric, "A Year In, Osaka Gov. Hashimoto on a Roll," *Japan Times,* February
    27, 2009.
———, "Is Prefectural Alliance a Step toward Superstates?" December 14, 2010,
    http://search.japantimes.co.jp/cgi-bin/nn20101214i1.html
Kanai, Toshiyuki, "The Recent Decentralization Reform in Japan," *Journal of Law
    and Politics* (Tokyo University) 5 (Spring 2008): 66–85.
Kisa, Shigeo and Osaka Seiji, *Watashitachi no machi no kenpo* (Our Town
    Constitution) (Tokyo: Nihon Keizai Hyoronsha, 2003).
Kohara, Takaharu, "The Great Heisei Consolidation: A Critical Review," *Social
    Science Japan* (September 2007): 7–11.
Kume, Ikuo, "The Agency-Delegated Function and Its Implications," in Michio
    Muramatsu, Farrukh Iqbal, and Ikuo Kume, eds., *Local Government Development
    in Post-war Japan* (Oxford: Oxford University Press, 2001).
Mabuchi, Masaru, "Municipal Amalgamations," in Michio Muramatsu, Farrukh
    Iqbal, and Ikuo Kume, eds., *Local Government Development in Post-war Japan*
    (Oxford: Oxford University Press, 2001).
MacDougall, Terry, "Political Opposition and Local Government in Japan: The
    Significance of Emerging Progressive Leadership" (PhD diss.), Yale University,
    1975.
———, "Toward Political Inclusiveness: The Changing Role of Local Government,"
    in Michio Muramatsu, Farrukh Iqbal, and Ikuo Kume, eds., *Local Government
    Development in Post-War Japan* (Oxford: Oxford University Press, 2001).

Minshuto, *Minshuto seiken koyaku* (DPJ manifesto) (Tokyo: Minshuto honbu, 2009).

Nagasu, Kazuji, *Chiho no jidai to jichitai kakushin* (Progressive Administrations in an Era of Localities) (Tokyo: Nihon Hyoronsha, 1980).

Niwa, Uichiro, "Chiho bunken ga katsuryoku aru Nihon wo tsukuru to iu kakushin: bunkeni wa zettai hikanai" (Decentralization as a Core to Japan's Vitality), in Bungei Shunju, ed., *Nihon no ronten* (Tokyo: Bungei Shunju, 2009).

Ohsugi, Satoru, "People and Local Government: Residential Participation in the Management of Local Governments," Papers on the Local Governance System and Its Implementation in Selected Fields in Japan, No. 1, Tokyo, CLAIR/COSLOG/GRIPS, 2007.

———, "Local Assemblies in Japan," Papers on the Local Governance System and Its Implementation in Selected Fields in Japan, No. 5, Tokyo, CLAIR/COSLOG/GRIPS, 2008.

Omori, Wataru, *Henka ni chosen suru jichitai* (Localities Facing the Challenges of Change) (Tokyo: Dai'ichi Hoki, 2008).

Ozawa, Ichiro, *Blueprint for a New Japan: The Rethinking of a Nation* (New York: Kodansha America, 1994).

Reed, Steven, *Prefectures and Policymaking* (Pittsburgh: Pittsburgh University Press, 1986).

Sasaki, Takeshi, "The Central Government vs Local Governments," *Japan Spotlight* (January/February, 2005).

Steiner, Kurt, *Local Government in Japan* (Stanford: Stanford University Press, 1965).

Steiner, Kurt et al., eds., *Political Opposition and Local Politics in Japan* (Princeton: Princeton University Press, 1980).

Stockwin, J. A. A., *Governing Japan: Divided Politics in a Resurgent Economy* (Oxford: Blackwell, 2008).

Takahara, Kanako, "Katayama; Empowering Local Government Is Key," September 30, 2010, http://search.japantimes.co.jp/cgi-bin/nn20100930f2.html

Takao, Yasuo, *Reinventing Japan: From Merchant Nation to Civic Nation* (New York: Palgrave Macmillan, 2007).

Tamura, Shigeru, *Jichitai kakusa ga kuni o horobosu* (National Disaster through Local Disparities) (Tokyo: Shueisha shinsho, 2007).

Tsujiyama, Takanobu, *Jichi kihon joreiwa naze hitsuyoka* (Why Are Local Charters Essential?) Tajimi City Booklet, No. 5 (Tokyo: Kojin no yusha, 2003).

Yokomichi, Kiyotaka, "The Development of Municipal Mergers in Japan," COSLOG Up-to-date Documents on Local Autonomy in Japan, No. 1, 2008, www.clair.or.jp/j/forum/honyaku/hikaku/pdf/up-to-date_en1.pdf (accessed December 25, 2009).

———, "Nihon ni okeru doshusei no donyu rongi" (The Debate on Ihe introduction of a Regional System in Japan), COSLOG Up-to-date Documents on Local Autonomy in Japan, No. 3, 2008.

10

Reporting with Wolves: Pack Journalism and the Dissemination of Political Information

Ofer Feldman

Introduction

One could say that Japanese society is flooded with information. Japan has a literacy rate of 99 percent, one of the world's highest newspaper consumption rates, and a publishing industry that churns out a large number of weekly and monthly magazines as well as journals and books. According to the World Association of Newspapers, Japanese daily newspapers circulation (67.2 million copies) in 2008 was the second highest in the world, after India (107 million copies; the United States came third with 51 million copies). In per capita terms, Japan ranked fourth, with an average of 613.1 newspapers circulating per 1,000 adults, following Iceland (817.4), Switzerland (627.4), and Luxembourg (619.3).[1] The television industry also flourishes in Japan. NHK (*Nippon Hoso Kyokai*) or Japan Broadcasting Corporation, the nonprofit state broadcasting corporation, reaches all of Japan with four TV channels: two using terrestrial broadcasting and two satellite channels. Another five major private TV stations and many local TV channels are available to audiences throughout the country, in addition to numerous cable and satellite broadcasters.

Most Japanese news organizations, particularly the daily newspapers, consider their publications to be of high quality; they claim to provide the widest and most in-depth political coverage possible, to be politically neutral, to maintain nonpartisan objectivity, and to adhere to a policy of "impartiality, political neutrality, and fairness" (*fuhen futo, churitsu kosei*). But this is not always the case. The news media generally present institutional perspectives that reflect their own approaches to the selection, reporting, composition, and relaying of symbols and images, and like every other aspect of Japanese society, they also reflect much of the social system in which they function. The peculiar sociocultural characteristics of Japanese society affect reporters' newsgathering methods, role definitions, interaction with information sources, and decisionmaking within and between news-rooms—all of which ultimately affects political communication in the country as a whole. For example, the traditional desire for group harmony and good relations with colleagues, including the wish to maintain solid, amicable relationships with news sources, are reflected in a willingness to conform to agreements about gathering and disseminating news, and to present political affairs through the eyes of the most influential politicians, even if doing so contradicts universally accepted journalistic standards.

In this chapter I detail selected aspects of Japanese news media, particularly those related to the interaction between news gatherers (reporters) and their information sources (members of the political or bureaucratic machinery). I also examine aspects of group behavior that affect reporters' interaction with officials who shape the scope and content of mainstream political journalism in Japan. First, I set the stage by providing an outline of major Japanese news organizations, their characteristics, and their role in society.

CHARACTERISTICS OF THE JAPANESE MEDIA

Types and Uses of Media

One important characteristic of the Japanese media is its highly concentrated nature. Media ownership is concentrated primarily among five major conglomerates. Each owns one of Japan's five nationwide daily newspapers: the *Yomiuri* (daily circulation, 13.58 million copies), *Asahi* (11.07 million), *Mainichi* (4.83 million), *Sankei* (2.17 million), and *Nihon Keizai* (4.63 million). Together, these conglomerates circulate 36.28 million newspapers every day (62.88 percent of the 57.69 million copies circulated by Japanese dailies).[2] They are tied by cross-media ownership agreements to the nation's five major commercial television networks, licensed on a prefectural basis: *Nippon News Network* (NNN) headed by *Nippon Terebi (Nittere* or NTV), affiliated with the *Yomiuri*; *Japan News Network* (JNN) headed by *Tokyo Hoso*, Tokyo Broadcasting System (TBS), affiliated with the *Mainichi*; *Fuji News Network* (FNN) headed by *Fuji Television* (Fuji TV), affiliated with the *Fujisankei Communications* conglomerate that includes the *Sankei*; *All-Nippon News Network* (ANN) headed by *Terebi Asahi*, affiliated with the *Asahi*; and *TV Tokyo Network* (TXN) headed by *Terebi Tokyo*, has ties with *Nihon Keizai*. Media ownership by these five media organizations extends to weekly and monthly magazines (i.e., *Shukan* [weekly] *Asahi, Shukan Yomiuri*, and *Sunday Mainichi*), sports tabloids, and local newspapers and television stations. The highly concentrated nature of Japanese media makes it easier to control the flow of information and to influence the public's attitudes and behavior.

In addition, there are five "bloc" regional newspapers: *Tokyo* in the *Kanto* area around the capital (daily circulation, 805,830 copies), *Chunichi* in the *Chubu* area in central Japan (3.29 million), *Nishi Nippon* on the island of *Kyushu* (943,146), *Hokkaido* on the northern island of *Hokkaido*

(1.74 million), and *Kahoku Shimpo* in the *Tohoku* region of northern Japan (575,020). Furthermore, there are more than 100 local newspapers—at least one in each of Japan's 47 prefectures. Some of these have larger circulations and more influence within their circulation area than any of the nationwide newspapers: examples are *Shizuoka Shimbun* in *Shizuoka* Prefecture (1.38 million copies daily), *Kyoto Shimbun* in *Kyoto* Prefecture (827,756 copies), and the *Chugoku Shimbun* in *Hiroshima* Prefecture (723,647 copies).[3]

Importantly, there are more than 2,750 weekly and monthly magazines ranging from intellectual periodicals reputed to be of high quality, such as *Chuo Koron, Bungei Shunju*, and *Sekai*; weekly publications of popular interest including *SPA!, Shukan Gendai*, and *Shukan Post*; weeklies devoted to social and political matters, like *Shukan Shincho* and *Shukan Bunshun*; women's magazines that focus on fashion, diets, and star scandals, including *Josei Seven* and *Shukan Josei*; and dozens of magazines that specialize in a particular topic such as cars, movies, music, sports, health, or electronics. Each of these journals sells between 400,000 and 900,000 copies. Their combined circulation is nearly eight times that of Japan's daily national newspapers.

According to the most recent (October 2009) nationwide survey conducted by the Japan Newspaper Publishers and Editors Association (*Nihon Shimbun Kyokai*, NSK) (sample: 6,000 people, aged 15–69), Japanese consider newspapers to be more important than other media.[4] More than TV (commercial and NHK), radio, magazines, and the Internet, newspapers are regarded as impacting society, sophisticated, containing detailed and valuable information on local affairs and community events, and instrumental in daily life and promoting education. The survey indicated that 99.0 percent of the respondents have regular contact with TV, 91.3 percent with newspapers, 57.1 percent listen regularly to radio, 77.4 percent read magazines, and 66.7 percent use the Internet. Of respondents, 80 percent said they have daily contact with a newspaper and 69.0 percent said they read a newspaper every morning. They reported average daily newspaper reading time of 24.8 minutes on weekdays and 29.1 minutes during weekends. Of respondents, 68.1 percent said they follow social events, 58.2 percent read political stories, 50.5 percent local and community issues, 30.9 percent about economics, 29.6 percent read about lifestyles, 27.6 percent about international affairs, and 20.3 percent about education. Newspapers were perceived by 81 percent of the respondents as influencing public opinion, 60 percent expressed satisfaction with their newspaper's content, and 45 percent were of the opinion that newspaper stories reflect society's conventional wisdom. Similar results were revealed in a survey conducted by the Japan Institute for Social and Economic Affairs (*Keizai Koho* Center) in March 2007 (sample: 3,913 people, aged 29 and up).[5]

Government Control

The second major feature of Japanese media is that although the news media is not specifically regulated by law in Japan, in contrast to the United Kingdom, the United States, and several other industrialized societies, the government does exert control through its licensing system. The constitution explicitly guarantees freedom of speech of the press, and discourages censorship and interference with the right to private communication. But laws governing broadcasting and the media (*Dempa-ho* and *Hoso-ho*, both enacted in 1950) require that all broadcasters, including cable TV systems with more than 500 subscribers, obtain a license from the Ministry of Posts and Telecommunications, to be renewed every five years. In effect, the networks must follow the specifications of the Ministry of Posts and Telecommunications in order to renew their broadcasting licenses. The government claims that this system is necessary to manage limited radio wave resources, and that it must make broadcasting companies responsible to the public interest. However, this is viewed as a convenient tool for the government to control the content of news broadcasts, with the potential for indirect control of newspapers as well, as each Japanese broadcasting company (except state-owned NHK) is partially owned by a newspaper company with which it collaborates in management and newsgathering efforts, suggesting that the licensing system also exerts indirect control on the newspaper companies. NHK, as a public network run by a public corporation, is subject to government control because the national Diet must approve its annual budget and senior personnel appointments.

Commercialism

The third feature distinguishing Japanese media is that all newspapers and commercial broadcasting corporations function as business enterprises. They depend on income from advertisements and sponsors, which is, of course, effected by the general economic situation. According to Advertising Expenditures in Japan 2009, published by *Dentsu* Inc., Japan's largest advertising agency,[6] total advertising expenditures declined for the fifth consecutive year in 2009 to 5.92 trillion yen (of the total expenditures, 47.8 percent went to four major media sectors: newspapers, 11.4 percent; magazines 5.1 percent; radio 2.3 percent; and TV 29.0 percent). Spending on television advertising totaled ¥1,713.9 billion, down 10.2 percent from the previous year, and spending on newspaper ads fell by 18.6 percent, to ¥673.9 billion. Expenditures dropped mainly due to the economic slowdown from the end of 2007, the global recession precipitated by the financial crisis in the United States from the latter half of 2008, and a slowing in the economy from the rapid appreciation in the value of the yen.

The dependency of the broadcast and the print media on advertisers has two consequences: The first is that news organizations compete with each other to increase circulation or viewer ratings, in order to attract and keep advertisers. The second is that reporters and editors must always consider the implication of stories that conflict with the views or interests of their sponsors. Editors know that as long as sponsors provide stable financial support for their company, structural changes are not needed. As happened when newspaper advertising was severely impacted by a floundering economy in 2007–2009, insufficient revenues can force newspapers to take such measures as discontinuing evening editions, raising subscription fees, and restructured divisions. To avoid being forced to take such measures, broadcasters and newspaper companies consider the possible impact of their stories on sponsors. Thus media organizations readily adjust the emphasis or the tone accorded to certain issues (particularly in areas important to their major sponsors, such as finance, insurance, real estate, and automobiles) and are liable to consider news items more from the perspective of large corporate advertisers than from that of the general public.

Self-Censorship

In addition to structural and economic factors, social and cultural dimensions also affect media coverage. Reporters and editors must always consider the possible impact of their stories on specific groups of readers. To avoid evoking an adverse emotional reaction from readers, editors have to carefully filter information. The result is that daily newspapers tend to be "fringe-exclusive." Anything controversial—basically anything that irritates the supposed harmony of Japanese society or culture—is very easily neglected or carefully filtered before publication. This includes stories about taboo subjects like the imperial family, the nation's flag and anthem, minority groups such as the roughly 2 million *burakumin*, descendants of a former outcast group, and certain religious groups and cults, including the *Aum* Supreme Truth cult and its campaign to spread deadly sarin gas in Tokyo's subway system in 1995.

Newspapers pledge to maintain "impartiality, political neutrality, and fairness," but these ideas are not always applied to views arising from society's fringes, especially from the far right or left of the political spectrum. This is partly due to fear (as indeed have happened in the past) that either political extreme could resort to intimidation or even violent attacks against reporters or the offices of news organizations if they do not like certain stories. One way that editors avoid this type of intimidation is by refraining from touching on delicate issues. They may prefer to accept an incomplete story rather than risk upsetting cultural harmony or inviting intimidation of a media organization.

Journalists' tendency to self-censor is more pronounced when they belong to a press club, a newsgathering mechanism that encourages collaborative relationships with political figures or the government agencies to which they are attached.

KISHA KURABU AND THEIR ORGANIZATION

In Japan, political information sources and media representatives interact on a daily basis, mainly through Japanese-style press clubs called *kisha kurabu* (literally "reporters' clubs").[7] The *kisha* club system is a major cause of "pack journalism," whereby most reporters pursue identical targets most of the time. This system has relegated political reporters to the role of messengers who passively convey information from politicians and bureaucrats to the general public, resulting in the homogenization of political news.

A *kisha kurabu* is a formal association of reporters assigned to a common beat. A reporter from each news organization is assigned to each of hundreds of government agencies (including those of the prime minister, the Diet, and ministries), courts, police headquarters, large firms and major economic organizations, political party headquarters, and the Imperial Palace. *Kisha kurabu* reporters receive news releases and attend formal and informal press conferences held by top economic leaders, government officials, and leading Diet members. The convenient access to information and the cozy relations with sources discourage "club" reporters from doing investigative reporting and make them reluctant to criticize authorities. I say more about this below.

Officially, *kisha* clubs number about 800 in Japan, although the actual number is thought to be about 1,500. Each division of a government agency or a major private organization allocates a large room in its building for the use of reporters assigned to cover that entity for their respective news organizations. This room is where the "club" meets: it is where reporters gather to receive briefings, handouts, press releases, and other communications, interact with information sources, and write stories about the organization they cover.

A *kisha* club may have as few as a dozen reporters or as many as 400, depending on the nature and importance of the agency. Press clubs in most other countries are organized and sponsored by information sources; Japanese *kisha* clubs are organized and managed by the Japan Newspaper Publishers and Editors Association (NSK), according to its guidelines.[8] Membership in the association is a prerequisite for membership in the *kisha* clubs, hence access to important news sources has traditionally been limited to mainstream journalists, which means the representatives of the 133 companies belonging to the NSK (including 106 daily newspapers, 4 news agencies, and 23 broadcasters, as of November 1, 2010),[9] and nonmember media organizations with a similar standing. The nine major newspapers mentioned above (i.e., the big five plus four of the five "bloc" newspapers, *Tokyo, Chunichi, Nishi Nippon,* and *Hokkaido*), the nation's six television networks (NHK, NTV, TBS, Fuji TV, *Terebi Asahi,* and *Terebi Tokyo*), and the two news agencies (*Kyodo* News and *Jiji* Press) together comprise the 17 companies whose reporters belong to almost every major *kisha* club and dominate these clubs as a whole.

Kisha clubs are often criticized for barring foreign and Japanese magazine reporters, including reporters who work for unions, periodicals, Web media, and freelance journalists, from joining the clubs, and shutting out news conferences, briefings and off-the-record chats with senior government officials. However, in recent years, as detailed below, a few *kisha* clubs have begun to allow representatives of foreign media organizations and freelancers to join major clubs either as members with seats and the same privileges, or as observers, which mean that they can attend press conferences but cannot ask questions.

"Pack Journalism" and the Homogenization of News

Within each *kisha* club, reporters generally have the same access to resources. All reporters witness the same events on their assigned beat, and receive the same briefings and handouts describing what is to take place on a particular day. All are exposed to news sources at the same time, either during formal press conferences or in background briefings held regularly by top officials. Reporters invariably talk with information sources in the presence of colleagues from other organizations. They often discuss the news among themselves and collectively compose a sketch of the story they will all file.

The result of this Japanese-style pack journalism is almost complete uniformity in coverage. Each newspaper, just like its brethren, addresses the same topics, employs the same perspectives, and emphasizes the same news items with almost the same words. The media is thus united in its collective interpretations of public events. And, if all the newspapers (and other news media channels as well) publish the same information and give a certain news item the same interpretation, it is natural for the public to believe that they portray reality, more so than if some of them printed different information.

Japanese reporters rely on very few—perhaps 15–20—key Diet members for their information. This circle includes the prime minister, the chief cabinet secretary, who is also the chief government spokesman, and the leaders and secretary-generals of the major political parties. Questions about what these leaders do, whom they meet with, and what they think are the main focus of political reporting.

1. *Nagata Kurabu*

There are over 40 press clubs in Tokyo alone. The largest and most important press club is the *Nagata* Club, called officially the *Naikaku Kishakai* and among journalists known as the *Kantei* ([Prime Minister's] Official Residence). The club is located on the first floor in the prime minister's new Official Residence, only a few meters away from the press conference room where the prime minister and the chief cabinet secretary hold important conferences. On the wall, just to the left of the entrance, there are two large boards labeled "Cabinet Secretariat Notice Board" (*naikaku kanbo keijiban*) with announcements and information related to the Office of the Prime Minister and the schedules of officials who work in the building, including the chief cabinet secretary and his deputies. On the wall to the right is an electronic display showing the names of the officials who work in the Office of the Prime Minister—including the prime minister, the chief cabinet secretary, the three deputy chief cabinet secretaries, and the five secretaries of the prime minister. When any of these officials enters his or her office, their name lights up and all the press club members can see that they are in the building. As soon as they leave the building, the lamp illuminating their name is turned off.

On the left side of the clubroom, there are desks, sofas, armchairs, two TVs, and beverage vending machines. This is where reporters rest, read the news, watch television, and nap. The right side of the room is partitioned into niches for the various news organizations in the club. Each niche has about 10 workspaces for reporters, and a TV set that is usually on whenever reporters are in the club so they can follow breaking news. The center of the room has a "common space" that reporters can also use when they write their stories.

Nagata Club has close to 400 members, representing about 104 agencies of the news media dominated (as of January 2011) by the members of 19 news organizations: *Yomiuri, Asahi, Mainichi, Sankei, Nihon Keizai, Tokyo, Nishi Nippon, Hokkaido, Chugoku, Kyoto, Japan Times*; NHK, NTV, TBS, Fuji Television, *Terebi Asahi*, and *Terebi Tokyo*; and *Kyodo* News and *Jiji* Press. In addition, representatives of 77 news organizations have the status of "observer." Among them are 10 companies from Japan (e.g., *Telebi Yamaguchi*), 8 from China (e.g., *Xinhua News Agency*), 14 from South Korea (e.g., *Chosun Ilbo*), 23 from the United States (e.g., *ABC, Washington Post*), 4 from the UK (e.g., *BBC, Reuters*), 6 from France (e.g., *AFP—L'Agence France-Presse*), and *Itar-Tass* of Russia.

2. Hirakawa Kurabu

Second in importance, until the August 30, 2009, election and the historic shift of power to the Democratic Party of Japan (DPJ) after a landslide election win was the *Hirakawa* Club, which has almost 150 reporters. The *Hirakawa* Club (also used to be called *Yoto* or "Ruling Party" Club, termed now the *Yato* [opposition parties] Club) is located in the Liberal Democratic Party (LDP) headquarters, facing the Diet building. When the Diet is in session, the club members shift their location to one of two press clubs in the Diet building: one covers the lower house and the other the upper house. As in the *Nagata* Club, each news company has its own niche.

At the top of the list of LDP politicians covered by *Hirakawa* Club reporters are the party's president (*sosai*), who also served as prime minister when the LDP ruled the government, the vice president (*fuku-sosai*), and the "three leading officials" (*sanyaku*): the secretary-general (*kanji-cho*), who is in charge of all party affairs from election-related issues to daily administration of the party; the chairman of the Executive Council (*somu-kaicho*), who manages the party's basic policies, which includes the adjustment of policies and decisions; and the chairman of the Party Affairs Research Council (*seimuchosa-kaicho*), who is charged with reviewing policies. The next objects of the reporters' attention is the chairman of the Diet Policy Committee (*kokkai taisaku iincho*), who focuses on the functioning of the Diet and negotiations with representatives of other parties, the LDP acting secretary-general (*kanji-cho dairi*), the acting chairman of the Policy Research Council (*seicho kaicho dairi*), and the chief secretary of the Election Strategy Headquarters (*senkyo taisaku kyokucho*).

Since the advent of coalition governments, reporters in the *Hirakawa* have also covered the LDP's coalition partners, mainly the New *Komei* Party, with particular focus on the top leaders in this party: the chief representative (*daihyo*), the secretary-general, and the chairman of the Policy Research Council.

Following the August 2009 general election and the resultant historic victory of the DPJ (who controls now 308 of the lower chamber's 480 seats), more media attention has focused on covering the DPJ and its partners to the 2009 administration, the Social Democratic Party (SDP) and the People's New Party (PNP).

3. Other Clubs and the Coverage of Diet Committees

Another noteworthy press club is the *Yato* (opposition parties) Club. It is located now on the third floor of the Diet building (the *Yoto* Club is located on the second floor), and has about 130 reporters. When the LDP controlled Japan until September 2009, each of the main news agencies assigned up to four reporters to cover the activities of all the opposition parties. Usually each reporter covered the activities of one party: the DPJ, the SDP, or Japan Communist Party (JCP). Within these political parties, reporters focused their attention especially on the chief representatives, secretary-generals, chairmen of the Diet Policy Committees, and the chairmen of the Policy Research Committees.

With the recent change in power more reporters are now assigned to cover, in particular, the activities of DPJ leaders (centered now in the *Yoto* Club). Naturally, the dominant position of the political party in Japanese politics dictates its dominant position in media attention and coverage. News media representatives heed now closely the activities of the DPJ's secretary-general, the party's acting secretary-general, the chairman and the acting chairman of the party's Policy Research Committee, the chairman and the deputy chairman of the party's Diet Affairs Committee, the chairman of the Election Campaign Committee, the chairman of the DPJ Caucus, House of Councillors (*saningiin kaicho*), the secretary-general of the DPJ Caucus, House of Councillors (*sanin kanjicho*), and the chairman of the Diet Affairs Committee, DPJ Caucus, House of Councillors (*sanin kokutai iincho*). Reporters in the *Yoto* Club are also responsible to cover the activities of the four leading members—the president, secretary-general, chairman of the Diet Affairs Committee, and chairman of the Policy Research Committee of the PNP, the DPJ coalition partner.

Another important *kisha* club covers the Ministry of Foreign Affairs: it is named the *Kasumi* Club, after the *Kasumigaseki* district where the ministry is located. It has 180 reporters who cover Japan's relations with other countries. In addition, there are up to 80 reporters in each of the clubs close to the Ministry of Education, Culture, Sports, Science and Technology (*Mombu kurabu*), and the Ministry of Defense (*Boei kishakurabu*). Reporters from the political desks of the leading newspapers and the wire services are also assigned to cover the Ministries of Finance, Health, Labor and Welfare, Justice, Public Management, Home Affairs, Posts and Telecommunications.

Kisha club reporters also cover the Diet committees related to the government agency they are assigned to; reporters who work at the Ministry of Foreign Affairs, for example, are responsible for covering the activities of the Foreign Affairs Committee; the meetings of the Education Committee are covered by reporters from the Ministry of Education, Culture, and Science.

Teamwork in the Press Clubs

Although *kisha* clubs accommodate reporters from various news media, the 17 companies permanently located in the clubs described earlier (especially those of the print media and news agencies) usually install a large staff of reporters in each of the main clubs in Tokyo. For example, *Yomiuri* and *Asahi*, the two largest of the big five national newspapers, each assign 11 reporters to the *Nagata* Club, whereas *Kyodo* assigns 13 reporters to cover the activities of the cabinet and prime minister through this club. *Kyodo* also appoints 13 reporters to cover the activities of the DPJ and its coalition partner, the PNP, and 10 reporters to the *Hirakawa* Club. In the *Yato* Club, *Asahi* has five reporters, *Mainichi* has four reporters, and *Kyodo* has six. Each reporter generally covers one opposition party.

To be able to immediately analyze many aspects of breaking events, the media often assign reporters from various sections—political, economic, or foreign affairs—to a single club. Reporters from the same company assigned to a given *kisha* club constitute a team (*chiimu*). One reporter, who usually has an average of 10 years' experience in two or three different clubs (a reporter is usually assigned to a press club for one to three years, and is then transferred to a different club), serves as "captain" (*kyappu*), and another with less experience fills the position of subcaptain (*sabu-kyappu*). These two are responsible for supervising the writing of articles that are sent either by telephone, facsimile machine, electronic compilation system, or messenger to the news agency's political desk.

METHODS OF GATHERING POLITICAL INFORMATION
Press Conferences

Kisha clubs facilitate the gathering of information through two main methods: press conferences and *ban* reporting. The most important press conferences for political reporters are held at the *Nagata* Club in the Prime Minister's Official Residence. There the prime minister holds press conferences that are broadcast live on television and radio before or after elections, following dissolution of the Diet, after the inauguration of a new cabinet, at the beginning of the year, and before leaving for important overseas meetings. Japan's top leader also meets the press when a special need to address vital issues or to announce major political decisions arises.

Nagata Club is also the venue for equally important press conferences with the chief cabinet secretary, who serves as the top spokesman for the cabinet and is considered to be better versed in Diet affairs than anyone else. The chief cabinet secretary meets reporters at least twice a day—at around 11:00 a.m. and around 4:00 p.m. The chief cabinet secretary starts news conferences by briefing reporters, and then answers any questions ranging from domestic politics to foreign policy.

Leaders of political parties regularly appear before reporters, who work in *kisha* club close to their parties' headquarters, to provide updates on the views of their organs, and cabinet ministers also hold press conferences for the reporters in the *kisha* club closest to their agency at least twice a week, usually after each cabinet meeting. Traditionally, parliamentary and administrative vice ministers from each government agency also met the press twice a week to discuss new developments. Following the 2009 general election and the shift of power to the DPJ, however, Prime Minister Hatoyama Yukio's government decided, on September 16, 2009—as a measure to ensure political control over the bureaucracy—to forbid civil servants, that is, administrative vice ministers, from holding news conferences. Only cabinet ministers, vice ministers, and parliamentary secretaries, whose posts are filled by politicians, are allowed now to disclose the views of their ministries to the news media.

Another principal media policy of the DPJ reflected Prime Minister Hatoyama's promise during the 2009 general election to extend access to information from central government offices by opening-up press conferences to representatives of all news organizations including magazines' writers, Web-based news sites journalists, and freelancers who were nonmembers of the *kisha* clubs. Foreign Minister Okada Katsuya was the first cabinet member who allowed nonclub members of the ministry, including magazine writers and online news reporters, to attend his regular news conferences and briefings, declaring in a press conference on September 29, 2010, that he did it for the sake of the "public right to know." In the few months after the regime changed about two-thirds of the ministries, including *Nagata* Club at the prime minister's office and 14 cabinet agencies (excluding the Cabinet Secretariat, the Ministry of Justice, and the Imperial Household Agency) opened up press conferences to nonmainstream media, even allowing online journalists and freelancers the right to pose questions to the spokespersons.

This DPJ-led coalition's new media policy that aimed to increase information disclosure to the public confirmed its preelection pledge to advance political transparency. Eventually, it assisted the government to reach a broader public than before throughout both the established mainstream news media channels and other news organizations including online media.

In addition to formal press conferences, reporters try to obtain further information through *ban kisha* activities.

Beat Reporting

Ban kisha (beat or literally "watch reporters") work in groups of 5 to 17, each from a different news organ. Most often a *ban* consists of seven reporters, representing the big five newspapers and the two wire services. In some situations, the *ban* increases to as many as 17 reporters, representing all the major newspapers and broadcasters in Japan. The group's objective is to cover closely and constantly—even after regular working hours—the movements of a leading politician whose activities are of great significance to the nation's political, economic, or social life.

Some of the most important *ban* are those connected to the *Nagata* Club. Among them are the *kanbo fukuchokan-ban* (the deputy chief cabinet secretary beat), the *kanbochokan-ban* (the chief cabinet secretary beat), and the *sori-ban* or *shusho-ban*, which covers the prime minister, the nation's top leader.

The structure of the *sori-ban* differs from that of other beats. Two reporters from the wire services—*Kyodo* and *Jiji*—follow the prime minister's car from the time he leaves home in the morning until he returns home, late at night. These two are called *ban-sha* (the car beat). They are obliged to inform all the other news agencies about where the prime minister went and what he did, who he met with at what times, and when he arrived back home. From the time the prime minister enters his official residence each morning until the moment he leaves the building, the *sori-ban* consists of representatives of all the major newspapers and other news media affiliated with the *Nagata* Club. The team captains from the major news media at *Nagata* Club each assign three to five reporters to the *sori-ban*. They alternate among themselves every few hours, so that at least one reporter from each news agency is always observing the prime minister's movements. At the old Prime Minister's Official Residence (just next to the new Official Residence), which remained in use until May 2001, members of the entire *sori-ban* were able to follow the prime minister whenever he left his private office, and while walking with him pelted him with questions that could give them an idea for a story. As they walked they hung on each other's shoulders in order to be able to hear the prime minister's words, a practice known in journalistic jargon as *burasagari* (hanging down). As he walked with 17 or so reporters in tow, the prime minister answered their questions in a rather spontaneous fashion. Since not all of the reporters could hear his words clearly, those closest to the prime minister later told the others what they had heard, and all of them confirmed their understanding by comparing notes in a practice known as *memo awase* (matching memo).

However, this practice changed during the administration of Prime Minister Mori Yoshiro, who began to dislike reporters' "dangling" questions in front of him as he walked the halls of his Official Residence. Eventually he declined to respond to reporters' questions while walking in his Residence or in the Diet building. When Koizumi Junichiro assumed the office of prime minister in April 2001, he immediately informed the *sori-ban* that he would "not talk to the press while walking." Instead, Koizumi conducted "daily television interviews" (*deiri terebi intabyu*), appearing each day, around noon and before he left his office for the day, at around 6:30 p.m., in front of reporters to briefly answer their questions about important issues of the day. Prime Minister Koizumi completely replaced the old, impromptu *burasagari* sessions with interactions in which reporters must submit their precise questions in advance. Koizumi knew what he would be asked and prepared himself accordingly, keeping the media focused on a specific set of issues. This type of media strategy gave Koizumi important opportunities to talk "directly" to TV viewers while appearing to be well-informed and in control of political events. His media strategy helped to improve his public image and lifted his cabinet's approval rating. This practice of the *burasagari* of reporters with the prime minister twice a day continued also during the following administrations of Abe Shinzo, Fukuda Yasuo, Aso Taro, Hatoyama Yukio, and Kan Naoto.

Faction Reporters

During the years that the LDP controlled Japan (1955–2009), each major news agency assigned a certain number of reporters, which was between six and eight at the *Hirakawa* Club that covers the LDP and the other coalition parties. The idea was to have at least one reporter covering each of the five or six main factions in the LDP, and other reporters covering the New *Komei* Party, the LDP's coalition partner since 1999. Traditionally, covering an LDP faction entailed close involvement with a group that possessed its own dynamism, customs, and its own formal structure that included regular meetings, a membership roster, and solid discipline.

Reporters assigned by different news agencies to cover a single faction of the LDP together made up a group called *habatsu kisha* (faction reporters). During the 2000s, there were between six and eight such groups. In practice, faction reporters focused on the activities of the leader ("boss") or a few top people in the faction, two or three of the leader's closest aides. In this way, faction reporters' work was similar to that of the *ban* reporters. Usually, the beats of the *ban* and the *habatsu kisha* overlapped. So a reporter who covered the LDP secretary-general's faction also belonged to the *kanjicho-ban* (secretary-general beat), where the main contact was with the secretary-general of the LDP. These reporters also covered the activities of the boss and other influential persons of the secretary-general's faction. This was also the case for reporters on the *somukaicho-ban* (covering the chairman of the LDP's Executive Council) and *seicho kaicho-ban* (the chairman of the LDP's Policy Affairs Research Council beat). The LDP's three top officials—the two council chairmen and the secretary-general—were usually from three different factions, which in the past facilitated the work of reporters, enabling one reporter to cover both the faction as a whole and the faction member who holds a key party position.

Informal Newsgathering Methods

Faction reporters and other beat reporters have several characteristics in common on how they gather information. A *ban* or *habatsu kisha* group is made up of representatives of the major news agencies, reporters from 5 to 17 news organs. As in the *kisha* clubs, *ban* reporters work as a group when meeting with sources. Ordinarily, the *ban* groups follow their target—such as the chief cabinet secretary—the entire working day. They wait near the source's office in the morning and pursue them wherever they go, even to private meetings with friends or family. The aim is to observe the target closely in order to pick up any hints that will lead to a story.

There are three newsgathering methods that *ban* reporters use much more frequently than other reporters. These are (1) informal chat sessions (*kondan*) in news sources' offices; (2) meetings in sources' homes before or after working hours; and (3) following sources as they move from one place to the other.

1. *Kondan*

In addition to press conferences where they brief tens or hundreds of reporters, Diet members also hold intimate talks in their own offices with small groups of reporters. During *kondan*, reporters obtain deeper and more detailed information than the same politician provides in press conferences. Diet members also disclose facts in *kondan* that they will not reveal at all in press conferences with many reporters present.

In many cases, *kondan* are conducted on a daily or weekly basis. The chief cabinet secretary holds a *kondan* with his *ban* almost every day after press conferences. This meeting is known as the *kanbochokan-kondan* (friendly talk with the chief cabinet secretary). The LDP and the DPJ secretary-generals also hold *kondan* with beat reporters almost daily. The minister of foreign affairs conducts formal press conferences twice a week at *Kasumi* Club, and meets representatives of the club in their office for *kondan* at least another two times. The vice minister in the same agency also holds a *kondan* twice a week on a regular basis. Most government agencies' ministers hold *kondan* after cabinet meetings and during budget deliberations in the Diet, enabling reporters to sense the "real" mood within a given ministry toward the issues being discussed.

2. *Yo-uchi* or *Yo-mawari* and *Asa-gake*

Access to *kondan* is only one of the privileges reserved for the *ban* group. Another is the ability to meet with news sources outside of their workplace, especially before or after the workday. These meetings are called "night attacks" (*yo-uchi*), "night rounds" (*yo-mawari*), or "morning visits" (*asa-gake*). Morning visits are gatherings of *ban* reporters held early in the morning at the private residence of the Diet member being covered, to receive briefings. Similarly, "night attacks" refer to gatherings of beat reporters at Diet members' homes after working hours, between 8 p.m. and 10 p.m. Meetings held in a leading Diet member's living room allow reporters and politicians to converse with each other in an intimate and relaxed atmosphere, as the politician provides reporters with essential information.

One significant aspect of these "night attacks" and "morning visits" is that all the reporters meet with a source together, as they do in many *kondan*. This means that all the reporters from the various news agencies enter and leave an official's residence together. They chat, ask questions, and receive answers from the Diet member in the presence of colleagues from other news agencies.

3. *Shachu-kon*

The *ban* reporters meet their information sources also when the sources are traveling to remote places, including to their home districts. These newsgathering sessions are called *shachu-kon* (literally, informal chat in the car). At times, reporters join influential politicians to lectures in the countryside. On their way in the train, politicians conduct *kondan* where reporters listen to their briefing, ask questions, and send stories immediately to their desks from their laptop computers by connecting via a mobile phone, or even through the phone, while the train is still moving.

4. *Kichu-kondan* and *Doko kisha*

A similar type of newsgathering is called *kichu-kondan* (literally, chat in the air). This is practiced by *doko kisha* (companion reporters: reporters assigned to accompany a source on a journey). High-echelon politicians who travel abroad to participate in international meetings (e.g., world summits) are escorted by *doko kisha*. A group of such reporters includes members of different news media and sometimes members of the same media drawn from several *kisha* clubs, such as *Nagata*, *Hirakawa*, and *Kasumi*, and from different sections of a single news organ, such as the foreign, political, and economic desks. Reporters from a single company constitute a team, like the company teams in each press club, with each reporter contributing parts of a story.

In recent years, it is not uncommon for up to 300 reporters to join the prime minister and his entourage on one of the two Boeing 747-400 jets that serve as official government airplanes. During such a flight the prime minister conducts *kichu kondan,* when he gathers the reporters on the airplane and talks about matters related to the current trip and also about other political issues.

THE RULES OF THE GAME

Press clubs give reporters ready access to sources, information, gossip, and leads, but this easy access to the heart of the political system comes at a price.

Press club reporters must depend on information from their club for the identification and interpretation of newsworthy events, and they must follow certain rules or they will not be able to do their work.

Dependency on Information Sources

Press club reporters rely on no more than 20 key Diet members for their information. This circle includes the prime minister, the chief cabinet secretary, and the leaders and secretary-generals of the major political parties. Reliance on a limited number of sources of information means that reporters from various news organizations all receive essentially the same information. Consequently, there is considerable uniformity in the political stories presented by different media.

Reliance on limited sources also gives a handful of people the power to manipulate the news. Aware of reporters' utter dependence, senior Diet members can and do take advantage by influencing the perspective from which the public will see, hear, and read the news. As high-echelon politicians become experts in the legislative process, they also become adept media manipulators who cultivate techniques for luring reporters into covering events as they wish, and know the importance of repeating their message to different media for maximum effect. Former Prime Minister Koizumi, as noted above, skillfully maneuvered reporters and succeeded in conveying messages of his choice on his own terms, thereby increasing public support for his administration.

Press Club Regulations

The rules that press club reporters are bound by are clearly a hindrance to ambitious, independent-minded reporters, who may be punished for damaging "the press club's friendship and honor" should they transgress. Each press club has its own rules for reprimanding members. Offenders might be asked to submit a letter of apology to the club, or may be ostracized or excluded from the club, which would render them unable to do their job.

Club rules vary, but are almost always aimed at preventing friction between news sources and reporters. They demand first that reporters respect story embargoes, and self-imposed news blackouts whereby all Japanese media collectively agree not to report certain information before a given time to protect a news source or avoid social or political turmoil. These included reporting that Emperor Showa was dying of cancer; detailing on the Crown Prince's search for a spouse; and exposing unethical activities and bribery scandals of high-echelon politicians and high government officials, including the HIV-tainted blood product scandal.

At important press conferences that are broadcast live, press club rules dictate that reporters pool their questions. From the politician's standpoint, the ideal scenario is to know the precise questions in advance. Press conferences often end up being staged events where a political figure is at little risk of being pulled into "uncharted waters."

Another example of the discipline imposed by press clubs is the requirement that reporters honor news sources wish to conceal their identity as the source of specific information. For example, information disclosed by the chief cabinet secretary is usually attributed in the newspapers as coming from "a senior government official"; information obtained from the three key officials of the LDP is attributed to "a top-level LDP official"; and ministerial or vice ministerial remarks during *kondan* are attributed to "a top-level official in the ministry." The identity of these news sources is known to politicians and reporters and is only masked from the general public.

Finally, reporters have to respect off-the-record (*offu reko* in Japanese journalistic jargon) requests from their sources. No matter how strongly an ambitious reporter may want to publish a bit of news obtained through an off-the-record *kondan*, the traditional desire to maintain a working relationship and harmony with sources almost always outweighs universal reporting instincts. Because editors often evaluate reporters in terms of their ability to get information, a source can even sway a reporter's promotion by doling out information, thus influencing the reporter's entire career. As a result, Japanese journalists always keep in mind the impact their stories might have on information sources.

Conclusion

As news outlets compete over prestige, status, and advertising revenues, most assert that their publication is of the highest quality, providing the widest and most thorough political coverage possible. Nevertheless, the coverage of important political news often ends up being insufficient and superficial due to structural features of the media business, the political and personal motives of politicians and government officials, and the cozy relationships that the press club system fosters between reporters and information sources. Self-censorship of issues discussed outside the political center, dependence on limited information sources, collaboration with colleagues from "rival" news organizations, and reliance on handouts and updates from Diet members or government officials—all relegate a reporter's role to that of a "messenger" who passively transmits information to the public. The results are almost complete uniformity of coverage, with news items being reported in almost the same words, and more importantly, a lack of investigation into the inner workings of Japanese politics. Individual reporters and politicians develop friendships over a span of years during which their careers are intertwined, with each climbing the ladder of their respective profession, and the reporter ends up functioning often more as a protector than an investigator or monitor. Consequently, investigative and critical political journalism are viewed as being beyond the scope of the national media.

Journalists in Japan face serious challenges, including pressure to survive as commercial entities amid declining newspaper readership, and tight control of information by news sources. Phasing out the constrictions that *kisha* clubs impose on reporters would be a good first step toward waking journalists up to their professional and social responsibility to provide the public with thorough accounts and informed interpretations of political activity. More courageous treatment of controversial issues and critical and investigative reporting by mainstream media, perhaps even by freelancers and others from nonmainstream media outlets who are given currently access to information provided by a growing number of government agencies and are allowed to attend conferences with senior officials, would certainly increase popular interest in (and knowledge of) social affairs, and consequently enhance the public's active participation in politics.

NOTES

1. Detailed data reported in *Nihon Shimbun Kyokai,* http://www.pressnet.or.jp /data/circulation/ ; and, http://www.pressnet.or.jp/data/01cirsekai.htm
2. The number of copies is the combined figures for both the morning and evening editions. The most recent data regarding the newspapers' average circulations per day (covering the period between January and June 2010), appears in *ABC,* p. 7.
3. Ibid., pp. 7–8.
4. Survey available at http://www.pressnet.or.jp/adarc/data/
5. Survey available at http://www.kkc.or.jp/society/survey.php?mode=survey _show&id=4
6. Available at http://www.dentsu.com/marketing/pdf/expenditures_2009.pdf
7. The following discussion draws on Feldman, *Talking Politics in Japan Today.*
8. *Nihon Shimbun Kyokai, Editorial affairs committee, Kisha Club Guidelines,* http://www.pressnet.or.jp/english/about/kishaclub.htm
9. *Nihon Shimbun Kyokai, Affiliate members of the organization,* http://www.press-net.or.jp/member/

BIBLIOGRAPHY

ABC (Audit Bureau of Circulations). *Shimbun,* August 10, 2010.
Advertising Expenditures in Japan, published by *Dentsu* Inc, http://www.dentsu. com/marketing/index.html (accessed January 15, 2011).
Feldman, Ofer, *Talking Politics in Japan Today* (Brighton, UK: Sussex Academic Press, 2004).
Keizai Koho Center, www.kkc.or.jp/society/index.html (accessed January 15, 2010).
Nihon Shimbun Kyokai, http://www.pressnet.or.jp (accessed January 15, 2011).

11

Revision of Administrative Law as Shortcut to Constitutional Revision

Helen Hardacre

The Historical Background[1]

During the administration of Junichiro Koizumi (2001–2006), Japan's Liberal Democratic Party (LDP) pushed its longstanding commitment to constitutional revision much more vigorously than previous administrations, issuing its draft for a new constitution in November 2005. The draft wording of the LDP on Article 9 was, in the end, considerably weaker than the LDP would have liked, owing to the opposition of its coalition partner, the New Komeito Party. Nevertheless, the LDP draft incorporated language calling for the schools to teach patriotism and respect for tradition, two items cherished by the most conservative elements of the party, and that greatly energized the parallel LDP initiative to revise the Fundamental Law on Education. Publication of the LDP draft constitution was followed in 2007 with passage of a law setting out the procedures for a referendum to adopt a new constitution.

It may be that *most* changes desired by revisionists could be accomplished by changing administrative law alone. If those changes could be enacted before a referendum on revising the constitution, the choice facing voters would not look like a decision for radical change. Hence, it would be easier to vote "yes." Moreover, even if the constitution is not revised, changes initiated by administrative law would still produce many of conservatives' desired results. However, this scenario could unfold only if the process is perceived to be reasonable and fair, and if the electorate likes the results.

Constitutional revision is seen by many conservatives as key to the goal of "closing the postwar era" (*sengo shori*), after which the nation could leave behind its problematic issues of historical memory, the humiliation of the Tokyo War Crimes Trials, and the legacy of wartime atrocities. To revise the constitution would be the capstone of that process, and a new constitution could provide a new focus for national identity.[2] By contrast, those who favor retaining the constitution as it is see in the conservatives' perspective a desire to return to the prewar period and a desire to roll back the progressive achievements of the postwar period. A number of civil society groups debate these issues in Japan today over the Internet; interested researchers may consult an archive of the websites of 57 such groups and individuals through the Constitutional Revision in Japan Research Project of the Reischauer Institute of Japanese Studies, Harvard University.[3]

Every sovereign nation has a right to revise its constitution, and some do so frequently. Italy has revised its constitution 14 times, France 16 times, and Germany dozens of times. Revision is a normal process, functioning to align fundamental principles and changing political reality. Although in the abstract, constitutional revision is a normal and unexceptional process, it can also become a vehicle for political parties to achieve their ideological agendas. This is true for the LDP in Japan, even though it is not alone in seeking constitutional revision. In 2000 the LDP established an internal research committee (*Kenpo Chosakai*) to study constitutional revision,[4] and both houses of the Diet established similar committees.[5] In 2004 the LDP issued a discussion paper announcing its stance on the issue. The paper expressed ongoing allegiance to the present constitution's adoption of such universal values as popular sovereignty, pacifism, and human rights. The document asserted that history has demonstrated Japan's unchanging commitment to the values of harmony, mutual assistance, love of peace, reverence for nature, and respect for life; this is Japan's *kunigara* (the character of Japan), a vague expression that the authors took particular care to distinguish from *kokutai* (national character or national essence), a word associated with prewar militarism and nationalism. The LDP paper described the process of constitutional revision as additive in nature, as starting with the expression of the universal values above and adding to them a further specification of the characteristically Japanese values summed up by the term *kunigara*.

The paper goes on to describe the problems that necessitate drafting a new constitution: "changed circumstances" (alluding to security issues); the "unilateral pacifism" of the current constitution; its excessive emphasis on rights and its failure to specify corresponding duties and obligations of the citizen; its failure to give expression to Japan's national character; and its fostering of such problematic attitudes as excessive individualism and regarding economic development as the highest good. Among the benefits that would flow from revising the constitution, the paper proposes that Japan would become more trusted by other nations, more dignified and "international." The people and their government would cooperate better in promoting the national interest.[6]

The LDP specified four main topics for revision in its 2005 draft constitution. The most significant change concerns Article 9. The first clause renouncing war was retained, but provisions for "the right of collective self-defense" (*shudanteki jieiken*, allowing Japan to go to the defense of an ally) were specified, and the Self-Defense Force (*Jieitai*, SDF) was to be renamed the Self-Defense Army (*Jieigun*). Second, a beefed-up section on the duty of the people (*kokumin no sekimu*) to protect the nation's independence and security was included. Third, the emperor was to be named head of state (*genshu*). Fourth, at the New Komeito's insistence new rights were specified: the right to privacy, freedom of information, environmental rights, rights of victims of crimes, and the right to protection from defamation or libel. [7]

The LDP also planned to revise the Japan-U.S. Joint Declaration on Security and the associated Guidelines for Japan-U.S. Defense Cooperation, to enable the security framework to meet China's new military capability, international terrorism, and the proliferation of weapons of mass destruction. The plans called for Japan to provide enhanced logistical support to the U.S. military.[8] A plan to relax the nonnuclear principles to permit U.S.-Japan cooperation in the construction of a missile defense system was broached.[9] The simultaneity of plans for enhanced military cooperation and constitutional revision led critics of the revision to protest that the LDP was trying to revise the constitution in response to pressure from the United States.[10] The extension through 2005 of the SDF's Iraq deployment strengthened this view.

WHY REVISE THE FUNDAMENTAL LAW ON EDUCATION?

Let us examine the reasons why the LDP wanted to revise the Fundamental Law on Education. Falling academic achievement, bullying, and youth crimes are the problems that the revised Fundamental Law on Education was supposed to address.[11] According to the Organization for Economic Cooperation and Development (OECD) statistics, Japan is considerably above the average for the OECD countries in science and math, most recently ranking third in science, behind Finland and Canada, and sixth in math, behind Finland and South Korea. If falling academic standards are truly a problem in Japan, Japan still remains in an enviable situation in these important areas. If there is a problem, it lies in the area of reading. In 2000 Japan ranked eighth, still far above average, but by 2006 it had fallen to the OECD average, behind South Korea, Poland, and other countries. By comparison with other OECD countries, Japan was described as having a more troublesome disciplinary climate, more trouble with teacher morale and commitment, and a lower quality of schools' physical infrastructure. Since at least 1995, Japan's total expenditure on educational institutions as a percentage of GDP has been below the OECD average.[12] The slump in reading evidently occurred during the Koizumi years.

As in the United States, school bullying (*ijime*) has long been recognized as a major problem of the Japanese schools, leaving some victims psychologically scarred for life and sometimes leading to suicide. For this chapter, two examples must suffice. In 1986 a middle school boy who had been bullied for years finally hanged himself after his classmates and four teachers publicly humiliated him by staging a mock funeral for him. In 2006 a 13-year-old male pupil in Fukuoka hanged himself, leaving a note explaining that he had consulted his teacher by writing a letter asking him how to deal with bullying. However, far from helping the boy, the teacher ridiculed him by reading his letter in front of the whole class. This further encouraged the bullies, who stripped him in front of the girls in the class. The worst of the bullies was bold enough to attend the dead boy's funeral and try to photograph him in his coffin with a cell phone camera, saying of him, "good riddance" (*sei-sei shita*). The teacher involved was allowed to continue working at the school even after his role in the suicide was made public.[13] These cases illustrate the way in which teachers can sometimes exacerbate bullying, with tragic results.

These revelations about bullying deeply shocked the public, but they paled by comparison with reaction to youth crimes. In June 1997 a youth was arrested in Kobe for the gruesome murder of a retarded boy, decapitating him, and leaving his head before the school gates with a letter taunting the police. "Youth A," as he came to be known, had previously attacked several girls with hammers, killing one of them. The influence of these brutal and unmotivated murders on society's attitudes to youth crime has been enormous. Several other spectacularly heinous youth crimes have occurred since then, even through to late 2009.[14]

Japanese civil society has been so deeply and continuously concerned about youth problems that it is difficult to summarize the discussion, but as anyone who has casually perused a Japanese newspaper, at almost any point, in the past 30 years can attest, many different interpretations and proposed solutions abound. Working mothers, absent fathers, liberal teachers, and permissive educational policies are the easy targets, followed by macrolevel discussions of the shrinking size of the family, the aging of the population, and a lack of character among the young. These are the "usual suspects."[15]

It is noteworthy that although these problems of youth are the source of much anxiety in Japan, the scale of the problem may be inflated in public opinion by a saturation of media coverage. Youth crime in Japan cannot begin to compare to that in the rest of the developed world. Even within Japan, a gap between public perception and statistical trends exists. For example, the number of bullying cases referred to the police peaked in 1985 and has been in a long-term decline since then. The years 2003–2007 were a short-lived exception, and youth crime showed an increase during this period, but thereafter the trend to decline has reappeared.[16]

With this brief review of some of the problems about youth and a small slice of the public discussion, let us next examine how youth problems are connected to the revision of the Fundamental Law on Education.

THE REVISED FUNDAMENTAL LAW ON EDUCATION[17]

Authored by the Occupation, the original Fundamental Law on Education (*Kyoteki kihon ho*) was enacted by proclamation in 1947 and was not revised until 2006. In the interim, the number of "fundamental laws" (*kihon ho*) has increased, and these laws have assumed distinctive functions. Fundamental laws are treated as a bridge between ordinary laws and the constitution, providing an overview of government policy in a particular area. They tend to be somewhat abstract statements of principle or the direction of policy, a charter for the subject, and they are accorded precedence over more specific laws. The Fundamental Law on Education was the first to be adopted; there are 35 other fundamental laws, including on nuclear energy (1955), science and technology (1995), and gender equality (1999). The 2006 revision of the Fundamental Law on Education took place through this process: a committee recommendation for specific revisions, a period for public comment, committee recommendation to adopt revision proposals, and presentation of the revision to the Diet.[18]

Step 1: When the old Ministry of Education was restructured to become the Ministry of Education, Culture, Sports, Science and Technololgy (MEXT) in January 2001, the Central Council on Education (*Chuo Kyoiku Shingikai*), an advisory board reporting to the minister, was charged to report on educational reform. Its 2002 interim report specified the problems as follows:

> Among the trials of this time of great change, a vicious cycle has emerged of wavering values [*kachikan ga yuragi*], loss of self-confidence, and decline of morality. In the field of education, children are becoming feeble [*hinjyaku*] in the midst of material affluence, unable to formulate a clear dream or goal for the future. Their sense of standards and will to learn are declining. We are anxious in the face of increasing, heinous youth crime and issues of academic ability. And in the schools we are faced with profound and dangerous problems like bullying, truancy, school leaving, and disruption [*gakkyu hokai*] so severe that teachers cannot control the classroom.[19]

The report recommended reform of the universities, establishment of a system of lifelong learning, and a host of measures affecting primary and secondary education. Changes evoking public comment included an increase of classroom hours by 10 percent and a requirement that teachers renew their licenses every 10 years. A call for the schools to inculcate patriotism (*aikokushin*) was the most controversial proposal. In April 2004 after much rancorous discussion, the Liberal Democratic and New Komeito Parties formulated a definition of *patriotism* that both could live with: "to value customs and culture, and to love our country." With that, parties submitted reform proposals to the Diet. The proposed reforms reflected the ideas that the family should bear primary responsibility for children's education, and that problems like bullying and youth crime can be dealt with through strengthening morality education (*dotoku kyoiku*) and patriotic attitudes.

During the same period that the revision of the Fundamental Law on Education was going forward, the LDP issued its draft for a new constitution in August 2005. One of the proposed new articles bears on the issues examined above.

Article 12: The Duties of the People

> The rights and freedoms guaranteed to the people under this constitution must be protected by the ceaseless efforts of the people. The people must not misuse these rights and freedoms. The people have a duty to exercise their

rights recognizing that they are accompanied by duties and responsibilities, and that they are to enjoy freedoms in a way that does not contravene public order or the public good.[20]

The emphasis of Article 12 *before* revision fell on rights, not duty, and much of the prose in the revised version is entirely new. In short, the proposals for revising the *constitution* in this area amount mainly to a shift in emphasis from rights to duties.

Returning to the revisions that the government proposed for the Fundamental Law on Education, we see significant differences in the Preambles of the 1947 and 2006 laws. The 1947 law upheld an ideal of "education which aims at the creation of culture, general and rich in individuality," while the revision called for "education which transmits tradition and aims at the creation of a new culture." The 2006 law is longer than the original and charges the educational system with goals not anticipated in 1947, such as fostering attitudes "valuing equality between men and women" (Article 2, iii), to "contribute to the protection of the environment" (Article 2, iv), and "to respect our traditions and culture, love the country and region that nurtured them, together with respect for other countries and a desire to contribute to world peace and the development of the international community" (Article 2, v). A new clause requiring that education be made available to persons with disabilities has been added (Article 4, (2)).

Continuing the theme seen in proposals to revise the *constitution* to emphasize the duties of the people, a new article (10) on Education in the Family has been added, specifying that the family has the "primary responsibility" for children's education.[21]

Article 10:

Mothers, fathers, and other guardians, having the primary responsibility for their children's education, shall endeavor to teach them the habits necessary for life, encourage a spirit of independence, and nurture the balanced development of their bodies and minds.

(2) The national and local governments shall endeavor to take necessary measures supporting education in the family, by providing guardians with opportunities to learn, relevant information, and other means, while respecting family autonomy in education.[22]

One implication of this new article is to place responsibility for youth problems on parents and thereby to dilute government responsibility for problems arising in the schools.

We see an enhancement of central authority in Article 16(2): "The national government shall comprehensively formulate and implement education measures in order to provide for equal opportunities in education and to maintain and raise education standards throughout the country." Article 17 mandates the government to "formulate a basic plan covering basic principles [and] required measures" for promoting education, to report the plan to the Diet and make it public. The Japan Teachers' Union interprets this clause as a move to transfer all initiative in setting educational policy to the ministry, thus undermining the mandate of local school boards.[23]

Step 2: Public Comment. The government solicited public comment on its proposed revisions through 2006, receiving some 13,100 communications from the public (letters, faxes, emails, etc.), with presentation of experts' opinions (7 individuals and some 31 organizations represented), and 5 "Town Meetings," at which 46 persons spoke from a total audience of 1,245 persons. But when it came to light in late 2006 that the government had paid agents to speak in support of the revision proposal at these town meetings, Prime Minister Shinzo Abe and others in his cabinet apologized and returned the agents' salaries to the public purse. The prime minister declared, however, that the revision itself was not the problem, and the government pressed on.[24]

Step 3: Committee Recommendation to Accept Revision Proposals. Following the period for public comment, a multiparty Special Committee on the Fundamental Law on Education (*Kyoiku Kihonho ni kansuru Tokubetsu Iinkai*), chaired by Hirofumi Nakasone, was convened to reach a decision on whether to forward the revision to the full Diet. The Committee concluded its discussions on December 14, 2006, with passage of the revision forwarded to the Diet, but not before the prime minister endured a severe tongue lashing from opposition parliamentarians.

When Mitsuru Sakurai of the Democratic Party asked Abe to explain the basis on which he claimed that the people wished the Fundamental Law on Education to be revised, and when Abe had presented the revision as a means of addressing the list of youth problems we have surveyed above, Sakurai said that rigged town meetings hardly constitute credible evidence, and furthermore, that the revision measures provide no solution at all to the problems of youth. To this, Abe replied that since implementation of the current law, the size of families has shrunk, the nuclear family has become the norm, and, as a result, morality, standards, and public spirit have been vitiated. Pupils must learn to restrain their urges to violence and disruption of the classroom. Morality must be instilled in order to inculcate the much-needed capacity for self-control.[25]

Minister of Education Fumiaki Ibuki responded to questioning from Mieko Kamimoto of the Democratic Party, affirming that in the process of formulating the revisions of the Fundamental Law on Education, his ministry had "checked" that nothing in the proposal contravened anything the government had in mind for revision of the constitution. Kamimoto interpreted this response to mean that the revision of Fundamental Law on Education must, therefore, violate the *current* constitution. The prime minister took offense at her implication that the project to revise the Fundamental Law on Education was merely a part of the government's plan to revise the constitution, and a heated exchange ensued, but the revisions were nevertheless forwarded to the Diet.[26]

Step 4: Presentation to the Diet. In Diet discussion, lower house representatives of the opposition parties chastised the government on December 15,
2006, for resorting to rigging its own town meetings and then presenting
the canned remarks of stooges as evidence of popular support for revision.
Keiji Karata of the Communist Party called the revision a naked attempt to
infringe on freedom of conscience and push patriotism on the people.[27] He
declared that the government was trying to ram through the revision even
though the public saw no need for it. Naoto Kan of the Democratic Party
criticized the government's revision for lacking any measure to address bullying and falling academic achievement, adding icily that since the prime minister had attended private school, it was hardly any wonder that he showed so
little insight into the problems of public school classrooms. Nobuto Hosaka
of the Socialist Party said that *all* the legislation pushed so aggressively by the
government, including the revision of the Fundamental Law on Education,
raising the SDF to a ministry, and a bill on a referendum for constitutional
revision, sought mainly to enlarge government authority, threatening popular sovereignty, and infringing on freedom of conscience. To summarize,
there was a complete lack of opposition party support.[28]

Implementing the Revised
Fundamental Law on Education

Once the Fundamental Law on Education had been revised, implementation
began. The Central Council on Education issued a report calling for reform
of the ministry's official Curriculum Guidelines (*Gakushu shido yoryo*) in
January 2008. The report cited declining academic achievement, especially
in Japanese language reading and writing skills, science, and math, as a reason for reform, and expatiated at length on the need to enhance pupils' mas-
tery of, and appreciation for, Japanese literature, music, and tradition. In the
area of morality education, the report made extensive comments on the need
to nurture a respect for humanity, to develop powers of judgment, a spirit of
public participation, and a sense of integrity. Throughout these remarks, the
report repeatedly cited a need to develop appropriate curricular materials and
lamented the tendency for morality instruction to become less appealing to
students as they grow older.[29]

Two months later, in March 2008 (3.28.2008) MEXT issued revised
Curriculum Guidelines, with class time increased by 10 percent, incorporat-
ing the goals for morality education set out in the report just examined, and
mandating that an emphasis on tradition and culture be established in all
possible subject areas.[30] It seems that patriotism will be addressed under the
rubrics of morality education, although neither document offers specifics.
Concrete details are still lacking for morality education, but the intention to
strengthen this area, and perhaps elevate it to a graded subject, is clear.[31]

Nevertheless, specific measures linked to ethics and patriotism education
began to be implemented in 2007, and standardized morality tests began
to be carried out in primary and middle schools around the country. The

Curriculum Guidelines had specified that patriotism would *not* be graded, but in fact parents found that primary and middle school children were being assessed. According to the *Asahi* newspaper, in 2007 at least 1,200 primary and 1,100 middle schools administered the tests of one commercial company to some 380,000 pupils, at a cost of 430 yen per student. One sample question was, "How do you feel when you see graffiti written on a temple?" presumably on the assumption that all pupils of whatever religious affiliation could be expected to be outraged, and also that it is permissible to grade children on questions designed to evoke religious sentiments.[32] Clearly, no one with an understanding of the constitution was in charge—either at the company that produced the test or in the 2,300 schools that administered it.

In May 2008 MEXT Minister Tokai stated that the Occupation prohibition on school visits to the Yasukuni Shrine is null and void.[33] Strangely, this change was not widely reported by the Japanese media, but a South Korean newspaper noticed, wondering what the Japanese government expected school pupils to learn from such visits.[34] The change has come about so recently that it is difficult to know what impact, if any, it will have, but the lack of media attention is striking, even alarming. It seems unlikely that this could have happened if the Fundamental Law on Education had not been revised.

In these ways, the revision of the Fundamental Law on Education has made possible the intensification of morality education, the reinstitution of patriotic education (even if the curriculum and evaluation techniques are still to be worked out), and school trips to Yasukuni Shrine. Whether these measures go any distance toward raising academic achievement or to reducing bullying and violent crime among youth is another question, but the link to constitutional revision is clear.

DISCUSSION

We can recognize that revising the Fundamental Law on Education and implementing it through revised curricula responded to genuine concerns of the public about youth crime and falling educational achievement, and that it would have been irresponsible of bureaucrats and politicians *not* to respond. The response followed the outlines of the dominant party's conservative principles *and* its blueprint for constitutional revision, due in part to the role of fundamental laws as bridges to the constitution. But this strategy of linking educational and constitutional revision greatly embittered the opposition parties, who came to view both as measures being rammed down their throats without adequate public vetting. Some will find simplistic the idea that longer school hours and patriotism tests will solve the problems of the schools and society that were given as the reasons for revising the education law. One might also question, as many Diet members did, whether the government really even intended its revision of the Fundamental Law on Education to address those problems. What the government mainly seems to have accomplished was a populist move, pleasing to the most conservative section of its supporters and others happy to see youth blamed for large-scale social problems with complex origins. Not coincidentally, the move also accomplished a further centralization of authority over educational policy and struck a blow at the Japan Teachers' Union, the LDP's longtime antagonist. The government responded predictably, and the electorate had the option either to moderate that response at the local level and/or elect different politicians next time. In August 2009 the Japanese electorate had their chance, and they chose to reject the LDP decisively, although neither educational reform nor constitutional revision was a prominent issue of the campaign.

Opposition parties have found the revision process problematic. The rigged town meetings suggest above all that the LDP was not actually confident that the public wished to see the law revised. Resorting to this underhanded strategy (which was also illegal, given that tax money was used to pay the stooges) suggests that the government had reason to fear that its proposals were not, after all, what the public wanted. That the revision was pushed through in spite of these revelations does not necessarily mean that the public was unperturbed by the incident.

If one were to guess what the public wanted to see here, smaller classroom sizes would probably be high on the list. Like "No Child Left Behind" in the United States, Japan has begun investing heavily in standardized testing as a means of identifying underperforming schools. In 2008, for the second year in a row, Akita and Fukui prefectures ranked at the top, with the highest student scores, whereas Okinawa was at the bottom.[35] I cannot claim to have investigated education in those prefectures to be certain of this hypothesis, but one benefit of the sparse population of rural prefectures, such as Akita and Fukui, may be that their classrooms are small, and teachers can give children more individualized attention. This issue is at the center of opposition party criticism of the revised Fundamental Law on Education. Opposition party politicians demand a reduction in class size to a number under 30 students to afford teachers more time for individualized instruction and to help maintain order in the classroom.

Opposition MPs point out that one need look no further to find the main cause of Japan's faltering academic standards than this depressing fact: Japan's per-capita expenditure for education is now the lowest in the OECD.[36] A paraphrase of remarks in the lower house on April 17, 2007, by Nobuto Hosaka directed to Prime Minister Abe conveys the way in which a host of issues are coming together.

No sooner had you incorporated patriotism and love of community in the revised Fundamental Law on Education, than we find that the ministry's textbook approval machine has excised reference to the military's coercion of group suicides in the Battle of Okinawa. This shows us better than anything that your notion of patriotism spreads a narrow nationalism. Your insistence on standardized testing is creating administrative pyramids and a monolithic evaluation process, exacerbating the differences among schools. You are abandoning the children who attend the lower-performing schools. You shouldn't be trying to pin medals on the elite schools but instead raise the performance of *all* children. Tests alone will never deliver a full picture of a school or a group of teachers. You deny the whole system of local school boards in your rush to strengthen central authority. Does the Prime Minister imagine that these measures are addressing the problem of bullying?[37]

Mr. Hosaka's reference to the portrayal in school textbooks of the Battle of Okinawa derived from the announcement on March 30, 2007, that MEXT's textbook screening committee had decreed that textbooks should not include mention of Japanese troops forcing civilians to commit mass suicide in the face of the Allied invasion. However, by the end of the year MEXT was forced to reverse this position. In July 2007 over 100,000 Okinawans protested this decision in the largest rally there since the return of the islands to Japan in 1972. The Democratic Party called for the decision to be struck down, and by December the ministry had to back down and reinstate some of the excised material.[38]

The rush at the local level to start testing pupils on patriotism and to grade them—in contravention of MEXT policy—suggests that pressure to do so came from the local level. This confused situation may be due to the issuance of new curricular guidelines *before* the ministry was ready to provide its own instructional and assessment materials, leaving an opening for commercial test companies to come up with rather ineffective devices. At 430 yen per test, per pupil, this rush to grade children on their morals or patriotism also costs the taxpayer in the end. But the greatest price is the effect on public confidence in the Japanese educational system, if parents become concerned that teachers' evaluation of pupil achievement and potential is colored by the child's response to such a question as, "How do you feel when you see graffiti on a temple wall?"

MEXT now also has reason to rethink its 2003 decision to require teachers to stand, face the flag, and sing the national anthem in school ceremonies. In February 2008 the Tokyo District Court ruled that the Tokyo metropolitan government owed 27.5 million yen to 13 former high school teachers denied reemployment for refusing to comply with this rule. From 2003 to 2008 MEXT had continued disciplining teachers, some 125 in 2004 and 64 in 2005.[39] Tokyo (whose Governor Shintaro Ishihara is a great proponent of disciplining teachers) continues to account for a disproportionate share of these totals down through March 2008, when the prefecture disciplined 20 teachers in the first three months of the year, down from 35 in 2007.[40] The court's verdict will certainly encourage some of them to seek damages.

As for bullying and youth crime since the revision, we are faced with fragmentary data. Some prefectures report an increase in bullying; others report that appropriations for dealing with the problem have been cut. Meanwhile, MEXT has introduced hotlines and online advice. Some cities have established a "Bullying Rescue Squad" or a city ombudsman for bullying. Some cities and prefectures have learned how to monitor student email and Internet activity, deleting offensive material before it is posted.[41]

To recapitulate briefly, through revision of the Fundamental Law on Education and implementation of it through a changed curriculum, the LDP was able to enact significant policy changes based on its goals of returning to stricter standards of morality and patriotism, enhancing central authority, and shifting responsibility for the behavior of youth to the family. This process is closely aligned with—and probably would not have happened without—the LDP's parallel process of drafting a new constitution. I believe we can see these developments in the field of education as a significant step that smoothes the path for constitutional revision by setting in place the concrete policies that a revised constitution would express in more abstract terms. However, against this is the entrenched opposition of the other political parties, which view the government's manner of revising education policy with deep mistrust. What stance the DPJ will adopt toward these issues is not clear at this time (early 2011).

NOTES

1. Much of the material in this section is drawn from my earlier article, "Constitutional Revision and Japanese Religions."
2. Tamamoto, "A Land without Patriots: The Yasukuni Controversy and Japanese Nationalism."
3. The archive is available online at www.fas.harvard.edu/~rijs/crrp/index.html. The website also provides extensive research aids in the form of bibliographies, a chronology covering debate on constitutionalism from the Meiji period to the present, and descriptions of the many groups debating the issue today.
4. The committee is formally called *Jiminto Shin Kenpo Kiso Iinkai* (Liberal Democratic Party New Constitution Drafting Committee), and the document it issued is formally titled *Kenpo kaisei yokoan* (Outline for Constitutional Revision).
5. Yakushiji, "Koizumi and the LDP March toward Constitutional Revision," Sven Saaler (trans.).
6. "Kenpo kaisei purojekuto chiimu," *Ronten seiri, Jiyu Minshu to Seimu Chosakai, Kenpo Chosakai* (Constitutional Revision Project Team, the Points at Issue: Liberal Democratic Party Administrative Research Group, Constitution Research Group).
7. In addition to these specific proposals, the Preamble would be redrafted, the national flag and anthem named; the division of the land into 47 prefectures would be redrawn to a smaller number of "states" (*shu*). The LDP's draft can be compared to the present constitution, article for article, available online at www.jimin.jp/jimin/shin/_kenpo/shiryou/pdf/01122_a.pdf.
8. The lack of specificity about the geographical extent of the area of SDF deployment is one point of opposition criticism. See www.yomiuri.co.jp/20050114w02.htm.
9. "Buki yushutsu 3 gensoku no kanwa, misairu boei shisutemu ni gentei e, 11" (Relaxation of the three principles of weapons export, limiting the system of missile defense).